TABLE O

How to Build It

Bert Thompson, Ph.D.

Apologetics Press, Inc.
230 Landmark Drive
Montgomery, Alabama 36117-2752

ISBN: 0-932859-37-2

DEDICATION

To my late father, Charles Albert Thompson, D.V.M., who showed me the incomprehensible love of God, and who taught me the importance of standing for the Truth regardless of the consequences.

And to my late mother, Mary Ruth Thompson, who possessed a rock-solid faith in the Lord that never wavered, and who loved her son so much that she dedicated her life—in word and in deed—to imparting that same kind of faith to him.

PREFACE

At Caesarea Philippi, situated at the base of Mount Hermon that rises several thousand feet above it, Christ asked His disciples how the public viewed Him. "Who do men say that the Son of man is?," He inquired (Matthew 16:13). The reply of the disciples was: "Some say, John the Baptist; some, Elijah; and others, Jeremiah, or one of the prophets" (16:14). But Jesus delved deeper when He asked the disciples: "But who say ye that I am?" (16:15). Ever the impulsive one, Simon Peter quickly answered: "Thou art the Christ, the Son of the living God" (16:16). Jesus' response to Peter was this:

> Blessed art thou, Simon Bar-Jonah: for flesh and blood hath not revealed it unto thee, but my Father who is in heaven. And I also say unto thee, that thou art Peter, and **upon this rock** I will build my church; and the gates of Hades shall not prevail against it (16:17-18, emp. added).

Jesus had come—"in the fulness of time"—to bring the one thing that all the Earth's inhabitants needed. From Cain, the first murderer, to the lawless men who eventually would put Him to death on the cross, mankind desperately needed the salvation that the heavenly plan would provide. When he wrote to the young evangelist Timothy, the apostle Paul observed that it had been God's plan to save men through Christ even before the foundation of the world. He wrote of God, "who saved us, and called us with a holy calling, not according to our works, but according to his own purpose and grace, which was given us in Christ Jesus before times eternal" (2 Timothy 1:9). Through His foreknowledge, God knew that man one day would need redemption from sin. In fact, throughout the history of Israel, God made both promises and prophecies concerning a coming kingdom and its King. The promise was that from David's seed, God would build a "house" and "kingdom" (2

Samuel 7:11-17—a promise, incidentally, that was reaffirmed in Psalm 132:11 and preached as reality by Peter in Acts 2:29-34 when the church began). Seven hundred years before Christ's arrival, the prophet Isaiah foretold:

> For unto us a child is born, unto us a son is given; and the government shall be upon his shoulder: and his name shall be called Wonderful, Counsellor, Mighty God, Everlasting Father, Prince of Peace. Of the increase of his government and of peace there shall be no end, upon the throne of David, and upon his kingdom, to establish it, and to uphold it with justice and with righteousness from henceforth even for ever. The zeal of Jehovah of hosts will perform this (Isaiah 9:6-7).

Thus, Christ's exclamation to Peter that the building of His church would be upon a "rock" was nothing more than what the Old Testament prophets had foretold hundreds of years before. Isaiah prophesied: "Therefore, thus saith the Lord Jehovah, Behold, I lay in Zion for a foundation a stone, a tried stone, a precious corner-stone of sure foundation: he that believeth shall not be in haste" (Isaiah 28: 16). Later, Peter himself—through inspiration, and no doubt with the events of Caesarea Philippi still fresh on his mind—would make reference to this very rock foundation when he wrote about the "living stone, rejected indeed of men.... The stone which the builders rejected, the same was made the head of the corner" (1 Peter 2:4,7). In fact, even Jesus Himself mentioned the "rejected stone" of Old Testament allusion. In Matthew 21:42, Mark 12:10, and Luke 20: 17, He made reference to the psalmist's statement about "the stone which the builders rejected is become the head of the corner" (Psalm 118:22), and applied the rejection of the stone by the builders to the Sanhedrin's rejection and repudiation of Him. The rock upon which the Lord's church eventually was to be built, and upon which His disciples' faith ultimately would have to stand, was the fact evinced by Peter's confession—"Thou art the Christ, the Son of the living God."

On another occasion during His earthly tenure, Jesus related a story to His followers about the importance of that rock. Toward the end of His soul-stirring "Sermon on the Mount" (Matthew 5-7), Jesus told a parable about two men who had constructed houses for themselves. One man built his house upon a foundation of sand; the other built his upon a foundation of solid rock. When the winds blew, the rains descended, and the floods came, the house built upon sand collapsed and "great was the fall thereof" (Matthew 7:27). But when those same forces of nature struck the other house, "it fell not, for it was founded upon the rock" (Matthew 7:25). Jesus then explained that the man who built upon the sand represented those who refuse to obey God's Word, while the man who built upon the rock represented those who place their faith in that Word and who, in obedience to the God Who gave it, live according to its commands and precepts.

This book—the first in a planned three-volume series—concentrates on how to build a biblical faith exactly like that of the man whose house "fell not, for it was founded upon the rock." To that end, it presents discussions of the many faces and causes of unbelief, evidence for the existence of God and the inspiration of the Bible, an examination of the proofs for the deity of Christ, the importance and singularity of Christ's church, biblically mandated steps for salvation, and the mercy and grace of a Sovereign God.

Volume two, *Rock-Solid Faith: How to Sustain It*, will concentrate on how to sustain a personal faith. Volume three, *Rock-Solid Faith: How to Defend It*, will provide ammunition that can be used to defend that personal faith against the attacks made upon it by a society that all too often is becoming increasingly unbelieving and frequently hostile. It is my hope that reading and applying the concepts found in each book in the *Rock-Solid Faith* trilogy will help you build a foundation upon which you can construct a genuine, abiding faith in God, His Word, and His Son. If, along the way, I may be of any assistance to you in attaining that goal, please call on me. I gladly will do whatever I can to help.

Bert Thompson
April 1, 2000

CHAPTER 1

THE MANY FACES OF UNBELIEF [PART I]

One of the most mind-numbing mysteries for those who believe in God is trying to understand the unbelief of those who do not. As one who writes and lectures often on the topics of apologetics and evidences, I frequently am asked, "What causes people **not** to believe in God?" Generally speaking, the motive behind the question is not derogatory, but complimentary. That is to say, the querist really is asking: "Why is it that **obviously intelligent** people do not believe in God?"

Neither inquiry is easy to answer because usually the person asking the question wants a simple, quick, concise response. It is difficult for the querist to understand why people who are "obviously intelligent" refuse to believe in God. It has been my experience that rarely is there a single reason for unbelief, because rarely is there a single reason that can explain adequately why people think, or act, as they do.

Surely, however, a part of the answer has to do with the fact that when God created humans, He endowed us with **freedom of choice** (often referred to as "personal volition" or "free moral agency"). This stands to reason, considering Who God is. The Bible describes Him as being, among other things, a God of love (1 John 4:8). Even a cursory survey of the Scriptures documents God's desire that man, as the zenith of His creation, possess, and employ, the freedom of choice with which he has been endowed. God did not create mankind as some kind of robot to serve Him slavishly without any personal choice in the matter.

For example, when Joshua—who had led the Israelite nation so faithfully for so long—realized that his days were numbered and his hours were few, he assembled the entirety of that nation before him and, in one of the most moving, impassioned pleas recorded within the pages of Holy Writ, admonished his charges to employ their personal volition in a proper fashion.

> And if it seem evil unto you to serve Jehovah, choose you this day whom ye will serve; whether gods which your fathers served that were beyond the River, or the gods of the Amorites, in whose land ye dwell: but as for me and my house, we will serve Jehovah (Joshua 24:15).

Joshua's point could not have been any clearer. The Israelites, individually and collectively, had the ability, and yes, even the God-given right, to choose whether they wished to follow Jehovah. As the text continues, it indicates that on this particular occasion they chose correctly.

> And the people answered and said, Far be it from us that we should forsake Jehovah, to serve other gods.... And Israel served Jehovah all the days of Joshua, and all the days of the elders that outlived Joshua, and had known all the work of Jehovah that he had wrought for Israel (Joshua 24:16,31).

Years later, however, the people of Israel—employing that same heaven-sent personal volition—freely chose to abandon their belief in, and obedience to, God. Judges 2:10-11 records:

> [T]here arose another generation after them, that knew not Jehovah, nor yet the work which he had wrought for Israel. And the children of Israel did that which was evil in the sight of Jehovah, and served the Baalim.

Within the pages of the New Testament, the principle is the same. When Jesus condemned the self-righteousness of the Pharisees in John 5:39-40, He made this observation: "Ye search the scriptures, because ye think that in them ye have eternal life; and these are they which bear witness of me; and ye **will not** come to me, that ye may have life." The Pharisees of New Testament times possessed the same freedom of choice as the Israelites of Old Testament times. But while the Israelites to whom Joshua spoke chose at first to heed his plea and obey Jehovah, the Pharisees to whom Christ spoke chose to ignore His plea and to disobey God.

Two chapters later, when Jesus addressed the Jews in their own temple, the text indicates that they marveled at His teaching (John 7:15). But Jesus demurred, and said: "My teaching is not mine, but his that sent me. If any man **willeth** to do his will, he shall know of the teaching, whether it is of God, or whether I speak from myself" (John 7:16-17). Jesus' point to the devout temple Jews was no different than the one He had made earlier to the legalistic Pharisees. God has imbued mankind with the ability to **choose**. If a person **wills**, he can accept God and His teaching, but God never will force Himself on that person. As the apostle John brought the book of Revelation to a close, he wrote: "He that will, let him take the water of life freely" (Revelation 22:17). The operative phrase here, of course, is "he that will."

But what of he that **will not**? Freedom is accompanied by responsibility. With freedom of choice comes the responsibility to think carefully, choose wisely, and act forcefully. Freedom of choice always works best when tempered with wisdom and good judgement. Thus, in every human activity the process of recognizing, believing, and properly utilizing truth is vitally important. Especially is this true in the spiritual realm. Jesus tried to impress this upon His generation when He said: "Ye shall know the truth, and the truth shall make you free" (John 8:32). What we as humans so often fail to realize is that we are not involved in a search for truth because **it** is lost; we are involved in a search for truth because without it **we** are!

Some, however, have elected to employ their freedom of choice to ignore the truth regarding God's existence and to disobey His Word. They are the spiritual descendants of the first-century Pharisees; they **could** come to a knowledge of the truth, but they **will not**. The simple fact of the matter is that we are responsible for what we choose to believe. Using the personal volition with which God has endowed each of us, we may choose freely to believe in Him or we may choose just as freely to disbelieve. The choice is up to each individual. And once that individual has made up his mind to disbelieve, God will not deter him, as Paul made clear when he wrote his second epistle to the Thessalonians. In that letter, he spoke first of those who "received not the love of the truth" (2:10), and then went on to say that "for this cause God sendeth them a working of error, that they should believe a lie" (2 Thessalonians 2:11).

What, exactly, was Paul suggesting? Was the apostle teaching that God **purposely** causes men to believe error? No, he was not. Paul's point in this passage was that we may choose to accept something as the truth when, in fact, it is false. Because God has granted man personal volition, and because He has provided within the Bible the rules, regulations, and guidelines to govern that personal volition, He therefore will refrain from overriding man's freedom of choice—even when that choice violates His law. God will not contravene man's decisions, or interfere with the actions based on those decisions. The prophet Isaiah recorded God's words on this subject many years before when he wrote:

> Yea, they have chosen their own ways, and their soul delighteth in their abominations: I also will choose their delusions, and will bring their fears upon them; because when I called, none did answer; when I spake, they did not hear: but they did that which was evil in mine eyes, and chose that wherein I delighted not (Isaiah 66:3-4).

Concerning the people who refused to have God in their knowledge, and who exchanged truth for error, Paul repeatedly stated that "God gave them up" (Romans 1:24,26,28). In his commentary on the Thessalonian epistles, Raymond C. Kelcy addressed the fact that men often prefer the consequences of a certain belief system, and that as a result

> God gives the man over to the belief of the lie which he prefers. In a sense it might be said that the means by which a person is deceived is God's permissive agency—not God's direct agency (1968, p. 157).

There is an exact parallel in the instance of the Pharaoh who sparred with Moses and Aaron over the release of the Hebrews from Egyptian bondage. When these two brothers arrived at Pharaoh's court as God's ambassadors to demand the release of the enslaved Israelites, they told the pagan potentate: "Thus saith Jehovah, the God of Israel, 'Let my people go.'" Pharaoh's response, preserved in Scripture for posterity, foreshadowed the attitude of millions of unbelievers who would imitate the militant monarch's demeanor of disbelief throughout the course of human history: "Who is Jehovah, that I should hearken unto his voice to let Israel go? **I know not Jehovah**, and moreover I will not let Israel go" (Exodus 5:1-2, emp. added).

Several times the biblical text records that it was God Who "hardened Pharaoh's heart" (Exodus 7:3; 9:12; 10:1,20,27; 11:10; 14:8). Are we to understand, therefore, that God **caused** Pharaoh's stubborn attitude of disbelief? Certainly not. The simple fact of the matter is that God did not cause Pharaoh to harden his heart and disobey, but instead **permitted** the ruler's actions. The Scriptures speak to this point when they acknowledge that Pharaoh himself "hardened his heart" (Exodus 8:15,32; 9:34-35). In their commentary on the Pentateuch, Keil and Delitzsch addressed Pharaoh's hardness of heart, even after he witnessed the miraculous plagues sent by God.

> After every one of these miracles, it is stated that Pharaoh's heart was firm, or dull, i.e. insensible to the voice of God, and unaffected by the miracles performed before his eyes,

> and the judgments of God suspended over him and his kingdom.... Thus Pharaoh would not bend his self-will to the will of God, even after he had discerned the finger of God and the omnipotence of Jehovah in the plagues suspended over him and his nation; he would not withdraw his haughty refusal, notwithstanding the fact that he was obliged to acknowledge that it was sin against Jehovah. Looked at from this side, the hardening was a fruit of sin, a consequence of that self-will, high-mindedness, and pride which flow from sin, and a continuous and ever increasing **abuse of that freedom of the will** which is innate in man, and which involves the possibility of obstinate resistance to the word and chastisement of God even until death (1981, pp. 454,455, emp. added).

Pharaoh's hard heart was not God's doing, but his own. God's **permissive agency** was involved, but not His **direct agency.** That is to say, He allowed Pharaoh to use (or abuse, as Keil and Delitzsch correctly noted) his freedom of will in a vain attempt to thwart God's plans. Throughout history, God's actions have been consistent in this regard. The psalmist wrote:

> But my people hearkened not to my voice; and Israel would not hear me. So I let them go after the stubbornness of their heart, that they might walk in their own counsels (81:11-12).

Concerning the rebellious Israelites, Paul wrote in Romans 11: 8 (quoting from Isaiah 29:10): "God gave them a spirit of stupor, eyes that they should not see, and ears that they should not hear." In every generation, God has granted mankind the freedom of self-determination to be blind to His existence, and in so doing to believe a lie. E.M. Zerr put it well when he said:

> The Bible in no place teaches that God ever forces a man to sin, then punishes him for the wrong-doing. Neither does He compel man against his will to do right, but has always offered him proper inducements for righteous conduct, then left it to his own responsibility to decide what he will do about it (1952, 5:159).

The same principles operate even today, almost two thousand years later. If an acknowledgment of God's existence and obedience to His Word make us free (John 8:32), surely, then, disbelief and disobedience make us captives of one sort or another. Set adrift in a vast sea of confusing and contradictory world views, we then find ourselves susceptible to every ill-conceived plan, deceptive scheme, and false concept that the winds of change may blow our way. We become captives to error because we have abandoned the one moral compass—the existence of God—that possesses the ability to show us the way, and thereby to set us free.

Throughout history, unbelief has worn many masks. But behind each is a Pharaoh-like spirit of rebellion that—in angry defiance—raises a clenched fist to God in a display of unrepentant determination **not** to believe in Him. An examination of the many faces, and causes, of unbelief is both informative and instructive.

Atheism

In his book, *If There's a God, Why Are There Atheists?*, R.C. Sproul noted in regard to theism that "literally, the word means 'Godism,' that is belief in God. It is derived from *theos*, the Greek word for God" (1978, p. 16). Chief among unbelievers, then, would be the **atheist** (*a*, without; *theos*, God)—the person who affirms that there is no God. As Sproul went on to observe: "Atheism involves the rejection of any form of theism. To be an atheist is to disavow belief in any kind of god or gods" (p. 18). In his thought-provoking book, *Intellectuals Don't Need God*, Alister E. McGrath noted:

> The atheist is prepared to concede—no, that is too negative a word, to **celebrate**—the need for commitment and the existence of evidence to move one in the direction of that commitment. In other words, the atheist recognizes the need to come off the fence and the fact that there are factors in the world of human experience and thought that suggest which side of the fence that ought to be. At present, the atheist happens to sit on the godless side of that fence (1993, p. 81, emp. in orig.).

Bruce Lockerbie, in *Dismissing God*, referred to atheism as "the abdication of belief," and described the person who falls into this category.

> For the ardent disbeliever, the hypothesis and its given propositions are one and the same: **God does not exist**.... All that has energized the human imagination and motivated the human spirit with prospects of nirvana, the Elysian Fields, the happy hunting grounds, paradise, or heaven—all that is meant when the Book of Ecclesiastes declares that God "has set eternity in the hearts of men"—must be invalidated by counterclaims of atheism (1998, pp. 225,227, emp. in orig.).

This, no doubt, explains why a famous unbeliever like the late Carl Sagan, the eminent atheist/astronomer of Cornell University, opened his television extravaganza *Cosmos* (and his book by the same name) with these words: "The Cosmos is all that is or ever was or ever will be" (1980, p. 4). Commenting on the exclusivity of that statement, D. James Kennedy wrote: "That is as clear a statement of atheism as one could ever hear" (1997, p. 61).

Declaring oneself to be an atheist, however, is much easier than defending the concept of atheism. Think of it this way. In order to defend atheism, a person would have to know **every single fact** there is to know, because the one fact that avoided detection might just be the fact of the existence of God. Theodore Christlieb noted:

> The denial of the existence of God involves a perfectly monstrous hypothesis; it is, when looked at more closely, an unconscionable assumption. Before one can say that the world is without a God, he must first have become thoroughly conversant with the whole world.... In short, to be able to affirm authoritatively that no God exists, a man must be omniscient and omnipresent, that is, he himself must be God, and then after all there would be one (1878, pp. 143,144).

Impossible task, that—since one would have to **be** God in order to state with certainty that there is no God! Yet, as apologist Dan Story has pointed out,

> ...[T]his fact stops few atheists from arguing against the existence of God. Rather than admitting (or even recognizing) the irrationality of their own position, many atheists attempt to remove the rationality of the Christian position.... These atheists argue that because they don't believe in God, because their belief is negative, they don't have to martial any arguments in their favor (1997, p. 20).

Evidence of such a stance abounds. Atheistic writer George H. Smith, in his book, *Atheism: The Case Against God*, wrote:

> Proof is applicable only in the case of a positive belief. To demand proof of the atheist, the religionist must represent atheism as a positive belief requiring substantiation. When the atheist is seen as a person who lacks belief in a god, it becomes clear that he is not obligated to "prove" anything. The atheist *qua* atheist does not believe anything requiring demonstration; the designation of "atheist" tells us, not what he believes to be true, but what he does **not** believe to be true. If others wish for him to accept the existence of a god, it is their responsibility to argue for the truth of theism—but the atheist is not similarly required to argue for the truth of atheism (1979, p. 16, emp. in orig.)

Such a view, however, is seriously flawed for at least two reasons. First, theists do not make the statement, "God exists," with wild abandon, expecting it to be accepted as if somehow it were spoken by divine fiat. Rather, when they defend God's existence, theists offer **evidence** to back up their case (e.g., the cosmological argument, teleological argument, moral argument, etc.)—which places the matter of the existence of God in an entirely different perspective. As Story properly noted:

> Christians have given ample evidence for the existence of the Judeo-Christian God. In light of this, if atheists claim God does not exist, they must be prepared to explain why. When Christians state that God exists and offer evidences to support this claim, they have moved the debate into a new arena—an arena in which atheists must prove that the Christian **evidences** are erroneous (1997, p. 20, emp. in orig.).

If **evidence** for God's existence has been set forth, the atheist has a responsibility (if he expects his world view to be considered seriously and accepted intellectually) to show **why** such evidence is not legitimate. After all, the Law of Rationality (one of the foundational laws of human thought) states that one should draw only those conclusions for which there is adequate and justifiable evidence. Indifference to such evidence—in light of the claim made by the atheist that God does not exist—could prove to be suicidal philosophically. The evidence just might document the theist's claim. And in the process, the atheist just might be proven wrong!

Second, in his book, *Dismissing God*, under the chapter heading, "When Disbelief Has Gone," Bruce Lockerbie rightly remarked:

> To **disbelieve** necessitates the possibility of a reasonable alternative, namely to **believe**. So "when disbelief has gone" means that the secular mind has passed even beyond this stage of contesting with Christian orthodoxy, no longer deigning to concern itself with the fantasies of faith (1998, p. 228, emp. in orig.).

While it may be the case that the modern-day unbeliever no longer deigns to concern himself with what he views as "fantasies of faith," such an attitude does nothing to address the evidence presented by the theist. Nor does indifference to the theist's evidence on the part of the atheist do anything to establish whatever type of unbelief the atheist wishes to recommend in its place. Lockerbie is correct: "To **disbelieve** necessitates the possibility of a reasonable alternative, namely to **believe**." Thus, the atheist shoulders two burdens: (1) to prove the theist's evidence is invalid; and (2) to establish—with attending evidence—a belief system that is a "reasonable alternative" worthy of acceptance by rational, thinking people.

Neither of these tasks is simple (nor, theists would suggest, possible). One problem that, by necessity, would have to be broached from the outset is this. For whatever reason(s), many atheists appear unwilling to consider the evidence in the first place. Robert

Gorham Davis is a retired professor of English at Harvard University who spends much of his time writing letters to the editor of the *New York Times* in order to take exception to any published reference to religion in that newspaper. In one such letter to the editor, he wrote:

> On no clear evidence theologians and philosophers declare God to be omniscient and omnicompetent. Plainly **if there were such a God who really wished to reveal Himself to mankind, He could do so in a way that left no doubt** (1992, emp. added).

That God **did** reveal Himself "in a way that left no doubt" is made clear from such evidence as: (1) the marvelous order and complexity of the macrocosm we call the Universe; (2) the intricate, delicately balanced nature of life; (3) the deliberate design inherent in the microcosm we know as the incomparable genetic code; (4) the astounding historical testimony attesting to the miracle-working Son of God; and (5) an otherwise unexplained (and unexplainable) empty tomb on a Sunday morning almost two thousand years ago. Each of these pieces of evidence (plus many more like them) helps form the warp and woof of the fabric whose purpose it is to document God's eternal existence.

That the atheist does not consider the evidence to be trustworthy or adequate to the task **does not negate the evidence**. A man's attitude toward the truth does not alter the truth. As Winfried Corduan stated in his book, *Reasonable Faith*:

> An argument, in order to be considered sound, must have true premises and valid logic. Because we think within the context of world views, someone may not be convinced by a perfectly sound argument. This is an everyday occurrence in all human reasoning and attempts at persuasion. **That is no fault of the argument**... (1993, p. 106, emp. added).

A good example of this point would be the late evolutionist and atheist, Isaac Asimov, who once admitted quite bluntly: "Emotionally, I am an atheist. I don't have the evidence to prove that God doesn't exist, but I so strongly suspect he doesn't that I don't want to waste my time" (1982, p. 9). Such a boast is easy enough to understand and requires no additional explanation. Yes, Dr. Asimov was indeed a committed atheist. However, he did not hold this view because he was able to offer legitimate reasons to justify his unbelief. Rather, his world view was an emotional response resulting from his personal freedom of choice. The fact remains that after everything is said and done, the atheist's first option—disproving the theist's evidence—is a difficult challenge that many choose not to accept.

What, then, about option number two—providing, with attending evidence, a belief system that is a "reasonable alternative"? That, too, apparently is beyond the pale of atheism. In 1989, Richard Dawkins, renowned atheist and evolutionist of Oxford University, authored a book by the title of *The Selfish Gene* in which he discussed at great length the gene's role in the naturalistic process of "survival of the fittest." Dawkins admitted that, according to the evolutionary paradigm, genes are "selfish" because they will do whatever it takes to ensure that the individual in which they are stored produces additional copies of the genes. In commenting on the effects of such a concept on society as a whole, Dr. Dawkins lamented: "My own feeling is that a human society based simply on the gene's law of universal ruthlessness **would be a very nasty society in which to live**" (1989b, p. 3, emp. added).

Michael Ruse, a Canadian philosopher, and Edward O. Wilson, a Harvard entomologist, had made the same point four years earlier when they wrote under the title of "Evolution and Ethics":

> Morality, or more strictly **our belief in morality, is merely an adaptation put in place to further our reproductive ends**.... Ethics is seen to have a solid foundation, not in divine guidance, but in the shared qualities of human nature and the desperate need for reciprocity (1985, 208:51-52, emp. added).

The eminent humanistic philosopher, Will Durant, went even further when he admitted:

> By offering evolution in place of God as a cause of history, Darwin removed the theological basis of the moral code of Christendom. And the moral code that has no fear of God is very shaky. That's the condition we are in.... I don't think man is capable yet of managing social order and individual decency without fear of some supernatural being overlooking him and able to punish him (1980).

Once again, the fact remains that after everything is said and done, the atheist's second option—providing, with attending evidence, a belief system that is a "reasonable alternative"—is an unattainable goal. Enter agnosticism.

Agnosticism

Perhaps the logical contradiction inherent in atheism (i.e., one would have to **be** God in order to **know** God does not exist) has caused many unbelievers to affirm agnosticism instead. The **agnostic** (*a*, without; *gnosis*, knowledge) is the person who says it is impossible to know if God exists, due to the fact that there simply is not enough credible evidence to warrant such a conclusion. Sproul has suggested that "the agnostic seeks to declare neutrality on the issue, desiring to make neither assertion nor denial of the theistic question.... The agnostic maintains that there is insufficient knowledge upon which to make an intellectual judgment about theism" (1978, pp. 19-20).

The term "agnostic" was coined by British scientist Thomas Henry Huxley, a close personal friend of Charles Darwin's and an indefatigable champion of evolution who frequently referred to himself as "Darwin's Bulldog" (see Leonard Huxley, 1903, 2:62). Huxley first introduced the word in a speech in 1869 before the Metaphysical Society, and later wrote of that occurrence:

> When I reached intellectual maturity and began to ask myself whether I was an atheist, a theist, or a pantheist; a materialist or an idealist; a Christian or a freethinker; I found that the more I learned and reflected, the less ready was the answer; until, at last, I came to the conclusion that I had nei-

> ther art nor part with any of these denominations, except the last. The one thing in which most of these good people were agreed was the one thing in which I differed from them. They were quite sure they had attained a certain "gnosis"—had, more or less successfully, solved the problem of existence; while I was quite sure I had not, and had a pretty strong conviction that the problem was insoluble....
>
> This was my situation when I had the good fortune to find a place among the members of that remarkable confraternity of antagonists, long since deceased, but of green and pious memory, the Metaphysical Society. Every variety of philosophical and theological opinion was represented there, and expressed itself with entire openness; most of my colleagues were *–ists* of one sort or another.... So I took thought, and invented what I conceived to be the appropriate title of "agnostic." It came into my head as suggestively antithetic to the "gnostic" of Church history, who professed to know so much about the very things of which I was ignorant; and I took the earliest opportunity of parading it at our Society.... To my great satisfaction, the term took.... This is the history of the origin of the terms "agnostic" and "agnosticism" (1894, pp. 239-240, italics in orig.).

Huxley cannot be accused of inventing the term "agnostic" in a cavalier fashion. Nor can he be accused of harboring a "hidden agenda." He knew exactly what he was doing, and went about doing it in a most public fashion. He spoke often to "working class folks," frequently presenting lunchtime lectures at factories. In a letter to a friend written on March 22, 1861, he remarked: "My working men stick by me wonderfully. By Friday evening they will all be convinced that they are monkeys" (see Leonard Huxley, 1900, 1: 205). He was passionate about referring to Charles Darwin as the "Newton of biology" (see Blinderman, 1957, p. 174) and did not hesitate to affirm that, so far as he was concerned,

> I really believe that the alternative is either Darwinism or nothing, for I do not know of any rational conception or theory of the organic universe which has any scientific position at all besides Mr. Darwin's.... Whatever may be the objections to his views, certainly all other theories are out of court (1896, p. 467).

Huxley worked diligently to convince those around him that agnosticism was a respectable philosophical position, and that it was quite **impossible** to know whether or not God existed. Yet he simultaneously advocated the position that it was quite **possible** to deny some theistic claims with certainty. He "knew," for example, that the Bible was not God's Word, and openly ridiculed anyone who believed it to be so. He heaped scathing rebukes upon those who believed in what he termed "the myths of Genesis," and he stated categorically that "my sole point is to get people who persist in regarding them as statements of fact to understand that they are fools" (see Leonard Huxley, 1900, 2:429).

That Huxley had in mind antagonistic views toward Judeo-Christian theism when he claimed to be "agnostic" has been made clear by those who would have no reason to be biased against him. For example, under the heading of "agnosticism," the authors of the British-produced *Encyclopaedia Britannica* wrote:

> Agnosticism both as a term and as a philosophical position gained currency through its espousal by Thomas Huxley, who seems to have coined the word "agnostic" (as opposed to "gnostic") in 1869 to designate one who repudiated traditional Judeo-Christian theism and yet disclaimed doctrinaire atheism, transcending both in order to leave such questions as the existence of God in abeyance.... But Huxley's own elaboration on the term **makes it clear that this very biblical interpretation of man's relation to God was the intended polemic target of agnosticism.** The suspension of judgment on ultimate questions for which it called was thought to **invalidate Christian beliefs** about "things hoped for" and "things not seen...." Huxley himself certainly rejected as outright false—rather than as not known to be true or false—many widely popular views about God, his providence, and man's posthumous destiny... (1997a, 1: 151; 1997b, 26:569, emp. added).

Rather than courageously embrace and defend atheism, Huxley opted to feign ignorance with his "I don't know, you don't know, nobody knows, and nobody **can** know" position. This cowardly compromise did not endear him to those who were quite willing to champion the more radical stance of apodictically affirming that God does not exist. In their discussion of agnosticism under the section on "religious and spiritual belief systems," the editors of *Encyclopaedia Britannica* noted that

> Huxley and his associates were attacked both by enthusiastic Christian polemicists and by Friedrich Engels, the co-worker of Karl Marx, as "shame-faced atheists," **a description that is perfectly applicable to many of those who nowadays adopt the more comfortable label** (1997b, 26:569, emp. added).

The fact is, the agnostic is far from indifferent. He takes his agnosticism extremely seriously when he affirms that nothing outside of the material world can be known or proved. But agnosticism is built upon a self-defeating premise. English philosopher Herbert Spencer (also a close personal friend of Charles Darwin, the man from whom Darwin borrowed his now-popular phrase, "survival of the fittest," and popularly regarded as one of the foremost apostles of agnosticism in his day) advocated the position that just as no bird ever has been able to fly out of the heavens, so no man ever has been able to penetrate with his finite mind the veil that hides the mind of the Infinite. This inability on the part of the finite (mankind), he concluded, prevented any knowledge of the Infinite (God) reaching the finite.

Such a premise is flawed internally because it wrongly assumes that the Infinite is equally incapable of penetrating the veil—a position that reduces the term "Infinite" to absurdity. An Infinite Being that is unable to express Itself is less finite than mortals who forever are expressing themselves. And an Infinite Being that is both capable of self-expression and aware of the perplexity and needs of mortal man, yet fails to break through the veil, is less moral than mortal man. As one writer expressed it:

> What **man** would stay in shrouded silence if he were the Infinite and knew that a word from him would resolve a thou-

> sand human complexes, integrate shattered personalities, mend broken lives, bring coveted light to baffled minds, and healing peace to disturbed hearts? (Samuel, 1950, p. 14, emp. added).

To be either correct or defensible, Spencer's proposition must work **both** ways. Finite man must be unable to penetrate the veil to the Infinite, but at the same time the Infinite likewise must be unable to penetrate the veil to the finite. By definition, however, the Infinite would possess the capability of breaking through any such veil.

Further, there is an important question that begs to be asked: Will the agnostic admit that it is at least **possible** for **someone else to know** something he does not? If he is unwilling to admit this point, is he not then attributing to himself (even if inadvertently) one of the defining characteristics that theists attribute to God—omniscience? In commenting on this very point, Nelson M. Smith wrote:

> Obviously, no agnostic can speak for anyone but himself and perhaps not then. What effort has he made to know God? Has he exhausted every effort to know God? Maybe he has not been as honest with himself and with the evidence as he ought to be? Maybe he is unconsciously hiding behind a screen of "can't know" to avoid responsibility as a being made in God's image of facing his Maker? (1975, 92 [6]:6).

Smith's point is well taken. Is it not possible that the agnostic is avoiding—purposely—the evidence for the existence of God? Rather than being **unable** to know, perhaps the agnostic is **unwilling** to know. Sir Hector Hetherington, principal emeritus of Glasgow University, addressed this concept when he said:

> There are issues on which it is impossible to be neutral. These issues strike right down to the roots of man's existence. And while it is right that we should examine the evidence, and make sure that we have all the evidence, it is equally right that **we ourselves should be accessible to the evidence** (as quoted in Samuel, 1950, p. 29, emp. added).

The agnostic is perfectly **capable** of making himself "accessible to the evidence." The question is—**will** he? Or will he choose instead to hide "behind a screen of 'can't know'"?

Skepticism

The **skeptic** is the person who doubts there is a God. The standard dictionary definition is quite revealing when it describes a skeptic as one who holds to "the doctrine that true knowledge or knowledge in a particular area is uncertain and who has doubts concerning basic religious principles." Notice that the skeptic does not claim knowledge of God's existence is **unattainable** (as in agnosticism), but only "uncertain." However, the skeptic does not stop at mere "uncertainty." In fact, skepticism "...confidently challenges not merely religious or metaphysical knowledge but **all** knowledge claims that venture beyond immediate experience" (*Encyclopaedia Britannica*, 1997b, 26:569, emp. added). The key words here are "**immediate experience**."

Translated into common parlance, this simply means that the skeptic is not prepared to accept **anything** that cannot be verified empirically (viz., via the scientific method). Corliss Lamont, famous twentieth-century skeptic and humanist, wrote:

> The development, over the past four centuries, of a universally reliable method for attaining knowledge is a far more important achievement on the part of science than its discovery of any single truth. For once men acquire a thoroughly dependable **method** of truth-seeking, a method that can be applied to every sphere of human life and by anyone who faithfully conforms to certain directives, then they have as a permanent possession an instrument of infinite power that will serve them as long as mankind endures. Scientific method is such an instrument (1949, pp. 236-237, emp. in orig.)

Paul Kurtz, another well-known skeptic and former editor of *The Humanist* (official organ of the American Humanist Association), put it like this:

> To adopt such a scientific approach unreservedly is to accept as **ultimate in all matters of fact and real existence the appeal to the evidence of experience alone; a court subordinate to no higher authority**, to be overridden by no prejudice however comfortable (1973, p. 109, emp. added).

Chet Raymo, in his book, *Skeptics and True Believers*, explained the dichotomy that exists between "Skeptics" and "True Believers" (capital letters are used throughout his book). Raymo, professor of physics and astronomy at Stonehill College in Massachusetts, has written a weekly column on science for the *Boston Globe* for more than a dozen years and was reared as a Roman Catholic. He began his book by suggesting that *Skeptics and True Believers* operate by different "made-up maps of the world." In chapter one he stated:

> We cannot live without some sorts of make-believe in our lives. Without made-up maps of the world, life is a blooming, buzzing confusion. Some elements of our mental maps (Santa Claus...) satisfy emotional or aesthetic **inner needs**; other elements of our mental maps (hot stove, nuclear-powered stars) satisfy intellectual curiosity about the world **out there**. We get in trouble when the two kinds of maps are confused, when we objectify elements of make-believe solely on the basis of inner need.
>
> The True Believer retains in adulthood an absolute faith in some forms of empirically unverifiable make-believe (such as astrology or the existence of immortal souls), whereas the Skeptic keeps a wary eye on firmly established facts (such as atoms). Both Skeptic and True Believer use made-up maps of the world... (1998, pp. 13-14, emp. in orig.).

Raymo then went on to ask:

> Is one map as good as any other? Since all knowledge is constructed, can the choice between two contradictory maps ...be a matter of personal or political expediency? Not unless we are willing to erect partitions between what we **know to be true on the basis of unambiguous, reproducible evidence** and what we merely **wish to be true**.

> Apparently, many of us are willing to do just that (1998, p. 14, emp. added).

With his strict dichotomy between the Skeptic (a person who **knows** about such things as atoms and nuclear-powered stars—"on the basis of unambiguous, reproducible evidence") and the True Believer (a person who **believes** in such things as Santa Claus, astrology, and an immortal soul—in spite of the evidence) firmly in place, Raymo then spent the remainder of his book laying out the Skeptic's case against: (a) the existence of God; (b) the Genesis account of creation; (c) the occurrence of biblical miracles; (d) etc. Eventually, however, he was forced to admit:

> The forces that nudge us toward True Belief are pervasive and well-nigh irresistible. Supernatural faith systems provide a degree of emotional security that skepticism cannot provide. Who among us would **not** prefer that there exists a divine parent who has our best interest at heart? Who among us would **not** prefer to believe that we will live forever? Skepticism, on the other hand, offers only uncertainty and doubt.... Science cannot rule out heaven and hell because they are beyond the reach of empirical investigation (1998, pp. 5,77, emp. in orig.).

Thus, in the end the skeptic does not say he **cannot** know that God exists. Rather, he says he **doubts** that God exists because He cannot be seen, felt, measured, weighed, or probed by the scientific method. Thirty-four years before Chet Raymo wrote about "Skeptics and True Believers," George Gaylord Simpson, the late evolutionist of Harvard, wrote: "It is inherent in any definition of science that statements that cannot be checked by observation are not really saying anything..." (1964, p. 769). Simply put, the point is this: If science cannot deal with something, that "something" either does not exist (worst-case scenario) or is completely unimportant (best-case scenario). Welcome to the make-believe world of the skeptic in which science reigns supreme and a cavalier attitude toward all things non-empirical rules the day.

But what about those concepts that, although non-empirical and therefore unobservable via the scientific method, nevertheless are recognized to exist, and are admitted to be of critical importance to the entire human race—concepts like love, sorrow, joy, altruism, etc.? Arlie Hoover accurately assessed the situation in which the skeptic finds himself in regard to the existence of such items when he wrote:

> Why does the scientific method reject subjective factors, emotions, feelings? Simply because it is not convenient! Because the method will not allow you to deal with the immense complexity of reality. The scientist, therefore, selects from the whole of experience only those elements that can be weighed, measured, numbered, or which lend themselves to mathematical treatment....
>
> This is a fallacy we call **Reductionism**. You commit the Reductive Fallacy when you select a portion of a complex entity and say the whole is merely that portion. You do this when you say things like: love is nothing but sex, man is just an animal, music is nothing but sound waves, art is nothing but color.... When it gets down to the real serious questions of life—origin, purpose, destiny, meaning, morality—science is silent....
>
> If science can't handle morality, aesthetics, and religion that only proves that the scientific method was reductive in the first place. Sir Arthur Eddington once used a famous analogy to illustrate this reductionism. He told of a fisherman who concluded from his fishing experiences with a certain net that "no creature of the sea is less than two inches long." Now this disturbed many of his colleagues and they demurred, pointing out that many sea creatures are under two inches and they just slipped through the two-inch holes in the net. But the ichthyologist was unmoved: "What my net can't catch ain't fish," he pontificated, and then he scornfully accused his critics of having pre-scientific, medieval, metaphysical prejudices.
>
> Scientific reductionism or "Scientism"—as it is often called—is similar to this fisherman with the special net. Since the strict empirical scientist can't "catch" or "grasp" such qualitative things like freedom, morality, aesthetics, mind, and

> God, he concludes that they don't exist. But they have just slipped through his net. They have been slipping through his net all the way from Democritus to B.F. Skinner to Carl Sagan (1981, p. 6, emp. in orig.).

In speaking of skepticism and its offspring of humanism, Sir Julian Huxley wrote: "It will have **nothing to do with absolutes**, including absolute truth, absolute morality, absolute perfection and absolute authority" (1964, pp. 73-74, emp. added). To that list, one might add absolute joy, absolute love, absolute freedom, absolute peace, etc. The skeptic has paid a high price for his scientism —the rejection and abandonment of some of the human race's most important, valuable, worthwhile, and cherished, concepts. Why? In order to be able to say: I **doubt** that God exists!

Infidelity

The **infidel** is the person who not only refuses to believe in God himself, but also is intolerant of, and actively opposed to, those who do. A study of human history provides a veritable plethora of men and women who made quite a name for themselves via their public display of infidelity. In the third century A.D., for example, Porphyry wrote a fifteen-volume series (*Against Christians*) in which he sought to lay bare alleged contradictions between the Old and New Testaments and to document how the apostles had contradicted themselves. He excoriated the book of Daniel, and charged Jesus with equivocation and inconsistency. He was recognized widely as one of the most celebrated enemies of God the world ever has known. McClintock and Strong have suggested that he "...became the most determined of heathen polemics the world ever beheld or Christianity ever encountered" (1879, 8:422).

Another infidel of the ancient past whose name is associated with vitriolic opposition to God was the Frenchman Voltaire. Beginning in 1765, he attacked Christianity with viciousness and vigor. He began with what today would be styled "higher criticism," by which he brought into question the authenticity and reliability of the Bible. He then alleged chronological contradictions in the narratives of the Old Testament. He challenged as incorrect many of the messianic prophecies of the Old Testament, and he stoutly denied any such things as miracles and the efficacy of prayer. He once boasted: "It took 12 men to originate the Christian religion, but it will take but one to eliminate it. Within fifty years from now the only Bible will be in museums" (as quoted in Key, 1982, 21[12]: 2). [Interestingly, not long after his death, the Geneva Bible Society purchased Voltaire's house and used his printing presses to print French New Testaments.]

David Hume, born in 1711 in Scotland, attacked the idea of the immortality of the soul and placed the origin of religion on par with the existence of things like elves and fairies. But no doubt he is most famous for his essay, "Of Miracles," which was tucked away in his work, *Enquiry Concerning Human Understanding*, published in 1748. The essay itself consisted of scarcely more than 20 pages, but concluded that from what we know about the laws of nature a miracle simply cannot occur. The treatise went on to suggest that historical testimony regarding miracles is specious, and never could be strong enough to override more important scientific considerations. For Hume, there was **no** evidence strong enough to prove that miracles actually had taken place. His attack upon biblical miracles had serious consequences upon religion generally, and Christianity specifically. Even today many refuse to believe in God because of David Hume's arguments.

One of Christianity's most ardent opponents in the 1800s was Joseph Ernest Renan. Born in 1823, he was a French historian who rejected any supernatural content in religion. In 1860, he wrote *The Life of Jesus*, in which he repudiated all supernatural elements in Christ's life and ministry. The book was a frontal assault upon the personal deity of Christ and received much attention throughout Europe, assuring Renan of instant fame. He subsequently authored a book on the apostle Paul, as well as a five-volume set on the history of Israel. Today, his place in history as an infidel has been guaranteed as a direct result of his strident attacks upon Jesus.

In more recent times, one of the most vicious attacks upon God, Christ, and the Bible was spearheaded by Robert Ingersoll. Born in Dresden, New York in 1833, he set up his law practice in Peoria, Illinois in 1858, and eventually was appointed as that state's Attorney General. The late Madalyn Murray O'Hair, while still director of American Atheists in Austin, Texas, once characterized Ingersoll as "a superb egotist. And, he engaged in more than one drunken public brawl.... Not withstanding all of the anomalies of his character, he was magnificent when he did get going on either religion or the church..." (1983, p. vi).

In *The Atheist Syndrome*, John Koster has suggested concerning Ingersoll that "what he hated was organized religion" (1989, p. 123). Shortly after Ingersoll went on the lecture circuit around 1877, he began to include in his repertoire such topics as "Heretics and Heresies" and "Ghosts"—both of which were undisguised attacks upon religion generally and Christianity specifically. By 1878, he had expanded his lectures to include "Hell" and "Some Mistakes of Moses," both of which were favorites of atheists of his day. He died in 1899, having established his reputation both as an atheist and an influential infidel.

John Dewey was born in Vermont in 1859. He completed a doctorate at Johns Hopkins and in 1884 began teaching at the University of Michigan. In 1894, he was appointed chairman of the department of philosophy, psychology, and education at the University of Chicago. In 1904, he left Chicago and moved to Columbia University where he remained until his retirement in 1930. More than any other individual before or since, Dewey's views have altered American educational processes. Durant wrote: "There is hardly a school in America that has not felt his influence" (1961, p. 390). Why did he have such an impact? Durant went on to explain:

> What separates Dewey is the undisguised completeness with which he accepts the evolution theory. Mind as well as body is to him an organ evolved, in the struggle for existence, from lower forms. His starting point in every field is Darwinian.... Things are to be explained, then, not by supernatural causation, but by their place and function in the environment. Dewey is frankly naturalistic... (1961, p. 391).

Dewey was a prolific writer, and eventually authored *A Common Faith* in which he discussed religion (and in which his infidelity was brought into full view). He made it clear that "he wished at all costs to be scientific; for him the processes of science are the most obvious and the most successful methods of knowing. Therefore if science neglects something, the something is nothing" (Clark, 1957, p. 519). Because he viewed religion as "unscientific," he thus considered it to be "nothing," which was why he vehemently opposed religion of any kind and insisted upon the teaching of organic evolution as fact, not theory. In his writings he stressed that "moral laws" were neither absolute nor inviolable and unabashedly advocated situation ethics.

Dewey died in 1952, having altered forever the landscape of American education and having ensured his reputation as one of the chief infidels of the twentieth century. Had he lived a few years longer, he would have seen his ideas on the naturalistic origin and basis of all things take hold in a way that perhaps even he never dreamed.

Madalyn Murray O'Hair was the most famous atheist/infidel in America for more than three-and-a-half decades. Her public saga began in 1963 when a suit to remove prayer from public schools was heard before the United States Supreme Court. Although the suit (in which Mrs. O'Hair was only a secondary litigant) originally had been filed in the name of Philadelphia Unitarian, Ed Schempp, she took over the battle and ultimately was victorious in the landmark decision of *Murray v. Curlett*. A writer in *Time* magazine once described her as

> ...a heavy woman with a strong voice and a jaw who even in repose resembled, as author Lawrence Wright once observed, "a bowling ball looking for new pins to scatter." She was an Army veteran and a law-school graduate and a big talker. Most important, she was an atheist.... "I love a good fight," she said. "I guess fighting God and God's spokesmen is sort of the ultimate, isn't it?" (Van Biema, 1997, pp. 56, 57).

She was the star of the first episode of Phil Donahue's television talk show. She filed lawsuits at what one journalist called "a near pathological level of pugnacity" for 32 years (Van Biema, 1997, p. 57). And once, while watching a female orangutan on television, she quipped, "The Virgin just made another appearance" (as quoted in Van Biema, p. 57).

In 1965, having worn out her welcome with state and local authorities in Maryland and Hawaii, she settled in Austin, Texas and formed the Society of Separationists, later adding the Atheist Centre in America and several other satellite groups. In the 1980s, she enjoyed a heyday as she ruled over her pet project that came to be known simply as "American Atheists," from which she published her pratings against God via books, posters, and bumper stickers (e.g., "Apes Evolved From Creationists"). She would debate anyone, anywhere, anytime on the existence of God and the "atrocities" of organized religion.

In fact, in the late 1970s, while I was serving as a professor in the College of Veterinary Medicine at Texas A&M University, I attended a debate she conducted with Bob Harrington, a denominational preacher from New Orleans known popularly as "the chaplain of Bourbon Street." Mrs. O'Hair was (and I say this not in any derogatory sense, but only from personal observation as a member of the audience) unkempt, haggard, slovenly, and bitter. During the course of the debate, she cursed wildly (frequently taking God's name in vain), belittled the audience for its "obvious" lack of intelligence, and mocked her opponent. She was on the lookout for, and seized, every possible opportunity to berate God and anyone who, in her considered opinion, was "stupid enough" to believe in Him. Little wonder that in 1964 *Life Magazine* headlined her as "the most hated woman in America." Bruce Lockerbie wrote regarding Mrs. O'Hair:

> When we begin to speak of O'Hair and others like her, we turn directly into the face of aggressively militant **disbelief**. Here is no lady-like apologist, no grandmotherly disputant; for O'Hair, the cause is nothing short of all-out war (1998, p. 231).

Then suddenly, without warning, she disappeared—vanished without a trace. On August 28, 1995 workers at the American Atheists building came to work, only to find a note taped to the front door that read: "We've been called out on an emergency basis, and we'll call you when we get back." But she (along with her son Jon and his daughter Robin who disappeared with her) never did call and never has been back. Curiously, about the same time over $600,000 turned up missing from the treasury of American Atheists. In 1995, tax forms submitted by the United Secularists of America (one of American Atheists' satellite groups) documented a $612,000 decrease in net assets and admitted:

> The $612,000...represents the value of the United Secularists of America's assets believed to be in the possession of Jon Murray, former Secretary. The whereabouts of Jon Murray and these assets have not been known since September 1995 and is not known to the organization at this time (as quoted in Van Biema, 1997, p. 59).

[In April 1999, Ron Barrier, national spokesman for American Atheists, announced that the group was moving its headquarters from Austin, Texas to Cranford, New Jersey, stating that "the Northeast is much more progressive than the South..." (*Montgomery Advertiser*, 1999, D-3). On Sunday, April 4, 1999 a dedication ceremony was held for the new offices in Cranford. Late in 1999, police indicted one of Mrs. O'Hair's co-workers, charging him with foul play in connection with her disappearance. That case was pending before the courts as this book went to press.]

It can be said without fear of contradiction that "the most hated woman in America"—who had made it her life's goal to oppose God—did not live **up** to anyone's expectations, but undeniably lived **down** to the level of her self-professed atheism. The history of infidelity, only a brief overview of which I have examined here, documents all too well that she has not been alone. In his novel, *The Brothers Karamazov*, Russian novelist Fyodor Dostoyevsky had one of his characters, Ivan, comment that if there is no God, everything is permitted. French atheist and existential philosopher, Jean Paul Sartre, opined:

> Everything is indeed permitted if God does not exist, and man is in consequence forlorn, for he cannot find anything to depend upon either within or outside himself.... Nor, on the other hand, if God does not exist, are we provided with any values or commands that could legitimize our behavior (1961, p. 485).

As essayist G.K. Chesterton once observed: "When men cease to believe in God, they do not believe in **nothing**; they believe in **anything**" (as quoted in Bales, 1967, p. 133, emp. added).

CHAPTER 2

THE MANY FACES OF UNBELIEF [PART II]

Deism

The concept of deism (from the Latin *deus*, god) had its beginnings among writers in seventeenth-century England, beginning with Edward Herbert (1581-1648) who later became the first Baron Herbert of Cherbury and who often is recognized as the "father of deism." In his 1624 book, *De Veritate* (*On Truth*), Lord Herbert laid out five basic principles of deism: "(1) The being of God; (2) that he is to be worshipped; (3) that piety and moral virtue are the chief parts of worship; (4) that God will pardon our faults on repentance; and, (5) that there is a future state of rewards and punishment" (see McClintock and Strong, 1879, 2:730). In the second edition of that work (1645), Herbert expanded his ideas as he dealt with the foundations of religion and critiqued the idea of direct revelation from God. That same year, he further elaborated his views in the book, *De Causis Errorum* (*Concerning the Causes of Errors*). An additional work, *De Religione Gentilium* (*The Religion of the Gentiles*) was published posthumously in 1663. He urged a quick and permanent abandonment of the idea that God intervened supernaturally in man's world in any way.

Herbert's views were propagated by a number of influential British writers such as his chief disciple, Charles Blount (1654-1693), Anthony Collins (1676-1729), Thomas Woolston (1670-1731), Matthew Tindal (1655-1733), and Peter Annet (1693-1769), who was the last of the old-line British deists. In the eighteenth century, deism flourished in France. In fact, "English deism strongly influenced later French deism and skepticism, of which Diderot and Voltaire are notable examples" (Geisler, 1976, p. 165). Shortly thereafter, deism spread to Germany and held sway in Europe for a hundred years. Norman Geisler has added:

> Along the way there were many philosophical figures who may not technically qualify as deists but who nonetheless gave impetus to and provided arguments for the movement. Bacon's scientific approach, John Locke's empiricism, and David Hume's skepticism about miracles definitely aided the deistic cause (1976, p. 152).

Eventually deism spread to early colonial America as well. The editors of *Encyclopaedia Britannica* noted:

> By the end of the 18th century, Deism had become a dominant religious attitude among intellectual and upper class Americans.... The first three presidents of the United States also held deistic convictions, as is amply evidenced in their correspondence (1997b, 26:569).

The evidence sustains such an assessment.

> In America deism flourished after it had declined in England. Thomas Jefferson, Benjamin Franklin, and Thomas Paine are classed as deists.... Perhaps more than anywhere else in the United States, deistic tendencies of naturalism and Biblical criticism have lived on in modernistic or liberal Protestantism... (Geisler, 1976, pp. 165-166).

But why was such a system necessary? Basically deism came into existence as men attempted to work around the contradictions and internal inconsistencies posed by atheism and agnosticism. The atheist was unable to disprove God's existence, and the agnostic was forced to admit that while **he** might not be able to **know** that God exists, someone else certainly might possess such knowledge. Enter deism.

> The best way out of the dilemmas posed by atheism and agnosticism would appear to be the following: let us say that there is a God. This God created the world. He issued to the world a moral law, a code of behavior which all of His creatures are supposed to follow. God will someday judge His creatures on how well they obeyed His commandments. In the meantime He does not interfere with His creation. He made it the way He wanted it to be, and He will not contradict His own will. For the moment, we worship God and try to live by His law, but we must not expect Him to do supernatural things for us (Corduan, 1993, p. 90).

What, then, are the exact tenets of deism? Truth be told, at times those tenets are not at all easy to decipher.

> In the late seventeenth and in the eighteenth century more than a few thinkers came to be called deists or called themselves deists. These men held a number of related views, but not all held every doctrine in common. John Locke, for example, did not reject the idea of revelation, but he did insist that human reason was to be used to judge it. Some deists, like Voltaire, were hostile to Christianity; some, like Locke, were not. Some believed in the immortality of the soul; some did not. Some believed God left his creation to function on its own; some believed in providence. Some believed in a personal God; others did not. So deists were much less united on basic issues than were theists (Sire, 1988, p. 50).

By way of summary, however, it may be said that the **deist** begrudgingly acknowledges that God exists, and even grants that God created the Universe and its inhabitants. But deism insists that since His initial miraculous act of creation, God has had nothing whatsoever to do with either the Universe or mankind. As the editors of *Encyclopaedia Britannica* have observed:

> At times in the 19th and 20th centuries, the word Deism was used theologically in contradistinction to theism, the belief in an immanent God who actively intervenes in the affairs of men. In this sense Deism was represented as the view of those who reduced the role of God to a mere act of creation in accordance with rational laws discovered by man and held that, after the original act, God virtually withdrew and refrained from interfering in the processes of nature and the ways of man (1997b, 26:567).

The basic idea behind deism often is discussed and clarified via the analogy of a clock, the idea being that God created the clock, wound it up, and then walked away to leave it operating on its own. In his book, *The Universe Next Door*, James W. Sire titled his chapter on deism, "The Clockwork Universe," and commented that according to the deist "God is thus not immanent, not fully personal, not sovereign over human affairs, not providential.... God is not interested in individual men and women or even whole peoples" (1988, pp. 50,56). The God of deism therefore has been called a "hermit God" (Dickson, 1979, 121[8]:118), an "absentee landlord" (Brown, 1984, p. 47), and a "God in absentia" (Coats, 1989, p. 61). The deist's position is not that God **cannot** perform miracles; rather it is that God **will not** perform miracles because "according to deism, it is contrary to God's nature to do miracles.... In deism God and the supernatural are considered to be incompatible" (Corduan, 1993, p. 91).

Such a position inevitably leads to the following. First, deism rejects both the triune nature of the Godhead and the deity of Christ. Geisler and Brooks assessed the matter by suggesting that deists

> ...believe that God never specially intervenes in the world to help mankind. Since this also means that Jesus was not God (that would be a miracle), there is no reason for them to believe that God is a Trinity. The idea of three Persons in one nature (the Trinity) is to them just bad math (1990, p. 40; parenthetical comments in orig.).

Or, as Hoover has noted: "Deists believed in a Supreme Being, but he was only one in number. They denied the doctrines of Trinity and Incarnation. Jesus Christ was merely a great moral teacher" (1976, p. 12). Thus, the deist denies "any supernatural redemptive act in history" (Harrison, 1966, p. 162).

Second, deism rejects the idea that God has given a special revelation of Himself in the Bible. For God to reveal Himself by speaking directly to man would be a miracle—an intervention into man's world. This is something the deist is not prepared to accept. Observation of the general revelation that God has left of Himself in nature, says the deist, is sufficient for understanding the Creator and His desires for mankind.

> What did a typical deist deny? In one word: **intervention**.... God didn't need to reveal anything about himself in a holy book like the Bible or the Koran. Nature itself is the only revelation God needs. A rational man could find out all that he needed to know about God from nature... (Hoover, 1976, p. 13, emp. in orig.).

In summarizing the aversion of the deist to the miraculous, Roger Dickson noted that "the principle point of concern here is the deist's denial of the inspiration of the Bible and miracles. If God does not intervene in the natural world, then both are impossible" (1979, p. 118).

Third, deism advocates that human reason alone is all man needs to understand God and His laws for humankind.

> Deism...refers to what can be called natural religion, the acceptance of a certain body of religious knowledge that is inborn in every person or that can be acquired by the use of reason, as opposed to knowledge acquired through either revelation or the teaching of any church... (*Encyclopaedia Britannica,1997b, 26:567*).

Sir Peter Medawar put it this way: "The 17th-century doctrine of the **necessity** of reason was slowly giving way to a belief in the **sufficiency** of reason" (1969, p. 438). Without special revelation from God (a miracle), deism had no choice but to advocate that **reason alone was sufficient**.

Fourth, deism rejects the notions of a prayer-hearing/prayer-answering God and a God Who works in men's lives through divine providence. As Hoover observed: "If you deny revelation you must also sweep out miracle, prayer, and providence. **Any** tampering with nature and her perfect laws would imply that nature had a defect" (1976, p. 13, emp. in orig.). Coats lamented:

> With his concept of God, there is no possible way for the deist to believe in the providence of God. Since God has taken a long journey and is "**at rest**," He leaves the affairs of men and nations to tick alone, as would the pendulum of a clock. There is no reason to pray to a deistic god for the system is completely fatalistic (1989, p. 61, emp. in orig.).

What response may be offered to deism? First, deism's flawed view of God's inability to work miracles must be addressed. Corduan has reasoned as follows:

> Now we can see that deism is actually irrational.... If God can perform the miracle of creation, there is no good reason why He cannot do other miracles. Thus deism has an inconsistency at its core. Two affirmations are at the heart of deism: (1) God performed the miracle of creation; and (2) God does not perform miracles. If you are a deist, you must believe both of them, and yet these affirmations cannot both be true. Therefore deism is not a believable worldview. It founders on the criterion of consistency (1993, pp. 91-92).

In speaking to this same point, Geisler added:

> Since God performed the miracle of creation *ex nihilo* (from nothing), it follows from the very nature and power of this kind of God that other lesser miracle are possible. Walking on water is little problem for a God who created water to begin with. To make a human through a female ovum (virgin birth) is not difficult for a God who made a world from nothing. And multiplying loaves is surely not a greater feat than creating matter in the first place. In short, it is self-defeating to admit the miracle of creation and to deny that other miracles are possible (1976, p. 169; parenthetical comments in orig.).

Second, if the deist believes supernatural Creation occurred, he cannot deny the only divine source of knowledge concerning that Creation—special revelation.

> The deistic arguments intended to eliminate the basis for belief in a supernatural revelation apply equally as well to elimination of the deistic belief in creation.... If the Bible cannot be trusted to teach one doctrine then there is no grounds for believing the other one is true.... Hence, the deist defeats his own case against revelation when he accepts from revelation the doctrine of creation (Geisler, 1976, p. 170).

Third, since God created the laws of the Universe, and since those laws are contingent upon God for their very existence, there is no good reason why an omnipotent God could not supersede those laws for the benefit of mankind. Furthermore, would not a God concerned enough to create humans likewise be concerned enough to intervene on their behalf on occasion—especially if they had fallen into grave (spiritual) danger? Geisler has suggested:

> "You have made your own bed, lie in it" is something less than the attitude a good Creator ought to have. If he had enough love and concern for man to create him, then it would seem to be most compatible with such a nature to believe that God would miraculously intervene to help him if he were in need. And surely a God strong enough to create the world is strong enough to help it. The laws of creation are not inviolable; they are created and contingent. And what is created and contingent can be laid aside if need be for the moral good of man. Hence, the nature of God, even as conceived by deists, would be compatible with miraculous intervention into the natural world when the situation calls for it (1976, p. 170).

As Corduan has said: "God is not just a disinterested spectator, but He is deeply interested in the moral progress His creatures are making" (1993, p. 90). God is not merely a "Master Universe Mechanic." He also is personal—a concept even deists accept. Is it not reasonable, then, to suggest that this personal Creator would desire communication between Himself and His creation—especially if the creation had been made "in His image"? Geisler has remarked:

> Miraculous commerce between the personal Creator and the persons created would not only be possible, it would seem to be most probable. If the desire to have personal communication between the supernatural and the natural realm flows from God as personal, then not to perform miracles of personal communication (viz., revelation) would show God to be something less than perfectly personal. It is inconsistent to disallow a personal communication from the supernatural realm to the natural realm once one has admitted God is personal (1976, p. 170).

Fourth, the idea that human reason alone is an adequate guide for mankind, and that the "natural world" can provide him with all that he needs to know in regard to behavior, ethics, response to God, etc., is severely flawed. Hoover noted:

> Deistic thinkers seldom agree on what God is like, even though he is supposed to be the same to all minds who simply reason properly. If you don't believe me, try it for yourself. Compare the Gods of (say) Aristotle, Spinoza, and Tom Paine. You'll be depressed at the different pictures of God that reason alone comes up with in different men! (1976, pp. 14-15, parenthetical item in orig.).

When man exalts "reason alone" as the final standard, and limits his knowledge of God to whatever he can discern from the natural world around him, he is destined to fail. As Sire has explained:

> In some ways, we can say that limiting knowledge about God to general revelation is like finding that eating eggs for breakfast makes the morning go well—and then eating **only** eggs for breakfast (and maybe lunch and dinner too) for the rest of one's life (which now unwittingly becomes rather shortened!). To be sure theism assumes that we can know something about God from nature. But it also holds that there is much **more to know** than can be known that way and that there are **other ways to know** (1988, pp. 49-50, emp. and parenthetical comments in orig.).

Consider such an admonition as it relates to the deist's belief that human ethics and morals may be fashioned by mere "reason alone" based on the "natural world." Hoover has commented:

> Especially puerile was the deistic belief that you could establish an ethical code by mere reason based only on nature. Which part of nature do we consult for this moral standard? What animal gives us the norm? Some spiders eat their mate after sexual intercourse—should we humans imitate this example? If not, which animal shall we follow? (1976, p. 14).

If, according to deism, the Universe is both normal and perfect, and nature is God's complete revelation of Himself, then obviously both would reveal what is right. This leads inevitably to the position that

> ...God, being the omnipotent Creator, becomes responsible **for everything as it is**. This world must then reflect either what God wants or what he is like. Ethically, this leads to the position expressed by Alexander Pope [in volume one, line 294 of his work, *Essay on Man*—BT]: "One truth is clear, **whatever is, is right**." This position really ends in destroying ethics. If whatever is, is right, then there is no evil. Good becomes indistinguishable from evil.... Or, worse luck, there must be no **good** at all. For without the ability to dis tinguish, there can be neither one nor the other, neither good nor evil. Ethics disappears (Sire, 1988, pp. 54-55, first emp. added, last two in orig.).

Fifth, deism became the easily crossed bridge from theism to out-and-out naturalism—the view that there is no God and that "nature" is all that exists. Sire summed up this fact when he wrote:

> Deism did not prove to be a very stable world view. Historically it held sway over the intellectual world of France and England briefly from the late seventeenth into the first half of the eighteenth century. **Preceded by theism, it was followed by naturalism** (1988, pp. 56-57, emp. added).

Roger Dickson has pointed out that for many of its adherents, "deism was the first step toward naturalism" (1979, 121[8]:118). In his monumental work, *Does God Exist?*, Hans Kung summarized the situation as follows:

> This Deism, not accepted by theology, which still needed God in the physical world...now developed consistently into a **scientific atheism**, which did not need God either physically for the explanation of the world or even morally for the conduct of life (1980, p. 91, emp. in orig.).

Today, it is rare to find a genuine deist. I mention the concept here, however, not merely from a historical perspective, but also to document the end result of accepting it. As Kung poignantly noted, deism "developed consistently into a **scientific atheism**, which did not need God."

Pantheism

In the above section on deism, Hans Kung observed that eventually deism led to scientific atheism. However, he also noted that it did not necessarily follow a direct path. He went on to say:

> Almost imperceptibly, over a long period, a significant change had come about in the intellectual climate and with it also a change in the understanding of God: **away from the deism of the Enlightenment to a basically pantheistic attitude** (1980, p. 133, emp. in orig.).

I now would like to discuss the concept of pantheism in this context.

Both theists and deists hold to a view which suggests that God is "out there." In other words, He is **transcendent**—i.e., beyond the world. Pantheism (*pan*, all; *theos*, God), on the other hand, teaches that God is "in here." He is not in the least transcendent, but merely **immanent**—i.e., in the world. Put in the bluntest possible terms, "God and the world are so closely intertwined that you cannot tell them apart" (Corduan, 1993, p. 92). The central tenet of pantheism is that all is God and God is all. The seventeenth-century philosopher, Baruch Spinoza (1632-1677), was an outspoken advocate of the concept. In commenting on Spinoza's influence in this regard, Kung wrote:

> Spinoza's God does not live apart from the universe: God is in the world and the world is in God. Nature is a particular way in which God himself exists; human consciousness is a particular way in which God himself thinks. The individual self and all finite things are not autonomous substances but only modifications of the **one and only divine substance.** God, then, all in all—[is] a purely immanent, not a transcendent God (1980, p. 133, emp. in orig.).

While pantheism long has been associated with eastern religions such as Hinduism, Taoism, and some forms of Buddhism, in recent years it has made serious inroads into western thinking, as is evident from the teachings of the Christian Science religion, Scientology, and certain others. Its best-known public forum today is the teachings of the New Age movement, most noticeably the writings of Oscar-winning actress, Shirley MacLaine. In her book, *Out on a Limb*, she told of her discussions with a friend by the name of Kevin Ryerson who allegedly was able to "channel" John—a disembodied spirit from the days of Jesus' earthly sojourn. Once, when Ms. MacLaine was speaking with "John," he allegedly said to her: "[Y]our soul is a metaphor for God.... **You** are God. **You** know you are divine" (1983, pp. 209, emp. in orig.). In addressing what she refers to as her "higher self" in her book, *Dancing in the Light*, MacLaine said: "**I am God**, because all energy is plugged in to the same source. We are each aspects of that source. We are all part of God. We are individualized reflections of the God source. God is us and we are God" (1991, p. 339, emp. added). In her 1989 book, *Going Within*, she wrote: "I, for example, do a silent mantra with each of my hatha yoga poses. I hold each yoga position for twenty seconds and internally chant, 'I am God in Light'" (1989, p. 57).

In the book he authored refuting MacLaine's views, *Out on a Broken Limb*, lawyer F. LaGard Smith stated:

> The heart and soul of the New Age movement, which Ms. MacLaine embraces along with her reincarnation ideas, is nothing less than **self-deification**.... But it really shouldn't be all that surprising. All we had to do was put the equation together: We are One; God is One; therefore, we are God. The cosmic conjugation is: I am God, you are God, we are God.... Surely if someone tells herself repeatedly that she is God, it won't be long before she actually believes it! (1986, pp. 178,179-180,181, emp. in orig.).

In trying to comprehend the thinking behind such concepts, it is essential to understand that although pantheism sounds like a theory about the cosmos, actually it is a theory about self—the individual human being. Since each individual is a part of the Universe, since God is "in" the Universe and the Universe is "in" God, and since each individual shares the "divine nature" of the Universe, each individual **is God**. When Shirley MacLaine stands on the sands of the beach and yells out loud, "I am God" (1983), she literally means just what she says!

There are different varieties of pantheism, to be sure. In his book, *Christian Apologetics*, Norman Geisler has devoted an entire chapter to a discussion of these variants (1976, pp. 173-192).

But perhaps one of the most important threads running through each is the identification of God with the world. Winfried Corduan addressed this topic when he observed:

> In this worldview, God and the world are identical, not just in the sense of identical twins, who merely resemble each other strongly, but in the sense of being one and the same thing. The words "world" and "God" are then used as two different expressions for one thing (1993, p. 92).

Think about the implications of such a view. If pantheism is correct, then there no longer is a need for we humans to "look beyond ourselves" for solutions to whatever problems it is that plague us. Instead, we simply may "look within." We, being God, are our own source of truth. We, being God, can decide what is right and what is wrong. All the power that we need to cope with life and its vagaries lies within the untapped reservoir of human potential we call "self."

Sounds good—at first glance. But carry this kind of thinking to its logical end. First, if we are God, sin and its associated concept of redemption become unnecessary. Second, because God is not beyond the world but in it, there can be no miracles (as we normally would employ that term—i.e., **supernatural** events). While there may be **supernormal** events (e.g., channelings, healings, the ability to resist pain while walking on a bed of hot coals, etc.), since these things are not accomplished by any power outside the Universe, but instead are the result of people realizing and employing their divine potential, then "miracles" do not and cannot occur. Third, in pantheism there is neither need of, nor allowance for, divine providence. The consensus of pantheism is that, since God is all and all is God, and since God is good, then anything evil must not, and cannot, really exist. After all, if it existed, it would be God. As the pantheists themselves put it:

> ...Every action, under certain circumstances and for certain people, may be a stepping-stone to spiritual growth, if it is done in a spirit of detachment. All good and evil are relative

> to the individual point of growth.... But, in the highest sense, there can be neither good nor evil (Prabhavananda and Isherwood, 1972, p. 140).

If, "in the highest sense" neither good nor evil exists, then obviously mankind has no need of providence. Why should man want God to "look out for" him if there is no evil with which he has to be concerned and if he is all-powerful himself? Fourth, when pantheism is reduced to its basic, core concepts, it becomes clear that God does not have a personality, as depicted within Scripture; thus, He is not a "person" but an "it." As Geisler observed: "In the highest and absolute sense God is **neither personal nor conscious**. The Absolute and Supreme is not a He but an It" (1976, p. 185, emp. in orig.). Erich Sauer wrote of how pantheism "teaches the immanence of the Deity in the universe but denies the personality of God" (1962, p. 163). Fifth, pantheism advocates the view that there is one absolute, unchanging reality—God—and that humans, given time and proper teaching, can come to the realization that they, too, are God. This is exactly the position that Shirley MacLaine takes in her books, *Out on Limb*, *Going Within*, and *Dancing in the Light*. Eventually, she was able to stand on the sands of the beach and proclaim, "I am God!"

How should Christians respond to the concept of pantheism? First, we must point out that the pantheistic concept of "all is God and God is all" is wrong because it attempts to sustain itself via a contradiction. In logic, one of the fundamental laws of human thought is the basic Law of Contradiction, which, stated succinctly, says: "Nothing can both be and not be" (Jevons, 1928, p. 117). Aristotle, expressed it more fully when he said: "That the same thing should at the same time both be and not be for the same person and in the same respect is impossible" (see Arndt, 1955, p. x). Another ramification of the Law of Contradiction is the concept that "nothing can have at the same time and at the same place contradictory and inconsistent qualities" (Jevons, p. 118). A door may be open, or a door may be shut, but the same door may not be both open and shut at the same time. The entire system of pantheism, however, sustains itself via a logical contradiction. Corduan commented on this as follows:

> Pantheism is built around a contradiction, and a contradiction can never be true. No matter how spiritual or profound or enticing a message may appear it must be false if it contradicts itself. The primary contradiction of pantheism is that the two descriptions "world" and "God" are irreconcilably mutually exclusive.... Who (or what) is God? Pantheists agree that God is **infinite**, which includes that He is eternal, omnipotent, unchanging, and so forth. This understanding of God is at the heart of pantheism.... In pantheism, God is infinite.... What is the world? The world is **finite**. It is temporal, limited, and changeable. Yet pantheism tells us that this description of reality as finite world and the description of reality as infinite God are both true. Can this be? Can something be both finite and infinite? The answer is clearly no.... The point here is not to ridicule but to show that the pantheists' attempts to identify God and the world with each other cannot work. **It is not just too hard, it is impossible**. There is a categorical distinction between God and the world (1993, pp. 93,94, emp. added, parenthetical comment in orig.).

This is where the Law of Contradiction sets itself against pantheism. Since it is true that "nothing can have at the same time and at the same place contradictory and inconsistent qualities," then one cannot say that God and the world are identical while at the same time asserting that God is infinite and the world finite. If words mean anything, such a dichotomy is the death knell to pantheism.

Second, we need to stress that, so far as God's Word is concerned, everything is not "one." The Bible clearly distinguishes between two different realms: the material and the spiritual. Solomon wrote: "Then the dust will return to the earth as it was, and the spirit will return to God who gave it" (Ecclesiastes 12:7). The writer of the book of Hebrews said: "Furthermore, we have had human fathers who corrected us, and we paid them respect. Shall we not much more readily be in subjection to the Father of spirits and live?" (12:9). Jesus was even more explicit when He affirmed that "God is Spirit" and then later stated: "Handle me and see, for a spirit does not have flesh and bones as you see I have" (John 4: 24; Luke 24:39).

The Bible not only teaches that there is a distinction between the material and spiritual realms, but also notes that there is an essential difference among the various orders of creation. The Genesis account of creation reports how God created plants, animals, and men separately. Thus, in a very real sense it is erroneous to speak of man as "one" with nature—for he most certainly is not. Paul wrote: "All flesh is not the same flesh, but there is one kind of flesh of men, another flesh of beasts, another of fish, and another of birds" (1 Corinthians 15:39). Far from "all being one," nature's inhabitants actually were created by God to fulfill separate roles. The idea that "all is one" simply does not fit the available facts—scripturally or scientifically. Furthermore, the Scriptures speak to the fact that God existed prior to, and apart from, that which He created. As he began the book of Revelation, the apostle John described God as "the Alpha and the Omega...who is and who was and who is to come" (1:8). The psalmist wrote: "Before the mountains were brought forth, or ever thou hadst formed the earth and the world, even from everlasting to everlasting, thou art God" (90:2).

Third, we need to expose the illogical and unscriptural position within pantheism which teaches that God is an "impersonal It" rather than a personal God. As Sauer remarked: "It is also *a priori* impossible to accept an **unconscious intelligence**. This is a contradiction in terms. Similarly it is impossible to speak of unconscious ideas, for ideas demand a conscious, rational principle which produces them" (1962, p. 157, emp. added). In commenting on the same problem, Geisler wrote:

> [G]ranting that there are no real finite selves or "I's," then there is no such thing as an I-Thou relationship between finite selves nor between man and God. Both fellowship and

> worship become impossible. All alleged I-Thou or I-I relations reduce to I.... Religious experience is impossible in any meaningful sense of the term since all meaningful experience involves something or someone other than oneself with whom one enters the changing experience (1976, pp. 187-189).

How, we must ask, is it possible to communicate (physically or spiritually) with an impersonal, unconscious "It"?

Fourth, pantheists believe that God is the one absolute, unchanging reality. Yet they also believe it is possible for humans to come to realize that they are God. But if humans come to realize something, then they have changed along the way. A process has occurred that brought them from a point where they **did not know** they were God to a point where they **now know they are God**. That is to say, a "change" has occurred. As Geisler and Brooks put it: "But God cannot change. Therefore, anyone who 'comes to realize that he is God' isn't! The unchanging God always knew that He is God" (1990, p. 46). The pantheist cannot have it both ways.

Fifth, the concept of self-deification inherent in pantheism (e.g., MacLaine's sandy beach proclamation, "I am God!") must be opposed. It is here that the conflict between pantheism and Christianity is most obvious. Through the prophet Ezekiel, God told the king of Tyre: "Thou hast said, 'I am a god, I sit in the seat of God, in the midst of the seas'; yet thou art man, and not God, though thou didst set thy heart as the heart of God" (Ezekiel 28:2). In the Bible, only the wicked elevate themselves to the status of deity. King Herod flirted with self-deification—and died in a horrific manner as a result. Luke reported the event as follows:

> So on a set day Herod, arrayed in royal apparel, sat on his throne and gave an oration to them. And the people kept shouting, "The voice of a god and not the voice of a man!" Then immediately an angel of the Lord struck him, because he did not give glory to God. And he was eaten of worms and died (Acts 12:21-23).

This stands in stark contradistinction to the reaction of Paul and Barnabas when the heathens at Lystra attempted to worship them (Acts 14:8-18). Had they been pantheists, these two preachers would have encouraged the crowds in Lystra to recognize not only the preachers' deity but their own deity as well! Yet, consider the response they offered instead:

> They rent their garments, and sprang forth among the multitude, crying out and saying, "Sirs, why do ye these things? We also are men of like passions with you, and bring you good tidings, that ye should turn from these vain things unto a living God, who made the heaven and the earth and the sea, and all that in them is" (Acts 14:14-15).

The testimony of the creation is not that man is God, but rather that God transcends both this world and its inhabitants. In Romans 1, the apostle Paul spoke directly to this point.

> For the wrath of God is revealed from heaven against all ungodliness and unrighteousness of men, who hinder the truth in unrighteousness; because that which is known of God is manifest in them; for God manifested it unto them. For the invisible things of him since the creation of the world are clearly seen, being perceived through the things that are made, even his everlasting power and divinity; that they may be without excuse: because that, knowing God, they glorified him not as God, neither gave thanks; but became vain in their reasonings, and their senseless heart was darkened. Professing themselves to be wise, they became fools, and changed the glory of the incorruptible God for the likeness of an image of corruptible man, and of birds, and four-footed beasts, and creeping things. Wherefore God gave them up in the lusts of their hearts unto uncleanness, that their bodies should be dishonored among themselves: for that they exchanged the truth of God for a lie, and worshipped and served the creature rather than the Creator, who is blessed for ever (Romans 1:18-25).

The idea of self-deification that is so prevalent in pantheism effectively eliminates the entire scheme of redemption and negates 4,000 years of Heaven's interaction in men's lives. It denies the role of Jesus in creation (John 1:1-3), the amazing prophetic accuracy of the Old and New Testaments (1 Peter 1:10-12), the providential preservation of the messianic seed (Galatians 3:16), the miraculous birth of Christ (Isaiah 7:14; Matthew 1:21-23), the significance of His resurrection (1 Corinthians 15), and the hope of His second coming (1 Thessalonians 4:13-18). When man decides to declare his own deity, he foments rebellion against the legitimate Inhabitant of heaven's throne. And he will bear the consequences of that rebellion, just as angels of old did (Jude 6).

Sixth, and last, Christians need to help others see that pantheism is little more than "disguised atheism." As Sauer put it:

> Moreover, pantheism is, logically considered, only a polite form of atheism. For if one asserts that God and the world are the same, finally this comes to the same thing as saying "There is only one world, but there is no God." 'The statement of pantheism, "God and the world are one," is only a polite way of sending the Lord God about His business' (Schopenhauer) [1962, p. 157].

Geisler noted:

> ...if God is "All" or coextensive in his being with the universe, then pantheism is metaphysically indistinguishable from atheism. Both hold in common that the Whole is a collection of all the finite parts or aspects. The only difference is that the pantheist decides to attribute religious significance to the All and the atheist does not. But philosophically the Whole is identical, namely, one eternal self-contained system of reality (1976, p. 190).

Like atheism, pantheism offers no moral absolutes. Since each person is "God," each person does what is right in his own eyes. As in atheism, situation ethics rules supreme. The utopian hope of a planet and its inhabitants "united" or "one" with God is a pipe dream. In the concluding chapter of their book, *Apologetics in the New Age: A Critique of Pantheism*, Clark and Geisler succinctly wrote of what they called the "false hope" of pantheism, and then went on to say: "It lacks substance. The evidence that such a transformation will take place is sadly lacking. **Hope without realism is cruel**" (1990, p. 235, emp. added).

Pantheism is cruel indeed. In the truest tradition of Satan's temptation of Eve in the Garden of Eden, it convinces man to set himself up as God. The results then were tragic for the entire human race. The results of accepting pantheism in our day and age will prove to be no less so.

Panentheism

Although the names may sound somewhat familiar, pantheism and pan**en**theism actually are quite different. Whereas pantheism teaches that God **is** the world, panentheism teaches that God is **in** the world. In panentheism, God is neither beyond the world nor identical with it. Rather, the world is God's body. "Further, unlike the God of theism, the panentheistic god does not create the world out of nothing (*ex nihilo*) but out of his own eternal sources (*ex Deo*)" [Geisler, 1997, p. 19].

Kreeft and Tacelli, in their *Handbook of Christian Apologetics*, have suggested that panentheism is

> ...a kind of compromise between theism and pantheism. It does not identify God with the material universe (as pantheism does), but neither does it hold that there actually exists an eternal God, transcendent to creation (as theism does). Panentheists believe that the material universe constitutes God, but that God is more than the material universe.... Thus panentheism is one way of making God temporal (1994, p. 94).

Another way of expressing God's temporal nature is to say that He is "finite" (as opposed to infinite). In fact, panentheism often is referred to by the synonym, "finite Godism." Another phrase used to describe panentheism is "process theology"—a concept that needs to be explained here.

The idea of "process theology" as expressed in its current form essentially is the brainchild of philosopher Alfred North Whitehead who penned several influential books on the subject, including *Process and Reality* (1929), *Adventures of Ideas* (1933), and *Modes of Thought* (1938). For those of us who are non-philosophers (or not even very philosophically oriented), process theology can seem a little like wading into a gently flowing creek that unexpectedly turns into a raging torrent. The first few steps do not begin to prepare you for what is yet to follow. Allow me to explain.

According to Whitehead (and other eminent proponents of process theology like Samuel Alexander, Charles Hartshorne, and Schubert Ogden), God is composed of two "poles" (thus, He is "bipolar," which is why another synonym for panentheism is "bipolar theism"). First, there is what is known as His **primordial** pole, which is eternal, unchanging, ideal, and beyond the world. Second, however, there is what is known as His **consequent** pole, which is temporal, changing, real, and identical to the world. The primordial nature of God is His "potential" pole—i.e., what He **can be**. The consequent nature is his "actual" pole—i.e., what He **actually is** at any given moment. Geisler and Brooks have explained this as follows:

> So the world is not different from God; it is one of God's poles. His potential pole inhabits the world just like a soul inhabits a body. There it becomes actualized or real. So what the world is, is what God has become. As such God is never actually perfect; He is only striving toward perfection.... So God is always changing as the world changes. He in the **process** of becoming all that He can be (1990, pp. 48,47, emp. in orig.).

Since God is in the "process" of becoming all that He can be (sounds like the U.S. Army recruitment campaign slogan, doesn't it?), the concept is known as "process theology." And if you are wondering right about now if this is just a tad convoluted and thus a bit difficult to follow, let me set your mind at ease. Yes, it is! Therefore, in order to help explain what all of this means in "plain English," I would like to provide the following well-written, simplified summary from Winfried Corduan's book, *Reasonable Faith*.

> To understand the nature of God in Whitehead's system, we must come to terms with how Whitehead wants us to

think of the world.... Put briefly, rather than thinking of things that change, we ought to think of **changes that take on the forms of things**. Take the following example. Let us say we are watching a football game. We see players, referees, cheerleaders, and spectators. They are running, kicking whistling, clapping, and shouting. Whitehead would want us to reverse the picture and think of the actions first with the people second. We observe running, kicking, whistling, clapping, and shouting which has taken on the form of players, referees, cheerleaders, and spectators. The action is of first order. In fact, it would be correct to say that we are observing "the football game event." This is strange language intended to make the point that nothing is as fundamental to the world as change. Whitehead even wanted us to think of the whole universe as one big event.

What is change? Suppose we bake a cake. We mix together the ingredients and create a batter. Then we put the batter into the oven and out comes a cake. We changed the batter into a cake. The batter had the potential to become a cake, but it was only after the change took place that it actually was a cake. The potential cake became the actual cake; in other words, the potential of the batter to become a cake was actualized. All change can be understood in this way. When something changes, a potential has been actualized.

So when Whitehead says that the world is one big event, we need to picture it in terms of constant change. Thus the world must consist of two parts—or poles—an actual pole and a potential pole. The actual pole is everything that is true of the world at a given moment. The potential pole is the vast reservoir of everything that the world is not but can **become**. As the world is changing, potential is constantly being actualized. Picture an arrow in perpetual motion flowing from the potential to the actual side.

In this picture created by Whitehead, God watches over this process. Keep in mind that this God is supposed to be finite; He too changes. We must think of God in the same terms as the world: He has a potential pole and an actual pole (though Whitehead calls them God's "primordial" and "consequent" natures). Every moment some new potential in God is actualized; He changes in response to changes in the world.

> Like the God of deism, the process God does not intervene in the world. He is strictly finite. In the football game of reality, He is the cheerleader. He presents the world with ideals to aim for; He entices the world to follow His plans; He grieves if the world strays; but He cannot make the world do anything. As the world changes, He changes, too, in order to coax the world along. Whatever He wants done needs to be accomplished by the world apart from His direct help (1993, pp. 96-97, emp. in orig.).

According to its advocates, then, panentheism avoids the pitfalls of some its major counterparts while at the same time partaking of the beneficial essence of strict theism. For example, in deism God is supposed to be an infinite Creator, yet One that does not perform miracles. In panentheism, since God is finite and not seen as omnipotent, panentheists suggest that there would be no inconsistency between a supernatural (but finite) being and the denial of the possibility of miracles. In pantheism, God **is** the world. Not so in panentheism; The world merely is **in** Him (His potential is constantly being actualized/realized). But, like true theism, panentheism envisions a God Who is the Author of moral commandments, and Who gives mankind the freedom of will to obey or disobey.

What should be the response of Christians to panentheism? First, we should be quick to point out that a "finite" God is worthless. As Corduan lamented:

> Once we have denied that God is infinite, we do not have any reason to think that He should be any of those other wonderful things that we say He is. Then He lacks a rationale for His being all-knowing, all-loving, eternal, and the other attributes that are based on His infinity. Take away the infinity, and you take away the justification for believing any of the standard attributes of God. Thus the arbitrary denial of any one attribute does not yield a **finite** God but yields **nothing at all** (1993, p. 95, emp. added).

This is an extremely important point. Once God's infinity is removed, most of His other traits fall one by one like the proverbial row of dominoes. A finite God, for example, cannot be an omniscient God. Consider the following. Panentheists place great faith in modern physics. In fact, much of Whitehead's "process theology" was based on concepts from physics. But according to the laws of physics, nothing travels faster than the speed of light (186,317 miles per second). That being true, then God never would be able to comprehend the entire Universe at once because

> ...his mind could not travel across the universe any faster than 186,000+ miles per second. But by the time he has moved from one end of the universe to the other, the universe would have changed multimillions upon trillions of times. In this case, God would not really know the universe (his "body") at all. He could only know an infinitesimal portion at a time while all else is changing.... Of course, panentheists could solve their problem by affirming that God's mind transcends the universe and is not subject to the speed of light. But if they take this way out of the dilemma, they fall right into the arms of classical theism, which they strongly reject. So the painful alternative for panentheism is to retain an incoherent view or else return to theism (Geisler, 1997, p. 67).

Dr. Geisler is absolutely correct in this particular criticism of panentheism. One writer assessed the situation as follows:

> The incontestable fact is that if God moves necessarily in time he is limited to some rate of velocity that is finite (say, the speed of light, if not the faster rate of some hypothetical tachyon). This means, unfortunately for process theism, that it is impossible for such a finite deity to have a simultaneous God's-eye view of the whole universe at once, since it would take him millions of light years or more to receive requisite data from distant points and places (Gruenler, 1983, p. 58, parenthetical comment in orig.).

Thus, panentheism finds itself in the untenable status of positing a finite, non-omnipotent, non-omniscient God Who is best described in the following illogical manner. (1) He has the entire Universe as His body. (b) By definition, however, He is limited (because He is finite) by the physical laws of that Universe. (c) Therefore,

He cannot even know His own body because it extends over the entire Universe, yet He cannot extend Himself over the entire Universe because He is restrained by its physical laws. Corduan could not have been more correct when he wrote: "Thus the arbitrary denial of any one attribute does not yield a **finite** God but yields **nothing at all**."

Second, panentheism suggests that God is in the "process" of changing, yet the crucial element of change—causality—is conspicuously missing. While it is correct to say that every change is the actualization of some potential, such change does not occur by itself. There must be a **cause** involved in the process. Remember the cake analogy above?

> Try actualizing a bowl of batter's potential to become a cake without putting it into an oven. A coffee cup has the potential to be filled with coffee, so let us see if it will fill itself. Of course it won't. Cakes cannot bake themselves; coffee cups cannot fill themselves; **potentials cannot actualize themselves**. Where a change occurs, there must be a cause to bring about that change.... Panentheism attempts to circumvent the principle of causality. In its picture of God and the world there is constant change. Potentials are actualized, but the cause is missing. This is a particularly embarrassing deficiency when it comes to its understanding of God.... Either his or her God is the metaphysical impossibility of a potential that actualizes itself (akin to the coffee cup which fills itself) or there has to be a cause outside of God (a God behind God) that actualizes His potential. This would mean that God is no longer in any recognizable sense. Either an impossible God or a God who is not really God; this is the panentheist's dilemma. It boils down to practical atheism (Corduan, 1993, pp. 97,98, emp. and parenthetical comments in orig.).

In other words, panentheism needs theism's God in order to "actualize" its God—which turns out after all not to be God but instead some sort of giant "creature" that needs a more ultimate and real cause than itself. The entire panentheistic scenario becomes the old "which came first, the chicken or the egg" routine. If the potential pole came before the actual, how, then, was anything actualized? Yet the actual pole certainly could not have come first, because it had no potential to become. As Geisler and Brooks have pointed out, when it comes to "potential" poles and "actual" poles

> [p]anentheists would say that they always existed together, but then we have to face the fact that time cannot go back into the past forever. The only answer can be that something else created the whole ball of wax. It took a creator beyond the process.... It took a transcendent God to create a chicken who would lay eggs (1990, pp. 50,51).

Third, panentheism is the grand example of man creating God in **his** image, rather than the reverse (which no doubt is why Norman Geisler titled his book critiquing panentheism, *Creating God in the Image of Man?*). Panentheists make the mistake of confusing God's unchanging **attributes** with His changing **activities**. And once that fatal error has been committed, God then is viewed as what He **does** rather than what He **is**. As Geisler has warned, with such a system

> [t]here is activity but no Actor, movement but no Mover, creation but no Creator. Beginning with an anthropomorphic bipolar model of God, it is no wonder that the god of panentheism emerges finite, limited in knowledge, goodness, and power, and in possession of a physical body like the rest of us. Whatever else may be said of this whittling of God down to man's level and form, it is surely not the God presented in the Bible (1976, p. 210).

The God of panentheism most certainly is not the God of the Bible. Do the Scriptures speak of God engaging in temporal, changing **actions** on occasion? Certainly. In fact, the Bible uses a number of different metaphors drawn from specific human analogies. For example, God is said to "repent" (Jonah 3:10), to have "arms" (Psalm 136:12), to see with "eyes" (Hebrews 4:13), and to hear with His "ear" (Isaiah 59:1-2). Yet the Bible also speaks of God as a "rock" (Psalm 18:2), a "tower" (Proverbs 18:10), and as having "wings" (Psalm 91:4). If one wishes to use these metaphors to frame a personal concept of God (as panentheists attempt to do), two things first must be acknowledged. (1) The Bible uses metaphorical/anthropomorphic terminology that is intended to assist humans (who are finite) as they grapple with the spiritual nature of God (Who is infinite). (2) At times, the images that are used are mutually conflicting (some speak of minerals [a rock], some speak of animal characteristics [wings], and some speak of human traits [arms, ears, eyes, etc.]. It is not a proper use of Scripture to take these images and apply them in a literal fashion to make the Universe God's body. Furthermore, such an attempt ignores additional passages of Scripture which teach that God, as a Spirit (John 4:24), is both infinite (Psalm 147:5) and unchanging (Malachi 3:6; Hebrews 6:18; James 1:17).

Panentheism has little to recommend it, and much to dissuade us from accepting it. The "god" of panentheism can "coax" us, but not command us. He can fight evil, but never triumph over it. He allegedly intends to achieve a better world with human cooperation, yet most of the world is happily oblivious to His existence. He is supposed to be able to achieve a better world, but is limited by the physical laws of that world so that He never can achieve more than those laws will allow. As Norman Geisler put it:

> How can anyone worship a god so impotent that he cannot even call the whole thing off? Is not such a god so paralyzed as to be perilous?... [A]s a total world view, the God of panentheism does not fill the bill. The basic dipolar concept of God as eternal potential seeking temporal actualization is self-defeating. No potential can activate itself; and if there is some pure actuality outside the panentheistic God that actualizes it, then one must posit a theistic God of pure act in order to account for the panentheistic God.... By comparison a theistic God is more adequate both metaphysically and personally (1976, pp. 210,213).

CHAPTER 3

CAUSES OF UNBELIEF [PART I]

Most rational, reasonable people would agree that actions have consequences. If a man commits a crime, is pursued and apprehended by law enforcement officers, tried by a jury of his peers, and sentenced to life in the penitentiary or death in the electric chair, who is responsible? When an individual decides to act, is it not true that ultimately the consequences of those actions fall squarely on his or her shoulders? Indeed, actions **do** have consequences.

But so do beliefs and ideas. Is that not one reason why the spoken word is so powerful. The ability to elucidate an idea via a speech, lecture, or other oral presentation can produce astonishing consequences. Think, for example, of the late president of the United States, John F. Kennedy, who inspired Americans with his "Ask not what your country can do for you, but what you can do for your country" inaugural speech. On the heels of his idea—presented so eloquently by a dashing, young, newly elected, and extremely popular president—volunteerism in American grew at an unprecedented rate. Or, reflect upon another presentation in our nation's capital by the late, slain civil rights leader, Martin Luther King, Jr. The moving oratory in his "I have a dream" speech captured the attention of an entire nation and culminated in legislation aimed at protecting the rights of **all** citizens, regardless of their ethnic background, skin color, or religious beliefs.

Beliefs and ideas presented via the written word are no less powerful. Ponder such documents as the hallowed United States *Constitution* that serves as the basis for the freedoms every citizen enjoys. Or contemplate the beloved *Declaration of Independence* that guarantees every American certain "unalienable rights." Throughout the history of mankind, the written word has expressed ideas that manifested the ability either to free men and women (e.g., the English *Magna Carta*) or to enslave them (e.g., Adolf Hitler's *Mein Kampf*).

Indeed, beliefs and ideas—like actions—have consequences. Prominent humanist Martin Gardner devoted an entire chapter in one of his books to "The Relevance of Belief Systems," in an attempt to explain that **what a person believes** profoundly influences **how a person acts** (1988, pp. 57-64). In his book, *Does It Matter What I Believe?*, Millard J. Erickson, wrote that there are numerous reasons

> ...why having correct beliefs is important. Our whole lives are inevitably affected by the real world around us, so what we believe about it is of the utmost importance.... What we believe about reality does not change the truth, nor its effect upon us. Correct belief, however, enables us to know the truth as it is, and then to take appropriate action, so that it will have the best possible effect upon our lives. Having correct beliefs is also necessary because of the large amount and variety of incorrect beliefs which are about (1992, pp. 12,13).

Consider then, in this context, belief in the existence of God. Surely it is safe to say that practically no single belief in the thousands of years of recorded human history has produced as many, or as varied a set of, consequences as this one idea. It has been studied and debated from time immemorial. It has been responsible for some of the most impassioned speeches of which the human spirit is capable. It has engendered multiplied millions of pages of text upon which billions of words—both pro and con—have been written. And, ultimately, it has produced as a consequence either belief or unbelief—both of which have serious implications. Erickson was correct when he suggested that "having correct beliefs is important." In the past, I have examined reasons for **belief** in the God of the Bible (e.g., Thompson, 1995a, 1995b; Thompson and Jackson, 1982, 1996). I now would like to examine causes of **unbelief**.

Bias Against God

There is little doubt that in many instances of unbelief, nonrational factors are a primary influence. H.H. Farmer put it like this: "There can be no question that many people find belief in God difficult because there is in their mind a bias which predisposes them against it" (1942, p. 129). This built-in bias is what Stanley Sayers has referred to as "the prejudice of unbelief." Writing under that title in his book, *Optimism in an Age of Peril*, he said: "One of the significant and obvious reasons the unbeliever remains an unbeliever is that **he likes it that way**. In fact, any evidence of any source or to any degree fails to move him from his position if his heart is strongly bent **against** evidence and **toward** unbelief" (1973, p. 43, emp. in orig.).

Consider the well-documented case of Charles Darwin. James Bales wrote concerning the now-famous popularizer of organic evolution: "For some reason or another, Darwin was determined not to believe in God. Although he admitted more than once that it is reasonable to believe in God, and unreasonable to reject God, yet so determined was he not to believe that he slew reason when reason led him to God" (1976, p. 17). Bales' assessment is correct, as is evident from Darwin's own comments. He wrote, for example:

> This follows from the extreme difficulty or rather impossibility of conceiving this immense and wonderful universe, including man with his capacity for looking far backwards and far into futurity, as the result of blind chance or necessity. When thus reflecting I feel compelled to look to a First Cause having an intelligent mind in some degree analogous to that of man; and I deserve to be called a Theist. This conclusion was strong in my mind about the time, as far as I can remember, when I wrote the *Origin of Species*; and it is since that time that it has very gradually, with many fluctuations, become weaker. But then arises the doubt, can the mind of man, which has, as I fully believe, been developed from a mind as low as that possessed by the lowest animals, be trusted when it draws such grand conclusions? (as quoted in Francis Darwin, 1898, 1:282).

Apparently, a singular event in Darwin's life set him irreversibly on the road to unbelief. In 1850, Charles and Emma Darwin's oldest daughter, Annie, fell ill. On April 23, 1851, she died at the tender age of ten. Darwin was devastated. Although Emma was a devout believer in God and Christianity, with Annie's death her husband no longer could stomach such concepts. In their massive, scholarly biography, *Darwin*, Desmond and Moore wrote:

> This was the end of the road, the crucifixion of his hopes. He could not believe the way Emma believed—nor **what** she believed. There was no straw to clutch, no promised resurrection. Christian faith was futile.... For him the death marked an impasse and a new beginning. It put an end to three years' deliberation about the Christian meaning of mortality; it opened up a fresh vision of the tragic contingency of nature.... Annie's cruel death destroyed Charles's tatters of belief in a moral, just universe. Later he would say that this period chimed the final death-knell for his Christianity, even if it had been a long, drawn-out process of decay.... Charles now took his stand as an unbeliever (1991, pp. 384,386,387, emp. in orig.).

In speaking of his now-abandoned belief in God, Darwin eventually admitted: "But I found it more and more difficult, with free scope given to my imagination, to invent evidence which would suffice to convince me. Thus disbelief crept over me at such a slow rate, but at last was complete. The rate was so slow that I felt no distress" (as quoted in Francis Darwin, 1898, 1:277-278; cf. also Greene, 1963, pp. 16-17). Bales therefore concluded:

> Darwin, so far as my research shows, never used doubt as to the reliability of human reason to discredit other positions. He did not say that since Darwinism was the product of his mind, therefore it could not be trusted. It was only when reason led him to God that he destroyed reason. What a strong bias against God he must have had. Is it not strange? Darwin said that the animal origin of man's mind keeps man from being fully able to trust his reasoning, and yet he said that **he fully believed** that man originated that way. Darwin should either have doubted all reasoning, including Darwinism, or have admitted that the human mind is not wholly an untrustworthy instrument. There are other things which could be said about these quotations from Darwin, but our purpose here is to show that he had a powerful bias against God.... [R]eason led him to God. So he got rid of reason (1976, pp. 17-18, emp. in orig.; cf. also R.E.D. Clark's, *Darwin: Before and After*, 1948, for other aspects of Darwin's flight from God).

Darwin's personal bias against God—brought to fruition when his ten-year-old daughter, Annie, died—ultimately allowed disbelief to root out belief. As Bales went on to observe, a person "cannot be coerced into accepting truth on any subject.... With reference to faith...as with reference to other things, man is still free to choose" (1976, pp. 94,95). Simply put, some people today carry within them a stubborn determination **not** to believe in God. It can have **little** to do with a lack of credible evidence and **much** to do with a built-in bias against belief in God in the first place. In the chapter, "Flight from an Indignant God," in his book *If There's a God, Why Are There Atheists?*, R.C. Sproul commented on this very point when he wrote:

> ...unbelief is generated not so much by intellectual causes as by moral and psychological ones.... Though people are not persuaded by the evidence, this does not indicate an insufficiency in the evidence, but rather an insufficiency in man. **This insufficiency is not a natural inability that**

> **provides man with an excuse.** Man's failure to see this general and universal revelation of God is not because he lacks eyes or ears or a brain with which to think. The problem is not a lack of knowledge or a lack of natural cognitive equipment but a moral deficiency.... The problem is not that there is insufficient evidence to convince rational human beings that there is a God, but that rational human beings have a **natural hostility to the being of God**.... Man's desire is not that the omnipotent, personal Judeo-Christian God **exist**, but that He **not exist** (1978, pp. 57, 58, emp. added).

In Northampton, Massachusetts in 1976, the famed preacher Jonathan Edwards presented a sermon titled, "Men are Naturally God's Enemies," in which he gave a lengthy exposition of Romans 5:10—"For if when we were enemies...." The point of the lesson was that men, by their behavior, have documented in an incontrovertible manner their inner hostility toward God. Edwards said:

> They are enemies in the natural relish of their souls. They have an inbred distaste and disrelish of God's perfections. God is not such a sort of being as they would have. Though they are ignorant of God, yet from what they hear of Him, and from what is manifest by the light of nature of God, they do not like Him. By His being endowed with such attributes as He is, they have an aversion to Him. They hear God is an infinitely holy, pure, and righteous Being, and they do not like Him upon this account; they have no relish of such kind of qualifications; they take no delight in contemplating them. It would be a mere task, a bondage to a natural man, to be obliged to set himself to contemplate these attributes of God. They see no manner of beauty or loveliness nor taste any sweetness in them. And upon the account of their distaste of these perfections, they dislike all the other of His attributes. They have greater aversion to Him because He is omniscient and knows all things; because His omniscience is a holy omniscience. They are not pleased that He is omnipotent, and can do whatever He pleases; because it is a holy omnipotence. They are enemies even to His mercy, because it is a holy mercy. They do not like His immutability, because by this He never will be otherwise than He is, an infinitely holy God (1879, 4:38).

In his book, *If There's a God, Why Are There Atheists?*, R.C. Sproul wrote in his chapter, "The Never-Ending Bias":

> The theme [of his book—BT] is that natural man suffers from prejudice. He operates within a framework of insufferable bias against the God of Christianity. The Christian God is utterly repugnant to him because He represents the threat of threats to man's own desires and ambitions. The will of man is on a collision course with the will of God. Such a course leads inevitably to a conflict of interests.... Men would apparently rather die in their sin than live forever in obedience (1978, p. 146).

Paul reminded the Christians in Rome of those who, "knowing God, glorified him not as God, neither gave thanks; but became vain in their reasonings, and their senseless heart was darkened. And even as they refused to have God in their knowledge, God gave them up unto a reprobate mind" (Romans 1:21,28). The problem about which the apostle wrote was not a failure to accept what was **unknowable** (the text in Romans clearly indicates that these were people who could, and did, know of the existence of God). Rather, it was a problem of refusing to accept what was **knowable**—i.e., God's reality. Those to whom Paul referred had such a built-in prejudice against God (what Sproul labeled "the never-ending bias") that they abjectly **refused** to have God in their knowledge. This situation, then, caused the apostle to write (by inspiration of the Holy Spirit) that "professing themselves to be wise, they became fools" (Romans 1:22).

In biblical usage, the term "fool" generally does not indicate a person of diminished intelligence, and it certainly is not used here in such a fashion. Instead, the term carries both a moral and religious judgment. As Bertram has noted:

> With reference to men the use is predominantly psychological. The word implies censure on man himself: his acts, thoughts, counsels, and words are not as they should be. The weakness may be due to a specific failure in judgment or decision, but a general deficiency of intellectual and spiritual capacities may also be asserted (1971, 4:832).

This is why the psalmist (again, writing by inspiration) said that "the fool hath said in his heart, there is no God" (14:1). If "the fear of the Lord is the beginning of wisdom" (Psalm 111:10), then, conversely, foolishness finds its origin in the rejection of God. Isaiah referred to a man as a fool whose "mind plots iniquity to practice ungodliness" and whose attitude of practical atheism causes him to "utter error concerning the Lord" (Isaiah 32:5, RSV). When Paul wrote his first epistle to the Christians in Corinth, he observed that "the natural man receiveth not the things of the Spirit of God: for they are foolishness unto him" (1 Corinthians 2:14). Bias against God thus has become one of the chief causes of unbelief, which no doubt explains why the Hebrew writer warned: "Take heed, brethren, lest haply there shall be in any one of you an **evil heart of unbelief** in falling away from the living God" (Hebrews 3:12).

Parents and Upbringing

In Romans 14:7, Paul stated that "none of us liveth to himself, and none dieth to himself." The essence of that thought has been perpetuated in the saying that "no man is an island." How true an observation that is. From the beginning to the end of this pilgrimage we call "life," we interact socially with those around us. But surely one of the most formidable influences upon any human being comes in the form of parents. Generally speaking, mothers and fathers have not only an initial, but a continuing effect upon their offspring. Children are born with sponge-like minds that begin basically as "blank slates" upon which parents have a grand opportunity (and an awesome responsibility!) to write. It has been said that a child's mind is like Jell-O® and that the parents' task is to put in all the "good stuff" before it "sets."

Sometimes that task is accomplished by instruction, which is why parents are admonished to teach and nurture their children "in the chastening and admonition of the Lord" (Ephesians 6:4).

Sometimes it is accomplished by discipline, which is why the Proverbs writer wisely observed that "the rod and reproof give wisdom; but a child left to himself causeth shame to his mother" (29:15). And sometimes it is accomplished by exemplary behavior that provides a proper example, which is why the apostle Peter discussed those very things in the context of a family relationship. He spoke of the potential effect a godly wife could have upon her unbelieving husband when he wrote: "In like manner, ye wives be in subjection to your own husbands; that, even if any obey not the word, they may without a word be gained by the behavior of their wives, beholding your chaste behavior coupled with fear" (1 Peter 3:1-2). What a sobering thought—that one person (e.g., a godly wife), through consistently impressive behavior tempered by a reverent fear of God, could set such a good example that another person (e.g., an unbelieving husband) might be convicted of God's existence and convinced to obey His will.

But consider the obvious corollary to this principle. If accurate instruction, timely discipline, and a proper example coupled with faithfulness can produce such wonderful results, what results might inaccurate instruction, a lack of discipline, and an improper example coupled with unfaithfulness produce? Does not practical experience answer that question in a thousand different ways? Although at times we wish they did not, the truth of the matter is that more often than not the decisions we make, and the actions that stem from those decisions, inevitably affect those we love the most. Certainly this is true in a spiritual context. One expert in child psychology put it this way:

> I believe that much atheism has the ground prepared for it in the disillusionment with the parent which has arisen in the child. Disbelief in life, skepticism about humanity, the denial of God—all sink their roots in the soil of emotion long before exposure to courses in philosophy and science. Life has scarred such people early and has made them unwilling to believe either in man or in God (Liebman, 1946, pp. 147-148).

Is it not the case that children often are influenced—rightly or wrongly—by the attitudes and actions of their parents? As proof of this point, consider the following real-life situation. One of the foremost unbelievers of our day is Harvard's famed paleontologist, Stephen Jay Gould. Dr. Gould—an indefatigable crusader on behalf of organic evolution—is a cogent writer and a gifted speaker, as well as one of the evolutionary establishment's most prolific and best-read authors. The January 1983 issue of *Discover* magazine designated him "Scientist of the Year," he often was featured as a special guest on Phil Donahue's television talk show, and through the past two or three decades his articles have appeared frequently not only in refereed scientific journals (e.g., *Science*, *New Scientist*, *Paleobiology*, etc.), but in popular science magazines as well (*Discover*, *Omni*, *Science Digest*, and others). In addition, he is the co-developer (with Niles Eldredge from the American Museum of Natural History) of the popular concept known as "punctuated equilibrium" that provides a new twist regarding the tempo and mode of evolution. All this being true, when Dr. Gould speaks, many people listen. Gould himself has suggested: "When we come to popular writing about evolution, I suppose that my own essays are as well read as any" (1987, 8[1]:67). One writer described him in these words:

> Stephen Jay Gould is as charming on television and in his popular essays about his atheism as he is about his love of baseball. Gould is almost jolly in his condescending remarks about religionists, patting such minor minds on the head with avuncular goodwill, as one might humor a foolish relative (Lockerbie, 1998, p. 229).

Interestingly, relatives and atheism share a common connection in Gould's life. In his 1999 book, *Rocks of Ages: Science and Religion in the Fullness of Life*, Dr. Gould discussed his early years

> ...in a New York Jewish family following the standard pattern of generational rise: immigrant grandparents who start-

> ed in the sweatshops, parents who reached the lower ranks of the middle classes but had no advanced schooling, and my third generation, headed for a college education and a professional life to fulfill the postponed destiny (p. 7).

His "New York Jewish family," however, was different than most, as he explained.

> I shared the enormous benefits of a respect for learning that pervades Jewish culture, even at the poorest economic levels. But **I had no formal religious education**—I did not even have a bar mitzvah—**because my parents had rebelled** against a previously unquestioned family background. (In my current judgment, they rebelled too far, but opinions on such questions tend to swing on a pendulum from one generation to the next, perhaps eventually coming to rest at a wise center.) But my parents retained pride in Jewish history and heritage, **while abandoning all theology and religious belief**.... I am not a believer (1999a, p. 8, emp. added, parenthetical comments in orig.).

While many no doubt are aware of the fact that Dr. Gould is **not** "a believer," they may not be aware of the fact that he **is** a devout Marxist. Exactly where did Gould develop his Marxism, and the atheism that inevitably accompanies it? Through one of his parents! As Gould himself admitted: "It may also not be irrelevant to our personal preferences that one of us learned his Marxism, literally, at his daddy's knee" (Gould and Eldredge, 1977, 3:145). In an article on "The Darwin Debate" in *Marxism Today*, Robert M. Young wrote that

> Aspects of evolutionism are perfectly consistent with Marxism. The explanation of the origins of humankind and of mind by purely natural forces was, and remains, as welcome to Marxists as to any other secularists. The sources of value and responsibility are not to be found in a separate mental realm or in an immortal soul, much less in the inspired words of the Bible (1982, 26:21).

Indeed, it may "not be irrelevant" that as a youngster Stephen Jay Gould was reared in a family who "abandoned all theology and religious belief," enthusiastically embraced Marxism in their place, and subsequently immersed him in the godless, dialectical materialism of that doctrine—thereby producing one of the foremost evolutionists of our generation.

If children witness callous indifference, skepticism, or outright infidelity on the part of their parents in regard to spiritual matters, more often than not those children will exhibit the same callousness, skepticism, or infidelity in their own lives. And is it not also extremely likely that **their** children will be reared in the same atmosphere? (Ask yourself—what do you think Dr. Gould's own son is being taught by his father, and likely will grow up believing?) Thus, in the end, the spiritual condition of not one, but several generations has been affected adversely as a direct result of the instruction/example of parents and the subsequent upbringing received at their hands.

Education

Surely one of the most important causes of unbelief in the world today relates to the kind of education a person receives. [Please notice that I did **not** say unbelief "relates to the education" a person receives; rather, I said unbelief "relates to the **kind** of education" a person receives. I do not mean to "throw the baby out with the bath water" by suggesting that **all** education results in unbelief, for that most certainly is not the case and is not representative of my position.] Generally speaking, the educational system in America is the end product of John Dewey's "progressive education movement." The renowned humanistic philosopher, Will Durant, wrote that "there is hardly a school in America that has not felt his influence" (1961, p. 390). But it was not just American schools that Dewey influenced. In his book, *The Long War Against God*, Henry Morris discussed how the progressive education movement "profoundly changed education not only in America but also in many other countries" as well (1989, p. 38).

Dewey, who was a socialist and materialistic pantheist, was one of the founders (and the first president) of the American Humanist Association, formed in 1933. I have discussed Dewey's atheistic views elsewhere (see Thompson, 1994, 1999). At this juncture, I simply would like to make the point that as a result of Dewey's efforts through the educational establishment, the **kind** of education now being offered in many public schools has the potential to discourage or destroy faith in God, while at the same time encouraging and promoting unbelief. One of the most important tools employed by Dewey and his intellectual offspring to cripple belief was, and is, organic evolution. As Samuel Blumenfeld stated in his classic text, *NEA: Trojan Horse in American Education*:

> An absolute faith in science became the driving force behind the progressives.... The most important idea that would influence the educators was that of evolution—the notion that man, through a process of natural selection, had evolved to his present state from a common animal ancestry. Evolution was as sharp a break with the Biblical view of creation as anyone could make, and it was quickly picked up by those anxious to disprove the validity of orthodox religion (1984, p. 43).

Morris quite correctly assessed the post-Dewey situation when he wrote:

> The underlying assumption of progressive education was that the child is simply an evolved animal and must be trained as such—not as an individual created in God's image with tremendous potential as an individual. A child was considered but one member in a group and therefore must be trained collectively to fit into his or her appropriate place in society (1989, p. 48).

The child's "appropriate place in society"—specifically the humanistic society that Dewey and his cohorts envisioned—neither included nor allowed for belief in the God of the Bible. Thus, every effort was made to use the educational system to gain new recruits. Alfred Rehwinkel discussed just such a situation.

> The shock received by the inexperienced young student is therefore overwhelming when he enters the classroom of such teachers and suddenly discovers to his great bewilderment that these men and women of acclaimed learning do not believe the views taught him in his early childhood days; and since the student sits at their feet day after day, it usually does not require a great deal of time until the foundation of his faith begins to crumble as stone upon stone is being removed from it by these unbelieving teachers. Only too often the results are disastrous. The young Christian becomes disturbed, confused, and bewildered. Social pressure and the weight of authority add to his difficulties. First he begins to doubt the infallibility of the Bible in matters of geology, but he will not stop there. Other difficulties arise, and before long skepticism and unbelief have taken the place of his childhood faith, and the saddest of all tragedies has happened. Once more a pious Christian youth has gained a glittering world of pseudo-learning but has lost his own immortal soul (1951, p. xvii).

Such a scenario is not merely theoretical, but practical. Consider as one example the case of renowned Harvard evolutionist, Edward O. Wilson, who is recognized worldwide as the "father of sociobiology." Wilson summarized his own youthful educational experience as follows:

> As were many persons in Alabama, I was a born-again Christian. When I was fifteen, I entered the Southern Baptist Church with great fervor and interest in the fundamentalist religion. I left at seventeen when I got to the University of Alabama and heard about evolutionary theory (1982, p. 40).

Chet Raymo serves as yet another example of a person who once cherished his belief in God, but who ultimately lost his faith as a result of the kind of education he received. Raymo is a professor of physics and astronomy at Stonehill College in Massachusetts, has written a weekly column on science for the *Boston Globe* for more than a dozen years, and was reared as a Roman Catholic. In his book, *Skeptics and True Believers*, he wrote:

> I learned something else in my study of science, something that had an even greater effect upon my religious faith. None

> of the miracles I had been offered in my religious training were as impressively revealing of God's power as the facts that I was learning in science (1998, p. 20).

Little wonder, then, that the thesis of Raymo's book is that there is an unavoidable dichotomy between educated people of science who empirically "know" things and those in religion who spiritually "believe" things—with the educated, scientifically oriented folks obviously being on the more desirable end of the spectrum (and winning out in the end).

There can be little doubt that many today believe in evolution because it is what they have been taught. For the past century, evolution has been in the limelight. And for the past quarter of a century or more, it has been taught as **scientific fact** in many elementary, junior high, and senior high schools, as well as in most colleges and universities. Marshall and Sandra Hall offered this summary.

> In the first place, evolution is what is taught in the schools. At least two, and in some cases three and four generations, have used textbooks that presented it as proven fact. The teachers, who for the most part learned it as truth, pass it on as truth. Students are as thoroughly and surely indoctrinated with the concept of evolution as students have ever been indoctrinated with any unproven belief (1974, p. 10).

In their book, *Why Scientists Accept Evolution*, Bales and Clark confirmed such an observation.

> Evolution is taken for granted today and thus it is uncritically accepted by scientists as well as laymen. It is accepted by them today because it was already accepted by others who went before them and under whose direction they obtained their education (1966, p. 106).

Further exacerbating the problem is the fact that evolution has been given the "stamp of approval" by important spokespersons from practically every field of human endeavor. While there have been men and women from politics, the humanities, the arts, and other fields who openly have defended evolution as factual, in no other area has this defense been as pronounced as in the sciences. Because science has produce so many successes in so many different areas, and because these successes have been so visible and so well publicized, scientists have been granted an aura of respectability that only can be envied by non-scientists.

As a result, when scientists champion a cause people generally sit up and take notice. After all, it is their workings through the scientific method that have eradicated smallpox, put men on the Moon, prevented polio, and lengthened human life spans. We have grown used to seeing "experts" from various scientific disciplines ply their trade in an endless stream of amazing feats. Heart surgery has become commonplace; organ transplants have become routine; space shuttles flying into the heavens have become standard fare.

Thus, when the atheistic concept of organic evolution is presented as something that "all reputable scientists believe," there are many people who accept such an assessment at face value, and who therefore fall in line with what they believe is a well-proven dictum that has been enshrouded with the cloak of scientific respectability. As atheistic philosopher Paul Ricci has written: "The reliability of evolution not only as a theory but as a principle of understanding is not contested by the vast majority of biologists, geologists, astronomers, and other scientists" (1986, p. 172). Or, as Stephen Jay Gould put it: "The fact of evolution is as well established as anything in science (as secure as the revolution of the earth around the sun), though absolute certainty has no place in our [scientists'—BT] lexicon (1987, 8[1]:64; parenthetical comment in orig). [In a guest editorial in the August 23, 1999 issue of *Time* magazine, Dr. Gould reiterated this point when he said that "evolution is as well documented as any phenomenon in science, as strongly as the earth's revolution around the sun rather than vice versa. In this sense, we can call evolution a 'fact'" (1999b, p. 59).]

Such comments are intended to leave the impression that well-informed, intelligent people dare not doubt the truthfulness of organic evolution. The message is: "All scientists believe it; so should you." As Marshall and Sandra Hall inquired: "How, then, are people with little or no special knowledge of the various sciences and related subjects to challenge the authorities? It is natural to accept what 'experts' say, and most people do" (1974, p. 10). Henry Morris observed: "...the main reason most educated people believe in evolution is simply because they have been told that most educated people believe in evolution" (1963, p. 26).

Huston Smith, a leading philosopher and professor of religion at Syracuse University has commented on this phenomenon as follows:

> One reason education undoes belief is its teaching of evolution; Darwin's own drift from orthodoxy to agnosticism was symptomatic. Martin Lings is probably right in saying that "more cases of loss of religious faith are to be traced to the theory of evolution...than to anything else" (1982, p. 755; Lings' quote is from *Studies in Comparative Religion*, 1970, Winter).

Sir Julian Huxley, the famous UNESCO [United Nations Educational and Scientific Organization] biologist, put it this way: "Darwinism removed the whole idea of God as the creator of organisms from the sphere of rational discussion" (1960, p. 45).

The simple fact is, however, that truth is not determined by popular opinion or majority vote. A thing may be, and often is, true even when accepted only by the minority. Furthermore, a thing may be, and often is, false even though accepted by the majority. Believing something based on the assumption that "everyone else" also believes it often can lead to disastrous results. As Guy N. Woods remarked: "It is dangerous to follow the multitude because the majority is almost always on the wrong side in this world" (1982, 124[1]:2). Or, as Moses warned the children of Israel: "Thou shalt not follow a multitude to do evil" (Exodus 23:2).

Pride

When the Lord asked in John 5:44, "How can ye believe, who receive glory one of another, and the glory that cometh from the only God ye seek not?," He summed up one of the main reasons why many are unprepared to believe in God. Man is so busy seeking and reveling in his own glory that he has neither the time nor the inclination to offer glory to His Maker. An unhealthy lust for power wrapped in a cloak of pride breeds unbelief. German philosopher Friedrich Nietzsche (he of "God is dead" fame) expressed such an attitude when he asked a friend, "If there were gods, how could I endure it to be no god?" In his famous composition, *Invictus*, infidel poet William Ernest Henley wrote: "I am the master of my fate; I am the captain of my soul." The famed Harvard evolutionist, George Gaylord Simpson, ended one of his books with these words: "Man is his own master. He can and must decide and manage his own destiny" (1953, p. 155).

One of the most famous apologists among Christian theists of the past generation was the renowned biblical scholar Wilbur M. Smith. In 1945 he authored *Therefore Stand*, which was then, and is now, a classic in the field of Christian apologetics. In chapter three, under the heading of "Some Reasons for the Unbelief of Men and Their Antagonism Against God," Dr. Smith listed numerous causes of unbelief, one of which was "The Pride of Man." Included in his discussion of that subject was this observation:

> When man says he believes in a Supreme Being...he at the same time, if he is honest, confesses that God is holy, and he himself, unholy, that God is independent and can do according to His own will, while man is dependent. All this is humiliating; it takes away any cause for pride, for if there is one thing that man has always liked to feel it is that he is sufficient for all things, that he is going to bring about a better world by his own ingenuity, that he is the greatest and highest and most important phenomenon in the world, and that beyond him there is nothing worth considering (1974 reprint, p. 151).

In their text, *A Survey of European Civilization: 1500-Present,* historians Walter Ferguson and Geoffrey Bruun discussed the "intellectual revolution" that had engulfed mankind. The following statement represents their assessment of the effects of this phenomenon: "The new learning offered man a more vain-glorious picture of himself, and rooted itself in his pride; whereas his religious beliefs had been the fruit of his humility" (1937, pp. 9-11). Forty years later, the accuracy of their assessment became clear when two eminent atheists of our generation, Richard Leakey and Roger Lewin, wrote:

> Unquestionably mankind **is** special, and in many ways, too.... There is now a critical need for a deep awareness that, no matter how special we are as an animal, we are still part of the greater balance of nature.... During that relatively brief span evolutionary pressures forged a brain capable of profound understanding of matters animate and inanimate: the fruits of intellectual and technological endeavour in this latter quarter of the 20th century give us just an inkling of what the human mind can achieve. The potential is enormous, almost infinite. **We can, if we so choose, do virtually anything**... (1977, p. 256; first emp. in orig., latter emp. added).

Smith's conclusion on "the pride of man" was this: "As pride increases, humility decreases, and as man finds himself self-sufficient he will discard his religious convictions, or having none, he will fight those of others" (1974, pp. 152-153).

In America, one of Nietzsche's intellectual offspring was Thomas J.J. Altizer, a professor at Emory University in Atlanta, Georgia. Through two popular books, *Oriental Mysticism and Biblical Eschatology* (1961) and *The Gospel of Christian Atheism* (1966), he affirmed—like his German counterpart—that "God is dead." His position was not exactly the same as Nietzsche's, however. Altizer had concluded that the God of traditional theism was "dead." A transcendent God was a useless, mythical, powerless figurehead Who had no authority over mankind. Almost forty years earlier, Walter Lippmann had addressed this same type of problem in his book, *A Preface to Morals.*

> This is the first age, I think, in the history of mankind when the circumstances of life have conspired with the intellectual habits of the time to render any fixed and authoritative belief incredible to large masses of men. The irreligion of the modern world is radical to a degree for which there is, I think, no counterpart.... I do not mean that modern men have ceased to believe in God. I do not mean that they no longer believe in Him simply and literally. I mean they have defined and refined their ideas of Him until they can no longer honestly say He exists... (1929, pp. 12,21).

In the mid-1960s, when Altizer's positions were receiving considerable publicity, James D. Bales authored an important and timely volume, *The God-Killer?* (1967), in which he reviewed and refuted Altizer's teachings. Almost a decade later, he still was exposing and opposing Altizer's views. In his book, *How Can Ye Believe?*, Dr. Bales wrote:

> Although some have been brought up in confusion, and have not had time to do much thinking, the ultimate roots of the refusal to face the meaning of human finitude are found in the pride and rebellion of man. Some have made a declaration of independence from God. They believe they are self-sufficient in knowledge. Through the unaided human mind they can answer all questions that can be answered, and solve all problems that can be solved. There is no need for the divine revelation. It would be a blow to the pride of man which says that unaided human reason is sufficient....
>
> For example, in our day Thomas J.J. Altizer has declared that God is dead. This was decreed by the pride of man. In his pride, Altizer maintained that man must be autonomous. He must be free to create his own nature and to formulate his own moral laws. If God is, and if God created man, man is not autonomous. He is not free to create his own nature, nor can he be left to his own will and whims as to what is right or wrong. He is not free to live his own life without being accountable to God. In his pride, Altizer wanted none of these things, so he decreed that God is dead in order that he might be free to live as it pleases him without being accountable to God. The arrogant heart cannot furnish fertile soil for seeds of truth... (1976, p. 73).

Bales' last statement—that "the arrogant heart cannot furnish fertile soil for seeds of truth"—is thoroughly biblical. Christ Himself warned: "For from within, out of the heart of men, evil thoughts proceed, fornications, thefts, murders, adulteries, covetings, wickednesses, deceit, lasciviousness, an evil eye, railing, **pride**, foolishness" (Mark 7:21-22, emp. added). The apostle John wrote: "For all that is in the world—the lust of the flesh, the lust of the eyes, and the **pride of life**—is not of the Father but is of the world" (1 John 2: 16, NKJV, emp. added).

Somewhere in time, Altizer lost his way. In his pride, **finite** man sought to rid himself of the **infinite** God. He forgot (if, indeed, he ever knew) that "Pride goeth before destruction, and a haughty spirit before a fall. Better it is to be of a lowly spirit with the poor, than to divide the spoil with the proud" (Proverbs 16:18-19). Henry Morris observed:

> The root of all sin...is the twin sin of unbelief and pride—the refusal to submit to God's will as revealed by His own Word and the accompanying assertion of self-sufficiency which enthrones the creature and his own will in the place of God (1971, pp. 214-215).

Imagine the position in which the devout unbeliever finds himself. He may be thinking: "I've been an unbeliever for a long time. If I alter my views now, I will lose face. My reputation is linked to my views. So is my conduct. Were I to change my mind, I would be condemning my whole past existence and altering my entire future life—in both word and deed."

Difficult scenario, to be sure. Not only is pride heavily involved, but personal integrity as well. Perhaps this is the very thing that Jesus had in mind when He said: "Anyone who **resolves** to do the will of God will know whether the teaching is from God" (John 7:17, NRSV, emp. added). If a person so desires, he or she **can** replace unbelief with belief. As the apostle John brought the book of Revelation to a close, he wrote: "He that will, let him take the water of life freely" (Revelation 22:17). The operative phrase, of course, is "he that will." It is one thing to let pride **get** in the way; it is entirely another to let it **remain** there.

Immorality

In his book, *If There's a God, Why Are There Atheists?*, R.C. Sproul titled one of the chapter subheadings "The Threat of Moral Excellence." In that section, he noted:

> It is a common occurrence among social human beings that a person who manifests a superior excellence is resented by his contemporaries. The student who consistently breaks the curve of the academic grading system is frequently treated with quiet hostility by his classmates.... The unusually competent person represents a threat not only to his peers but to his superiors as well, and is frequently treated as *persona non grata*.... **Competency at a moral level is perhaps the most unwelcome kind of competency** (1978, pp. 94, 95, emp. added).

Who among us has not endured taunts from associates because we steadfastly refused to participate in something immoral? Think about the teenager who rebuffs his friends' invitation to "do drugs," the employee who chooses not to "fudge" his time sheet, or the college student who elects not to cheat on the exam. Those who **are willing** to participate in immoral acts often react in hostile fashion to those who **are not**.

Consider the case of Jesus Christ. When He calmed the storm-tossed seas in Matthew 8, those around Him asked, "What manner of man is this?" (vs. 27). When those sent to spy on Him reported to the chief priests and Pharisees who had commissioned them, they admitted: "Never man so spake" (John 7:47). Christ was **morally** unique. He was the One Who taught:

> Ye have heard that it was said, "An eye for an eye, and a tooth for a tooth": but I say unto you, resist not him that is evil: but whosoever smiteth thee on thy right cheek, turn to him the other also. And if any man would go to law with thee, and take away thy coat, let him have thy cloak also. And whosoever shall compel thee to go one mile, go with him two.... I say unto you, love your enemies, and pray for them that persecute you (Matthew 5:38-41,44)

Practically everything Christ taught, and did, was in contradistinction to the common practices of His day—and of ours. As Sproul has suggested:

> The unique moral excellence of Jesus was a massive threat to His contemporaries, particularly to those who were considered to be the moral elite of His day. It was the Pharisees (those "set apart" to righteousness) who were most hostile to Jesus. Though the popular masses hailed the Pharisees for their moral excellence, Jesus exposed them as hypocrites. He "broke their curve," providing a new standard under which the old standard of morality dissolved. Jesus disintegrated the firm security of His contemporaries. **When the Holy appeared, the pseudo-holy were exposed** (1978, pp. 95-96, emp. added, parenthetical comment in orig.).

Little wonder, then, that "the chief priests and the scribes sought how they might put him to death" (Luke 22:2).

Now, multiply this angry attitude throughout a human race, the majority of which has become so vile that "it is written, 'There is none righteous, no, not one; there is none that understandeth, there is none that seeketh after God'" (Romans 3:10-11). If people reacted with downright disgust to the moral perfection of God's personal representative here on Earth, with what kind of dastardly disdain might they be expected to react to the moral perfection of the God Who inhabits eternity?

In his 1910 book, *Man's Need of God*, historian David Smith lamented not only the sorry state in which mankind found itself, but the fact that "[i]t is not intellectual aberration but moral depravity—the blight of uncleanness, the canker of corruption" that has brought humans to the precipice of moral bankruptcy (p. 98). One need not look long or hard to find corroborating evidence for such an assessment. For example, Aldous Huxley admitted:

> **I had motives for not wanting the world to have meaning**; consequently, assumed it had none, and was able without any difficulty to find satisfying reasons for this assumption.... The philosopher who finds no meaning in the world is not concerned exclusively with a problem in pure meta-

> physics; he is also concerned to prove there is no valid reason why he personally should not do as he wants to do.... For myself, as no doubt for most of my contemporaries, **the philosophy of meaninglessness was essentially an instrument of liberation**. The liberation we desired was simultaneously liberation from a certain political and economic system and **liberation from a certain system of morality. We objected to the morality because it interfered with our sexual freedom** (1966, 3:19, emp. added).

Huxley's admission leaves little to the imagination. Why did he, and so many of his contemporaries, abandon belief in God? It was to: (a) avoid the objective moral standards laid down by Heaven; and (b) provide legitimacy for indiscriminate sexual behavior of a wanton nature. In fact, this is one of the primary planks in the platform of modern-day humanism.

> In the area of sexuality, we believe that intolerant attitudes, often cultivated by orthodox religions and puritanical cultures, unduly repress sexual conduct. The right to birth control, abortion, and divorce should be recognized. While we do not approve of exploitive, denigrating forms of sexual expression, neither do we wish to prohibit, by law or social sanction, sexual behavior between consenting adults. The many varieties of sexual exploration should not in themselves be considered "evil." Without countenancing mindless permissiveness or unbridled promiscuity, a civilized society should be a **tolerant** one. Short of harming others or compelling them to do likewise, individuals should be permitted to express their sexual proclivities and pursue their life-styles as they desire (*Humanist Manifestos I & II*, 1973, pp. 18-19, emp. in orig.)

It should come as no surprise, then, that "as man finds himself self-sufficient he will discard his religious convictions, or having none, he will fight those of others" (Smith, 1974, pp. 152-153). The psalmist addressed this very point when he wrote: "The fool hath said in his heart, 'There is no God.' **They are corrupt, they have done abominable works**; There is none that doeth good" (14:1, emp. added).

Some might object on the grounds that not **all** unbelievers lapse into moral decay. Bales addressed this objection in his book, *How Can Ye Believe?*

> First, men are sometimes glad to get away from the moral authority of the Christian faith not because they want to do some things that it forbids, but **because some of the things which it sanctions and commands they do not want to do**. Second, the sinful attitude of heart may not be of the type that we generally associate with immorality, but such as the pride of individuals who do not want to admit that they are a long way from what they ought to be. Such an individual may welcome unbelief because it removes from his sight the accusing high standard of the faith which passes judgment on his life.... Third, the collapse in moral conduct may not come immediately because...the habits of the individual and his attitudes have been constructed by Christian morality and he finds it difficult to break away from them and to get over the idea of the shamefulness of certain types of conduct.... Fourth, it has not been suggested that this is the **only** cause of unbelief (1976, pp. 99,100, emp. added).

As this section on immorality as a cause of unbelief draws to a close, I believe it is appropriate to conclude with the following quotation from Wilbur M. Smith:

> The point I am making is this: one of the reasons why men refuse to accept the Christian Faith is because the very principles of their lives are in every way contradictory to the ethical principles of the Bible, and, **determined to remain in the lawlessness of their own sensuality**, they could not possibly embrace a holy religion nor walk with a holy God, nor look for salvation to His holy Son, nor have any love for His holy Word. ...**one of the deepest, profoundest, most powerful causes for unbelief**, holding men back from Christ **is a life of sin** (1974, p. 170, emp. added).

Scientific Materialism

Let's face it. We are living in an era where science reigns supreme and where we view daily its astonishing accomplishments. Today, citizens of most civilized countries are better fed, better clothed, and healthier than they ever have been. Science has increased life spans, improved planetary transportation, and altered forever methods of global communication. It has eradicated smallpox and is on the verge of eliminating polio. Scientific research has improved radically such things as educational, medical, and recreational facilities, especially when compared to those of previous generations. It even stands at the brink of decoding the entire human genome.

Pretty impressive stuff, to say the least. And therein lies the problem. Because of the tremendous strides that have been, and are being, made, science has become somewhat of a sacred cow and the laboratory a sort of "holy of holies." As Smith put it:

> The very word "laboratory" has in it the connotation of certainty, of wonder, of the discovery of secrets. Millions of people are living today because of the development of medicine, and thank God for that! Many are able to walk the streets today because of insulin, who, otherwise, would long ago have been in their graves. One discovery drives men on to another. The eliciting of one secret is only the opening of the door into another realm of mystery and delight. There is a positiveness, definiteness, and promise about mathematical equations, physical laws, and chemical formulae, which make men feel that here their feet are on solid rock, that their minds are grappling with realities (1974, pp. 162-163).

While we should be grateful for the great strides that science has made, we also should acknowledge all that science owes to God. During a seminar on origins at Murray, Kentucky on November 29, 1980, Russell C. Artist, former chairman of the biology department and professor emeritus at David Lipscomb University, commented: "The statement, 'In the beginning God created the heavens and the earth,' is the cornerstone of all scientific thinking." Dr. Artist was doing what far too many scientists are unwilling to do—"give credit where credit is due." If Genesis 1:1 is the **cornerstone** of science, then surely Genesis 1:28—wherein man is commanded to "subdue and have dominion over" the Earth—is the **charter** of science.

Yet undoubtedly one of the greatest obstacles to belief in God is the attitude that science somehow has made belief in God obsolete. Philosopher A.J. Ayer put it this way: "I believe in science. That is, I believe that a theory about the way the world works is not acceptable unless it is confirmed by the facts, and I believe that **the only way to discover what the facts are is by empirical observation"** (1966, p. 13, emp. added). Or, as humanistic philosopher Paul Kurtz suggested: "To adopt such a scientific approach unreservedly is to accept as ultimate in all matters of fact and real existence the appeal to the evidence of **experience alone; a court subordinate to no higher authority**, to be overridden by no prejudice however comfortable" (1973, p. 109, emp. added).

At the conclusion of the third annual Conference on Science and Philosophy and Religion in Their Relation to the Democratic Way of Life, a formal statement was framed to summarize the participants' conclusions. In that statement was this declaration:

> A world which has gained a unique sense of power through its inventive ability and its scientific knowledge, which has been trained to think in concrete terms and their immediate ends, and which enjoys the thrill of a continually changing panorama of obtainable knowledge is peculiarly resistant to the teachings of religion with its emphasis on ultimate objectives, and absolute truths (as quoted in Smith, 1974, p. 152).

In commenting on this assessment, Wilbur M. Smith wrote: "The result of such preoccupations is the snuffing out, as it were, of spiritual thoughts, or, a turning away from spiritual values. **Material contentment often makes for spiritual indifference**" (1974, p. 160, emp. added). Edward Watkin, in his book, *Theism, Agnosticism and Atheism*, opined:

> Man today is fixing his attention wholly upon a horizontal plane to the exclusion of the vertical. As this movement of exclusive outlook, this naturalism and religious humanism, has grown in power and self-confidence, it has produced an increasing blindness to religious truth. Those whose minds

> it has formed, and they are the majority of civilized mankind today, have their attention fixed so exclusively upon the phenomena visible along the **horizontal** line of vision that they can no longer see the spiritual realities visible only in the depths by a **vertical** direction... (1936, pp. 23-24, emp. added).

Approximately two decades after Dr. Watkin made that statement, its truthfulness was borne out by a prominent member of the scientific community. While attending the Darwinian Centennial Convocation at the University of Chicago in 1958, Sir Julian Huxley stated that, so far as he was concerned, Darwinian science had "removed the whole idea of God as the creator of organisms from the sphere of rational discussion" (1960, p. 45). After almost another four decades had passed, evolutionist Richard Lewontin expressed even more forcefully the unbeliever's attitude toward both science and God.

> Our willingness to accept scientific claims against common sense is the key to an understanding of the real struggle between science and the supernatural. We take the side of science **in spite** of the patent absurdity of some of its constructs, **in spite** of it failure to fulfill many of its extravagant promises of health and life, **in spite** of the tolerance of the scientific community for unsubstantiated just-so stories, because we have a prior commitment, a commitment to naturalism. It is not that the methods and institutions of science somehow compel us to accept a material explanation of the phenomenal world, but, on the contrary, that **we are forced by our *a priori* adherence to material causes** to create an apparatus of investigation and a set of concepts that produce material explanations, no matter how counter-intuitive, no matter how mystifying to the uninitiated. Moreover, **that materialism is absolute, for we cannot allow a Divine Foot in the door** (1997, p. 31, emp. in orig. except for last two sentences).

Notice what Lewontin has admitted. Neither he, nor his scientific cohorts, bases unbelief on "the methods and institutions" of science. Rather they are "forced" by their "*a priori* adherence to material causes" to accept an absolute materialism. Why? Because they resolutely refuse to "allow a Divine Foot in the door." Thus, scientific materialism has fostered unbelief.

In his book, *Intellectuals Don't Need God and Other Modern Myths*, Alister E. McGrath asked: "But what of the idea that science has rendered God unnecessary? As scientific understanding advances, will not God be squeezed out from the gaps in which Christian apologists have tried to lodge him?" (1993, p. 166). While Dr. McGrath expressed hope that this will not happen, he likewise acknowledged that, in fact, all too often it has. Smith wrote:

> But **science is no synonym for spirituality**, and the life of men is made up of more things than can be measured with test tubes and balances. Yet, man is so absorbed in the pursuit of nature's secrets that he is increasingly ignorant of his inner spiritual life, and this is one of the tragedies of our day. Men engaged in science are themselves partly to blame for this. They devote days and nights, months, and sometimes years, to the discovery of some scientific fact, but they will not give twenty minutes a day to pondering the Word of God, nor five minutes a day to the exercise of their soul in prayer to God.... Of course if men are going to lift such a miserable thing as humanity to a pedestal, then a holy and invisible God must be not only ignored, but despisingly rejected and hated, which is why many of our intellectual leaders today who look upon **humanity** as divine, must irritatingly and scornfully declare their conviction that a transcendent, omnipotent, sovereign and eternal Being can, for them, have no meaning (1974, pp. 163,164, emp. added).

Intellectual Intimidation

Some time ago, I received a heart-rending letter from a young Christian who was a graduate student in the applied sciences at a state university. His major professor was a man he termed "a giant in his field...rocket-scientist intelligent...and a devout evolutionist." In his letter, the student went on to say:

> Working this closely with one who thinks as he does is beginning to cause not a small amount of cognitive dissonance in my own mind. Hundreds of thousands of scientists

> can't be wrong, can they? Consensual validation cannot be pushed aside in science. How can that many people be following a flag with no carrier, and someone not find out? **I do not want to be a fool!**

This young writer expressed what many people experience, yet are unable to enunciate so eloquently. It is not an enjoyable experience to be exposed to the slings and barbs of infidelity. Nor is it pleasant to be labeled as dumb, stupid, or ignorant because you hold to a belief different than your opponent's. Yet it is those very labels that have been applied to those of us who are willing to defend the existence of God or the concept of creation. Several years ago, the famous atheist/evolutionist of Oxford University, Richard Dawkins wrote: "It is absolutely safe to say that if you meet somebody who claims not to believe in evolution, that person is **ignorant**, **stupid**, or **insane** (or **wicked**, but I'd rather not consider that)" (1989a, p. 34, emp. added, parenthetical comment in orig.). The old adage, "Sticks and stones may break my bones, but words can never hurt me," may be easy to parrot in such instances, but it is difficult to believe and does not offer much comfort. Truth be told, words **do** hurt. No one enjoys being thought of (or actually called) ignorant, stupid, insane, or wicked.

In this day and age, it is increasingly common to encounter those who once knew what they believed and why they believed it, yet who end up dazed, confused, and faithless because they have been intimidated intellectually. The "cognitive dissonance" mentioned by the young man is the label for the internal struggle one experiences when presented with new information that contradicts what he believes to be true. As the student struggled for consistency, he realized that he had only two choices. He either had to: (1) alter what he previously believed; or (2) disregard the new in formation being presented to him by "a rocket-scientist intelligent" professor whom he respected. This young Christian—like so many before and after him—once knew what he believed, and why. But by the time his letter arrived in my office, he no longer knew either. He pleaded: "I am a confused young man with some serious questions about my mind, my faith, and my God. Please help me."

That agonizing plea—"please help me"—has been echoed countless times through the centuries by those who languish in the "cognitive dissonance" that results from replacing the wisdom of God with the wisdom of man. The young graduate student asked: "Hundreds of thousands of scientists can't be wrong, can they?" This question may be addressed as follows. First, any argument based on "counting heads" is fallacious. Philosophy professors instruct their students on the various fallacies of human thought, one of which is the "Fallacy of Consensus." In his book, *Fundamentals of Critical Thinking*, atheistic philosopher Paul Ricci discussed the "argument from consensus," and explained in detail its errors (1986, p. 175). Interestingly, however, in the pages immediately prior to his discussion, Ricci had offered the following as a "proof" of evolution: "The reliability of evolution not only as a theory but as a principle of understanding is not contested by **the vast majority** of biologists, geologists, astronomers, and other scientists" (1986, p. 172, emp. added).

Mr. Ricci thus fell victim to the very fallacy about which he tried to warn his readers—i.e., **truth is not determined by popular opinion or majority vote**. A thing may be, and often is, true even when accepted only by a small minority. The history of science is replete with such examples. British medical doctor, Edward Jenner (1749-1823), was scorned when he suggested that smallpox could be prevented by infecting people with a less-virulent strain of the disease-causing organism. Yet his vaccine has helped eradicate smallpox. Dr. Ignaz Semmelweis (1818-1865) of Austria provides another interesting case study. He noticed the high mortality rate among surgical patients and suggested that the deaths resulted from surgeons washing neither their hands nor their instruments between patients. Dr. Semmelweis asked them to do both, but they ridiculed him and refused to comply (thereby endangering the lives of thousands of patients). Today, the solutions posed by this gentle doctor are the basis of antiseptic techniques in surgery.

Scientific successes often have occurred **because** researchers rebelled against the status quo. Sometimes "consensual validation" must be set aside—**for the sake of truth**. The cases of Jenner and Semmelweis document all too well the fact that "the intellectuals," although in the majority, may be wrong. Just because "hundreds of thousands of scientists" believe something does not make it right. As Darrell Huff observed: "People can be wrong in the mass, just as they can individually" (1959, p. 122). If something is true, stating it a million times does not make it any truer. Similarly, if something is false, stating it a million times does not make it true.

Second, the prestige of a position's advocates has nothing to do with whether that position is true or false. Newspaper magnate William Randolph Hurst, Jr. once wrote about pressures from "fashionable ideas...which are advanced with such force that common sense itself becomes the victim." He observed that a person under such pressure then may act "with an irrationality which is almost beyond belief" (1971, p. A-4).

As proof of his point, consider the suggestion some years ago by renowned scientist (and Nobel laureate) W.B. Shockley that highly intelligent women be artificially inseminated using spermatozoa from a select group of Nobel Prize winners in order to produce what he felt would be quite obviously super-intelligent offspring. There can be no doubt whatsoever that Dr. Shockley happened to be "a giant in his field" with "rocket scientist" intelligence. If the intellect or prestige of a person is enough to guarantee the validity of the positions he (or she) espouses, then perhaps the human race should have taken Dr. Shockley up on his suggestion.

But intellectual prowess or prestige does **not** confer veracity on a person's position(s). Shockley's idea, for example, was based on nothing more than the narcissism of an over-inflated ego. As Taylor has commented: "Status in the field of science is no guarantee of the truth" (1984, p. 226). The soundness or strength of a claim is not based on: (a) the number of people supporting the claim; or (b) the intellect or prestige of the one(s) making that claim.

Third, the idea of strict objectivity in intellectual circles is a myth. While most scholars like to think of themselves as broad-minded, unprejudiced paragons of virtue, the fact is that they, too, on occasion, suffer from bouts of bias, bigotry, and presuppositionalism. Nobel laureate James Watson remarked rather bluntly: "In contrast to the popular conception supported by newspapers and mothers of scientists, a goodly number of scientists are not only narrow-minded and dull, but also just stupid" (1968, p. 14). Phillip Abelson, one-time editor of *Science*, wrote: "One of the most astonishing characteristics of scientists is that some of them are plain, old-fashioned bigots. Their zeal has a fanatical, egocentric quality characterized by disdain and intolerance for anyone or any value not associated with a special area of intellectual activity" (1964, 144: 373). No doubt the same could be said of intellectuals in other fields as well (e.g., philosophy, business, the arts, etc.).

Fourth, on occasion it has been the "intellectuals" who have championed what can only be called "crazy" concepts. Bales addressed this fact when he wrote:

> There is no unreasonable position, there is no weird idea, which has not been propagated by some brilliant man who has a number of degrees after his name. Some have argued that everything is an illusion, others have maintained that they are nothing but a mess of matter or just a living mass of meat, others maintain that there is no realm of the rational and thus the very concept of an intellectual is an illusion... (1976, p. 91).

Space would fail me were I to try to provide a comprehensive listing of the "weird" ideas proposed by those esteemed as "intellectuals." For example, the eminent astrophysicist of Great Britain, Sir Fred Hoyle, proposed in his book, *Evolution from Space,* that life was planted here by creatures from outer space, and that insects are their representatives here on Earth (1981, p. 127). The celebrated philosopher René Descartes, in his *Meditations on First Philosophy* (1641), propounded the view that it is impossible to **know** anything (which makes one want to ask, "How does he **know** that it is impossible to **know**?"). And so on.

The majority ultimately will abandon God's wisdom in favor of their own. But the wisdom with which we **are** impressed is not always the wisdom with which we **should be** impressed. Christ, in His Sermon on the Mount, warned that "narrow is the gate and difficult is the way which leads to life, and there are few who find it" (Matthew 7:14). Guy N. Woods observed that this injunction

> ...was designed to guard the Lord's people from the corrupting influences of an evil environment, as well as from the powerful appeals of mob psychology to which so many in every generation succumb.... Man, by nature, is a social and gregarious being, tending to flock or gather together with others of his kind.... Man may, and often does, imbibe the evil characteristics of those about him as readily, and often more so, than the good ones (1982, 124[1]:2).

When the apostle Paul penned his first epistle to the Christians in Corinth, he warned:

> For it is written, I will destroy the wisdom of the wise, and the discernment of the discerning will I bring to naught. Where is the wise? Where is the scribe? Where is the disputer of this world? Hath not God made foolish the wisdom of the world? For seeing that in the wisdom of God the world through its wisdom knew not God, it was God's good pleasure through the foolishness of preaching to save them that believe (1 Corinthians 1:19-21).

It should not surprise us that many "intelligent" people view belief in God as the fool's way out. Paul also commented that

> not many wise after the flesh, not many mighty, not many noble, are called: but God chose the foolish things of the world, that he might put to shame them that are wise; and God chose the weak things of the world, that he might put to shame the things that are strong (1 Corinthians 1:26-27).

The most intelligent often are the least spiritual because "the god of this world" (2 Corinthians 4:3-4) has blinded their minds.

We must not fall prey to the type of mob psychology which suggests because "everyone is doing it," that somehow makes it right. The graduate student said, "I do not want to be a fool." It was a joy to tell him that he does not have to bear that stigma because "The fool hath said in his heart, there is no God" (Psalm 14:1). We need not be intimidated by the pseudo-intellectualism of those who esteem themselves with higher regard than they do their Creator. Lucy, the character in the *Peanuts* cartoon, was correct when she told Charlie Brown, "You're not right; you just **sound** right!"

CHAPTER 4

CAUSES OF UNBELIEF [PART II]

Evil, Pain, and Suffering

Surely it can be said without fear of contradiction that one of the most frequent, and thus one of the most important, causes of unbelief is the existence of evil, pain, and suffering in the world. But before we explore this concept, let us take a momentary diversion to separate the **genuine** problem from the **counterfeit**. When an individual claims not to believe in God because of the problem of evil, pain, and suffering, the person **making** such a claim may mean something entirely different than what the person **hearing** the claim thinks he means. Allow me to explain.

Admittedly, some people have difficulty believing in God because of what they consider to be **real intellectual obstacles** to such a belief. *Ex nihilo* creation, a virgin birth, or the bodily resurrection of Christ from the dead cause some to consider belief in God on par with belief in the Tooth Fairy or Santa Claus. Such concepts represent insurmountable barriers to the ultimate acceptance of God's existence.

Other people, however, face no such intellectual obstacles. Instead, they simply do not want to have to deal with the issue of the ultimate existence of a transcendent God. Their refusal to believe is not based necessarily on "this" barrier or "that" barrier. Rather, belief in God simply is inconvenient at best, or bothersome at worst. In a chapter titled "What Keeps People from Becoming Christians?" in his timely book, *Intellectuals Don't Need God*, Alister McGrath exerted considerable effort in an attempt to separate the claims of these two types of individuals when he wrote:

> "I could never be a Christian because of the problem of suffering" can mean two quite different things: (a) Having thought the matter through carefully, it seems to me that there is a real problem posed to the intellectual coherence of the Christian faith because of the existence of human suffering; (b) I don't want to get involved in a discussion about Christianity, which could get very personal and threatening. But I don't want to admit this, as it might seem to imply that I lack intellectual courage, stamina, or honesty. I can save face by letting it be understood that there are good grounds for my rejection of Christianity. So let me select a problem...suffering will do very nicely. Anyway, it will stall the efforts of this guy who's trying to convert me.
>
> For some, then, throwing intellectual problems at the Christian evangelist is like a warplane ejecting flares to divert heat-seeking missiles. It is a decoy meant to divert a deadly attack. But intellectual difficulties nevertheless constitute a real problem for some people, and answers must be given to their difficulties (1993, pp. 64-65, ellipsis in orig.).

It is not my intention in this section to deal with those in the second category who use the problem of evil, pain, and suffering merely as a ruse to hide their own cowardice in the face of overwhelming evidence regarding the existence of God. Likely, no evidence ever could convince them. They fall into the same category as Goethe, who said: "A voice from heaven would not convince me...that a woman gives birth without knowing man, and that a dead man rises from the grave" (as quoted in Smith, 1974, p. 175). Rather, I would like to discuss the unbelief of those who fall into the first category—i.e., people who view the co-existence of God and moral evil as an intellectual inconsistency that is incapable of being solved. Their number is legion, and their tribe is increasing.

For example, consider the following assessments offered by a variety of writers that runs the gamut from a Nobel laureate to a former well-known televangelist. The Nobel laureate is Steven Weinberg, author of *Dreams of a Final Theory*, which includes a chapter titled "What About God?" Within that chapter these comments can be found.

> I have to admit that sometimes nature seems more beautiful than strictly necessary. Outside the window of my home office there is a hackberry tree, visited frequently by a convocation of politic birds: blue jays, yellow-throated vireos, and, loveliest of all, an occasional red cardinal. Although I understand pretty well how brightly colored feathers evolved out of a competition for mates, it is almost irresistible to imagine that all this beauty was somehow laid on for our benefit. **But the God of birds and trees would have to be also the God of birth defects and cancer**....
>
> Remembrance of the Holocaust leaves me unsympathetic to attempts to justify the ways of God to man. **If there is a God that has special plans for humans, then He has taken very great pains to hide His concern for us** (1993, pp. 250-251, emp. added).

The former well-known televangelist is Charles B. Templeton, a high school dropout who, according to one writer, has "the natural flåre and fluidity of a salesman" (Lockerbie, 1998, p. 228). He served for many years as the pulpit minister for the Avenue Road Church (Toronto, Ontario, Canada) where his ubiquitous "Youth for Christ" rallies in the late 1940s were extremely popular. Eventually he became a world-renowned evangelist with the Billy Graham Crusade. Then, one day, he quit. He abandoned it all—not just the Billy Graham Crusade, but belief in God, belief in Christ, belief in the Bible, belief in heaven—everything! He explained why in his book, *Farewell to God*.

> I was ridding myself of archaic, outdated notions. I was dealing with life as it is. There would be an end to asking the deity for his special interventions on my behalf because I was one of the family.... If there is a loving God, why does he permit—much less create—earthquakes, droughts, floods, tornadoes, and other natural disasters which kill thousands of innocent men, women, and children every year? How can a loving, omnipotent God permit—much less create—encephalitis, cerebral palsy, brain cancer, leprosy, Alzheimer's and other incurable illnesses to afflict millions of men, women, and children, most of whom are decent people? (1996, pp. 221,230).

Almost a decade-and-a-half earlier, B.C. Johnson had given expression to the same kinds of concerns in *The Atheist Debater's Handbook*.

> A house catches on fire and six-month-old baby is painfully burned to death. Could we possibly describe as "good" any person who had the power to save this child and yet refused to do so? God undoubtedly has the power and yet...he has refused to help. Can we call God "good"? (1983, p 99).

It is not my intention here to provide an in-depth response to these (or similar) accusations. These matters have been dealt with elsewhere in detail (see: Jackson, 1988; Major, 1998; Thompson, 1990, 1993; Thompson and Jackson, 1992). Instead, I merely would like to document the role that evil, pain, and suffering have played, and still continue to play, as an important cause of man's unbelief.

Many have been those who, through the ages, have abandoned their belief in God because of the presence of evil, pain, and suffering in their lives or in the lives of those close to them. Earlier, I documented how, in 1851, Charles Darwin abandoned once and for all any vestige of belief in God after the death of his oldest daughter, Annie (see Desmond and Moore, 1991, pp. 384,386-387). But Darwin was not the only one so affected. Nine years later, on September 15, 1860, Thomas Huxley was to watch his oldest son, four-year-old Noel, die in his arms from scarlet fever. In their massive, scholarly biography, *Darwin*, Desmond and Moore wrote that Noel's death brought Huxley "...to the edge of a breakdown. Huxley tried to rationalize the 'holy leave-taking' as he stood over the body, with its staring blue eyes and tangled golden hair, **but the tragedy left a deep scar**" (1991, p. 503, emp. added).

At Noel's funeral, the minister briefly referred to 1 Corinthians 15:14-19 in his eulogy. When he quoted the passage from that section of Scripture which mentions, "if the dead be not raised," Huxley was outraged. Eight days after Noel's death, on September 23, he wrote to his close friend, Charles Kingsley, about the minister's words: "I cannot tell you how inexpressibly they shocked me. [The preacher—BT] had neither wife nor child, or he must have known that his alternative involved a blasphemy against all that was best and noblest in human nature. I could have laughed with scorn" (see Leonard Huxley, 1900, 1:151-152). In the equally scholarly (and equally massive) companion biography that he authored, *Huxley*, Adrian Desmond wrote of the man known as "Darwin's Bulldog" on the day of his son's death:

> He sat in the study facing the tiny body. His emotions were unleashed as he looked back to that New Year's Eve 1856, when he had sat at the same desk and pledged on his son's birth to give "a new and healthier direction to all Biological Science." He had found redemption on his son's death. There was no blame, **only submission to Nature**, and that brought its own catharsis (1997, p. 287, emp. added).

"Submission to Nature" became Huxley's watchword. Belief in God—however feeble it may have been prior to Noel's death—now had evaporated completely. All that remained was to give "a new and healthier direction to all Biological Science." And so it was to "Nature" that Huxley devoted the remainder of his life.

But not all such events have occurred in centuries long since gone. Modern-day parallels abound. Samuel Langhorne Clemens (a.k.a. Mark Twain) became implacably embittered against God after the death, in 1896, of his favorite daughter, Suzy. Famed English novelist, W. Somerset Maugham, recounted in his autobiography, *The Summing Up*, how that as a youngster he had prayed to God one night that he might be delivered from the terrible speech impediment that afflicted him. The next day he arose, only to find that the impediment still was present. So profound was his grief and disappointment at the failure of God to cure him overnight that from that point forward he pledged never to believe in God again.

In the mid-1960s, a devoutly religious young man from Chattanooga, Tennessee was a role model for all of his classmates. He led a prayer group, and planned to become a foreign missionary—until his sister died of leukemia and his father committed suicide. The boy's belief in God collapsed, and he subsequently became one of America's most outspoken unbelievers, humanists, and pro-abortion advocates. That boy's name?—Ted Turner, founder of world-famous CNN, the Turner Broadcasting System, and other well-known media enterprises.

But, of course, it is not just the famous who abandon their belief in God because of evil, pain, and suffering in their lives. The "man (or woman, as the case may be) on the street" is no less affected. A case in point is that of Judith Hayes, a senior writer for *The American Rationalist*. In 1996, Mrs. Hayes authored an acrimonious tirade titled, *In God We Trust: But Which One?*, in which she explained why she left the Lutheran Church (Missouri Synod) and became an atheist. First, as a youngster she had a good friend named Susan who was a devout Buddhist. Judith, however, simply could not accept the teachings of Scripture that Susan would be lost if she did not obey the biblical scheme of redemption set forth so plainly in God's Word. Thus she made, not a rational decision based upon the evidence, but an emotional decision based on her own "inner desires." Neither Christianity, she said, nor its God, could be accepted as true.

Second, Judith eventually married. But the relationship soured and disintegrated due to the fact, Mrs. Hayes reported, that her husband became verbally abusive. Instead of considering the possibility that **she** had made a poor choice of mates, or that **her husband** had misused his own personal freedom of choice, Judith blamed God. "[H]ow could I possibly have wound up married to a tyrant?," she wrote. "Why had God forsaken me?" (1996, p. 15).

Again, time and space would fail me were I to attempt merely to enumerate, much less discuss, all those who have abandoned belief in God because of evil, pain, and suffering in their lives or in the lives of those close to them. But what shall we say in regard to their accusations against their Creator? How shall we respond to their recalcitrant charge that—as a result of such epidemic, universal suffering—unbelief in God is both justifiable and justified?

Briefly, I would like to respond as follows. At the end of His six days of creation (Genesis 1:31), God surveyed all that He had made and proclaimed it "very good" (Hebrew terminology representing that which was both complete and perfect). Pestilence, disease, and death among humans were unknown. Man existed in an idyllic paradise of happiness and beauty where he shared such an intimate and blissful covenant relationship with his Maker that God came to the garden "in the cool of the day" to commune with its human inhabitants (Genesis 3:8). Additionally, Genesis 3:22 records that man had continual access to the tree of life that stood in the garden, the fruit of which would allow him to live forever.

The peacefulness and tranquility of the first days of humanity were not to prevail, however. In Genesis 3—in fewer words than an average sportswriter would use to discuss a high school football game—Moses, through inspiration, discussed the breaking of the covenant relationship between man and God, the entrance of sin into the world, and the curse(s) that resulted therefrom. When our original parents revolted against their Creator, evil entered the world. Moses informs us that as a direct consequence of human sin, the Earth was "cursed" (Genesis 3:17). Paul, in Romans 8:19-20, declared that the entire creation was subjected to "vanity" and the "bondage of corruption" as a result of the sinful events that took place in Eden on that occasion. Things apparently deteriorated rapidly. Just three chapters later, Moses wrote:

> And Jehovah saw that the wickedness of man was great in the earth, and that every imagination of the thoughts of his heart was only evil continually. And it repented Jehovah that he had made man on the earth, and it grieved him at his

> heart. And Jehovah said, I will destroy man whom I have created from the face of the earth; both man and beast, and creeping things, and birds of the heavens... (Genesis 6: 5-7).

From this assessment, one writer correctly concluded: "...the cause of all that is wrong with the earth is **not** godliness but rather **un**godliness" (Porter, 1974, 91[30]:467, emp. in orig.). The matter of man's personal volition has much to do with this. The Scriptures speak to the fact that since God is love, and since love allows freedom of choice, God allows freedom of choice (cf. Joshua 24:15; John 5:39-40). God did not create men and women as robots to serve Him slavishly without any kind of free moral agency on their part. Mankind now reaps the consequences of the misuse of freedom of choice (i.e., the sin) of previous generations. Surely one of the lessons taught here is that it does not pay to disobey the Creator. In his second epistle, Peter referred to "the world that then was," prior to its destruction by the Great Flood (3:6). That world no longer exists, however. Today we inhabit a once-perfect-but-now-flawed Earth. Man—not God—must bear the blame.

Furthermore, God created a world ruled by natural laws established at the Creation. If a man steps off the roof of a five-story building, gravity will pull him to the pavement beneath. If a boy steps in front of a moving freight train, since two objects cannot occupy the same space at the same time, the train will strike the child and likely kill him. The same laws that govern gravity, matter in motion, or similar phenomena also govern weather patterns, water movement, and other geological/meteorological conditions. **All** of nature is regulated by these laws—not just the parts that we find convenient. These natural laws are both inviolable and non-selective. **Everyone** (believer and unbeliever alike) must obey them or suffer the consequences. In Luke 13:2-5, Jesus told the story of eighteen men who perished when the tower of Siloam collapsed. Had these men perished because of their sin? No, they were no worse sinners than their peers. They died because a natural law was in force. Fortunately, natural laws work continually so that we can understand and benefit from them. We are not left to sort out some kind of haphazard system that works one day but not the next.

In the end, the most important question is not, "Why did 'this' or 'that' happen to me?," but instead, "How can I understand what has happened, and how am I going to react to it?" As McGrath put it:

> The sufferings of this earth are for real. They are painful. God is deeply pained by our suffering, just as we are shocked, grieved, and mystified by the suffering of our family and friends. But that is only half of the story. The other half must be told. It is natural that our attention should be fixed on what we experience and feel here and now. But faith demands that we raise our sights and look ahead to what lies ahead. We may suffer as we journey—but where are we going? What lies ahead? (1993, pp. 105-106).

As much as the unbeliever hates to admit it, there **are** times when suffering actually is **beneficial**. Think of the man whose chest begins to throb as he enters the throes of a heart attack. Think of the woman whose side begins to ache at the onset of acute appendicitis. Is it not true that pain often sends us to the doctor for prevention or cure? Is it not true also that at times suffering helps humankind develop the traits that people treasure the most? Bravery, heroism, altruistic love, self-sacrifice—all flourish in less-than-perfect environments, do they not? Yet people who exhibit such traits are cherished and honored as having gone "above and beyond the call of duty." Was this not the very point Christ was making when He said: "Greater love hath no man than this, that a man lay down his life for his friends" (John 15:13)?

Instead of blaming God because evil, pain, and suffering exist, we should turn to Him for strength, and let tragedies, of whatever nature, remind us that this world never was intended to be a final home (Hebrews 11:13-16). Our time here is temporary (James 4:14), and with God's help, we are able to overcome whatever comes our way (Romans 8:35-39; Psalm 46:1-3). With Peter, the faithful believer can echo the sentiment that God, "who called you unto his eternal glory in Christ, after that ye have suffered a little while, shall himself perfect, establish, strengthen you" (1 Peter 5:10). As McGrath went on to say:

> Suffering and glorification are part of, but represent different stages in, the same process of growth in the Christian life. We are adopted into the family of God, we suffer, and we are glorified (Rom. 8:14-18). This is not an accidental relationship. They are all intimately connected within the overall pattern of Christian growth and progress toward the ultimate goal of the Christian life—being finally united with God and remaining with him forever.
>
> We are thus presented with a glorious vision of a new realm of existence. It is a realm in which suffering has been defeated. It is a realm pervaded by the refreshing presence of God, from which the presence and power of sin have finally be excluded. It lies ahead, and though we have yet to enter into it, we can catch a hint of its fragrance and hear its music in the distance. It is this hope that keeps us going in this life of sadness, which must end in death....
>
> It is here that the resurrection of Christ becomes of central importance. The Resurrection allows the suffering of Christ to be seen in the perspective of eternity. Suffering is not pointless but leads to glory. Those who share in the sufferings of Christ may, through the resurrection of Christ, know what awaits them at the end of history. It is for this reason that Paul is able to declare with such confidence that "our present sufferings are not worth comparing with the glory of what will be revealed in us" (Rom. 8:18). This is no groundless hope, no arbitrary aspiration. It is a hard-headed realism, grounded in the reality of the suffering and resurrection of Christ and in the knowledge that faith binds believers to Christ and guarantees that we shall share in his heritage....
>
> Just as suffering is real, so are the promises of God and the hope of eternal life. This is no spiritual anesthetic, designed merely to enable us to copy with life's sorrows while they last. The death and resurrection of Christ...are pledges, sureties, and guarantees that what has been promised will one day be brought to glorious realization. For the moment we struggle and suffer in sadness mingled with bewilderment.

> But one day all that will be changed for the people of God. "God himself will be with them; he will wipe away every tear from their eyes, and death shall be no more, neither shall there be mourning nor crying nor pain any more, for the former things have passed away" (Rev. 21:3-4).
>
> In that hope, we go forward into life in faith. We may not know exactly where that faith will lead us. But we **do** know that, wherever we go, the God of all compassion goes a-head of us and journeys with us, consoling and reassuring us, until that day when we shall see him face to face, and know him just as he knows us (1993, pp. 106-107,105-106,108, emp. in orig.).

Finally, no one can suggest—justifiably—that suffering per se is contrary to the existence or goodness of God in light of the series of events that transpired at Calvary almost two thousand years ago. The fact that **even the Son of God**, was subjected to evil, pain, and suffering (Hebrews 5:8; 1 Peter 2:21ff.) shows conclusively that God loves and cares for His creation. He is not the unloving, angry, vengeful God depicted by atheism and infidelity. Rather, "while we were enemies, we were reconciled to God through the death of his Son, much more, being reconciled, shall we be saved by his life" (Romans 5:10). God could have abandoned us to our own sinful devices but instead, "God commendeth his own love toward us, in that, while we were yet sinners, Christ died for us" (Romans 5:8). The apostle John stated the matter beautifully when he wrote:

> Herein was the love of God manifested in us, that God hath sent his only begotten Son into the world that we might live through him. Herein is love, not that we loved God, but that he loved us, and sent his Son to be the propitiation for our sins (1 John 4:9-10).

The unbeliever, for reasons known only to himself, either is unable, or unwilling, to concede the love of God. That—not the current evil, pain, or suffering that he is enduring—is the greatest tragedy of his life.

Hypocrisy or Misconduct of Believers

As much as those of us who believe in God hate to admit it, the truth of the matter is that on occasion our own actions have the potential to drive others toward unbelief. Try as we might, we still make mistakes. And sometimes our errors are egregious. There always have been sad stories of graphic hypocrisy and sordid misconduct on the part of believers (witness the drama of Ananias and Sapphira in Acts 5). But those cases have not always been publicized in such a global fashion as they now are. Today, when Jimmy Swaggart is photographed in a midnight tryst with a prostitute, or when Jim Bakker is tried in a court of law and found guilty of fraud involving church funds, it is a dream come true for evening network television programs. And what self-respecting news anchor or late-night comedian can resist the temptation to point out that these indiscretions and crimes have been committed by "believers"? Juicy, salacious tidbits, these—made all the more prurient by the fact that they fly in the face of everything pure and holy that such people are supposed to emulate in their lives.

Such hypocrisy and misconduct are hard pills to swallow even for fellow believers. But put yourself in the place of the person who already is struggling with doubts not only about the **system** of belief, but about the **God behind the system**. From their vantage point, when the system "fails" (i.e., when its adherents are unable to conform to it successfully in their own lives), what, then, shall be said about the God behind the system? As Bales observed:

> The corruptions, or shortcomings, or the hypocrisy in the lives of some believers have been used to justify the rejection of Christianity. They are viewed as adequate samples of the faith, and since the samples are not good, the faith is viewed as bad (1976, p. 49).

The Proverbs writer emphasized: "Confidence in an unfaithful man in time of trouble is like a broken tooth, and a foot out of joint" (25:19).

The unfaithfulness, hypocrisy, or misconduct of a single believer can have severe repercussions not just for other believers, but for unbelievers as well. Such circumstances provide "grist for the mill" of those who continually are searching for what they consider to be legitimate reasons not to believe in God. Perhaps Paul had this in mind when he wrote his first epistle to the young evangelist Timothy, urging that his instructions be carried out so that there would be "no occasion to the adversary for reviling" (1 Timothy 5:14). When believers become hypocrites, it supplies ammunition for those who have set themselves against God. And oftentimes the seed of potential disbelief blossoms into the flower of full-fledged unbelief. History is filled with sad-but-true accounts of those who plunged headlong into the embracing arms of infidelity as the result of unpleasant experiences with believers. Two of the most prominent examples that come to mind are H.G. Wells (see Clark, 1945) and Thomas H. Huxley (see Clark, 1948).

While we readily acknowledge the devastating effect that can result from the hypocrisy and/or misconduct of believers, and while we make no attempt whatsoever to justify or excuse such conduct, at the same time we must recognize the fact that it is sheer folly to blame God for the blunders of humanity. Rejecting God because of hypocrisy in the lives of some of His followers can become a two-edged sword. It has been said that "hypocrisy is the tribute that vice pays to virtue." Put another way, it is contradictory for an unbeliever to attempt to justify his unbelief by pointing out hypocrisy in someone else. The very fact that the unbeliever is willing to label the believer a "hypocrite" proves that he is aware of the fact that the believer is not measuring up to the high standards of the system he professes to follow. By suggesting that a believer is a hypocrite, the unbeliever implies that there is a system of belief that, when properly adhered to, would legitimize the conduct of the believer. Bales put it this way:

> When an individual accuses another of being a hypocrite, he is appealing to a standard of integrity. He is saying that it is **wrong** to be a hypocrite.... Those who hold to a world view which justifies the acceptance of moral law can consistently oppose hypocrisy. Those whose world view rules out moral law cannot be consistent and accept a standard which says that hypocrisy is wrong (1976, p. 50, emp. added).

No one condemned hypocrisy more than the Son of God Himself when, in Matthew 23, He pronounced the well-known "seven woes" on the religious leaders of His day and condemned them for their own hypocrisy. Additionally, the point needs to be made that, on occasion, the label of "hypocrite" is misapplied.

> A person is not a hypocrite because he is weak, and fails at times in his struggle against evil. He is not a hypocrite because he never perfectly achieves the perfect standard of life. In fact, he would be a hypocrite if he claimed that he **had** arrived at perfection. One is not a hypocrite because he is inconsistent. One may not be aware of the contradiction in his life. He may not be conscious of a particular clash between his profession and his conduct. Because the tares and the wheat may look alike for awhile does not mean that the wheat is made up of tares.... **Because weeds spring up in a garden, does this mean they were planted by the gardener**? (Bales, 1976, p. 50, emp. added).

The psalmist wrote: "It is better to take refuge in Jehovah than to put confidence in man" (118:8). Oh, that the unbeliever could learn that lesson.

Unjust Acts Committed by Believers in the Name of God

It has been said that perhaps the only thing that is consistent in this world is **in**consistency. Anyone who has tried to live according to a standard can attest to the fact that such a statement contains an element of truth. The refrain, "Ah, consistency, thou art a rare jewel," reverberates within the human soul on a daily basis. Likely, most people **want** to live a consistent (and, hopefully, a **consistently good**) life. But such a feat often falls under the category of "easier said than done." Especially is this true when the standard by which a person is attempting to live is itself a consistently high one.

Enter belief in God and His Word. Even when those of us who firmly believe in God, and who confidently accept the Bible as His inspired communication to mankind, strive diligently to conform our words and deeds to those set out in God's Word, we sometimes still fail. David, Israel's beloved king, was described as a man after God's "own heart" (1 Samuel 13:14), yet he committed adultery with Bathsheba and had her husband, Uriah, murdered (2 Samuel 11-12). Peter, one of the Lord's hand-chosen apostles, loved his Master dearly, yet denied Him publicly three times on the eve of His crucifixion (Matthew 26:34,69-75). Even the apostle Paul waged his own personal war against the frequent temptations to do evil rather than good. When he wrote to encourage the first-century Christians in Rome, he admitted:

> For the good which I would I do not: but the evil which I would not, that I practice. For I delight in the law of God after the inward man: but I see a different law in my members, warring against the law of my mind, and bringing me into captivity under the law of sin which is in my members (Romans 7:19,22-23).

Adding to the problem is the fact that we may be absolutely sincere in what we do or say, yet still be entirely wrong. For example, consider the case of Uzzah. God had instructed the Israelites in a most specific manner (Numbers 4:15,19-20) that they were not to touch the "holy things," among which was the Ark of the Covenant. In 2 Samuel, however, the story is told of the day that King David had the Ark loaded onto an oxcart in order to move it. During the trip, the text indicates that "the oxen stumbled." Uzzah reached to steady the Ark and the moment he touched it, God struck him dead (2 Samuel 6:6-8). There can be no doubt that Uzzah was sincere in his attempts to protect the Ark. But he was **sincerely wrong**. Note specifically the Bible's statement that "God smote him there **for his error**" (2 Samuel 6:7).

Unfortunately, throughout human history there have been those who have professed the high standard of Christianity, yet who have committed unjust acts in the name of God—acts that have been a blight to believers and a boon to unbelievers. For example, in the time period between A.D. 1095 and 1270, eight different crusades occurred, during which armies representing "Christendom" battled Muslims in and around Jerusalem to gain control of the "holy city" and force Mohammed's followers into submission to Christ.

In 1613, Galileo published his first musings about the possible truthfulness of the Copernican system of planetary movements (i.e., that the Earth moves around the Sun, not the reverse as the old, revered Ptolemaic system suggested). In 1616, a decree was issued by the Catholic Church that prevented Galileo from publishing any additional supportive evidence for his hypothesis. But in 1632, he published *Dialogue Concerning the Two Great World Systems—Ptolemaic and Copernican.* One year later, in 1633, he found himself in front of an Inquisition in Rome—which found him guilty of violating church doctrine (in spite of the fact that he had been right in his defense of Copernicus' views).

In modern times, we have witnessed things no less savory. In 1988, Salman Rushdie authored *The Satanic Verses*, a book that drew the ire of radical Iranian Muslim spiritual leader, Ayatollah Khomeini. On February 4, 1989 Khomeini issued a *fatwa* (religious decree) in the name of Allah (God), calling for the immediate assassination of Rushdie and offering a six-million-dollar reward to anyone carrying out the task successfully. Rushdie was forced to go into hiding in Britain, where he was given 'round-the-clock protection by Scotland Yard.

In Northern Ireland, Catholics and Protestants have battled each other for decades under the flags of their respective religions. Bullets rip through shopping centers and schoolyards. Snipers fire on passers-by. Innocent adults, teenagers, and children die by the hundreds—all in the name of God. In Yugoslavia, "Christian"

Serbs depart on "search and destroy" missions in an effort to rout opposing Muslim forces. "Ethnic cleansing" is carried out—again, in God's name.

Or, to bring the matter closer to home, militants bomb abortion clinics, maiming and killing patients and staff alike. These same individuals declare "open season" on medical doctors who perform abortions, and these practitioners subsequently are shot dead as they stand at their kitchen window or get in their car to drive to work. All in the name of the God of heaven.

And the unbeliever's case is made for him as he witnesses what he views as unjust, heinous acts carried out by people who are supposed to live daily by the Golden Rule and by the Word of the God Who established that Rule. The reaction is as swift as it is adamant. How could a good God sanction such barbaric inhumanity? And why would anyone want to serve such a God? While the unbeliever continues to ponder such questions and witness such atrocities, the roots of his unbelief grow ever deeper.

How should the believer respond to these things? First, let us admit forthrightly that such things as the brutality of the Crusades, the murder of abortionists, or the ethnic cleansing of non-Christians **are** unjust deeds that never should have occurred in the first place. The acts committed are abhorrent and the attitudes of those responsible are deplorable.

Neither God nor Christ ever has **forced** men to submit to the Divine Will. In fact, Christ specifically stated: "My kingdom is not of this world: **if** my kingdom were of this world, **then** would my servants fight" (John 18:36, emp. added). Nothing can justify the torture inflicted on so many Muslims during the Crusades in an attempt to "cram Christianity down their collective throats." And the very idea of eliminating through "ethnic cleansing" those who are considered by some to be "enemies" of God is as repugnant as it is contrary to God's nature. The same God Who said, "As ye would that men should do to you, do ye to them likewise" (Luke 6:31), also commanded:

> Love your enemies, do good to them that hate you, bless them that curse you, pray for them that despitefully use you To him that smiteth thee on the one cheek offer also the other; and from him that taketh away thy cloak withhold not thy coat also. Give to every one that asketh thee; and of him that taketh away thy goods ask them not again. And if ye love them that love you, what thank have ye? for even sinners love those that love them. And if ye do good to them that do good to you, what thank have ye? for even sinners do the same. And if ye lend to them of whom ye hope to receive, what thank have ye? Even sinners lend to sinners, to receive again as much. But love your enemies, and do them good, and lend, never despairing; and your reward shall be great, and ye shall be sons of the Most High: for he is kind toward the unthankful and evil (Luke 6:27-30,32-35).

Nor does God condone the lawlessness involved in such acts as bombing abortion clinics or killing doctors who perform abortions. The same God Who condemns the slaughter of unborn children via abortion (Proverbs 6:16-17) likewise condemns the illegal slaughter of those who wrongly murder such children (Matthew 10:19).

Second, it is unfair to blame God for unjust acts committed in His name by those who claim to believe in Him, yet who disobey His will. While a person may be sincere, he or she may be **sincerely wrong**. The fact that someone commits an act "in God's name" does not mean necessarily that the **act itself** is sanctioned by the One in Whose name it was committed. For example, when law-enforcement officers act "in the name of the law," but illegally and unjustly pistol-whip a suspect to obtain a coerced confession, or commit perjury under oath in order to "frame" a defendant, does the "law" bear the blame for their offenses? Certainly not! The law specifically **forbade** their actions. The fact that those actions were carried out "in the name of the law" does not reflect poorly on the law itself. An unjust act that stands in opposition to an objective moral standard does not impugn the standard. So should it be with God. Reprehensible acts carried out "in God's name" should not reflect upon the high moral standard of God.

Third, in this context it is important to separate the **real** believer from the **counterfeit** believer. Just because someone **claims** to be a believer does not necessarily mean that he or she actually **is** a believer. But how is that distinction to be made? God warned:

> Beware of false prophets who come to you in sheep's clothing, but inwardly are ravening wolves. **By their fruits ye shall know them**. Do men gather grapes of thorns, or figs of thistles? Even so every good tree bringeth forth good fruit; but the corrupt tree bringeth forth evil fruit. A good tree cannot bring forth evil fruit, neither can a corrupt tree bring forth good fruit.... Therefore by their fruits ye shall know them (Matthew 7:15-20).

A counterfeit remains a counterfeit regardless of the fact that it **claims** (or even **appears**) to be genuine. Its genuineness is determined by whether or not it successfully matches the list of characteristics for that which actually **is** real—the "genuine article" as we so often call it. The same is true of those who believe in God. The genuineness of both their claim and their actions is determined by whether or not what they say and do matches the list of characteristics for **true believers**.

Consider two modern-day analogies. Everything done in the name of "science" is not scientific. When a scientist says that in his professional opinion a nuclear bomb should be dropped on a certain country, he is not speaking as a scientist. He may have degrees in science and may even wear a white laboratory coat while peering into a microscope. But the fact remains that there is nothing inherent in the scientific method that would allow someone to determine whether nuclear energy should be employed to destroy cancer cells or entire cities. This is a decision that science is not equipped to make because it falls far beyond the pale of the scientific method.

And, not everything done in the name of "morality" is moral. Surely, one of the saddest events in American history occurred between 1932 and 1972 when the U.S. Public Health Service sanctioned the "Tuskegee Experiments," in which 399 poor African

American men from Macon County, Alabama—known to be infected with *Treponema pallidum* (the microorganism responsible for the dreaded venereal disease, syphilis)—were studied to determine the effects of this debilitating condition. The government doctors involved in the study never told the participants that they had syphilis. Nor did they obtain "informed consent" from the men for their experiments.

Even though the physicians knew that the disease was fatal if left untreated, and even though antibiotics were available that could have saved the lives of the test subjects, those subjects were denied access to such antibiotics. Instead, they were patronized, prodded, and poked in what can only be called one of the most shameful experiments ever perpetrated on Americans. What was the rationale offered in later years for the experiments, once the scheme finally was uncovered? Those responsible claimed that they wanted to provide knowledge of the disease in the hope that it might prevent the physical degradation and death so often associated with syphilis victims. And, of course, they wanted to secure information that could be used to slow, or halt, the "moral degradation" associated with contracting a venereal disease in the first place.

Counterfeit actions carried out "in the name of God" are just that—counterfeit. Just because someone "claims" that certain actions are sanctioned by God does not mean necessarily that they are. What is needed here is a "fruit inspector" who can compare the counterfeit to the original and thereby separate fact from fiction. J.M. Mathews stated it well: "We ask that the consequences which can be proved to flow from Christianity as the legitimate fruit of the system should be distinguished from those which have no true alliance with her teachings or her influences" (1857, pp. 73-78).

Fourth, speaking of consistency (the topic I used to introduce this section), we need to realize that it is not just the **believer** who should be held to such a standard. The **unbeliever** needs to comply as well. The colloquialism, "The sauce that's good for the goose also is good for the gander," applies here. As Bales observed:

> Atheism and other systems of unbelief, in applying the fruit test to Christianity, are inviting the application of this test to their systems of faith and practice. Atheistic systems undermine the dignity of man by reducing him to an evolved animal; they destroy morality by denying the reality of freedom and the moral law. Any system of strict determinism and moral relativism undermines human dignity and the value of man. When men live by such systems of unbelief, the fruits are destructive. And these destructive fruits are rightly charged to any system which makes man but matter in motion, destroys the moral law, and eliminates the reality of duty. What atheistic materialism does when it rules the lives of men has been demonstrated in our times.... Perhaps this explains why, so far as the author knows, in our country believers in God do not hypocritically put on the cloak of atheism and parade as atheists (1976, pp. 47-48,49).

Bales has made a good point. When you examine the **legitimate** teachings and fruits of a particular system, ask yourself: "Which one has more to commend itself—belief in God, or unbelief?" When Dr. Bales stated that "when men live by such systems of unbelief, the fruits are destructive," he was not speaking out of turn. No less of an authority on atheism than Oxford professor Richard Dawkins conceded as much. In his book, *The Selfish Gene*, Dr. Dawkins discussed at great length the gene's role in the naturalistic process of "survival of the fittest" and admitted that, according to the evolutionary paradigm, genes are "selfish" because they will do whatever it takes to ensure that the individual in which they are stored produces additional copies of the genes. In commenting on the effects of such a concept on society as a whole, he then lamented: "My own feeling is that a human society based simply on the gene's law of universal ruthlessness would be a very nasty society in which to live" (1989b, p. 3).

When men act consistently, when men act congruously, and when men act correctly—in keeping with the cardinal doctrines of their respective world views—which system has more to recommend itself, belief or unbelief? To ask is to answer, is it not? One system—belief—teaches that we should esteem others better than ourselves, love our neighbors, and be self-sacrificing even unto death. The other—unbelief—teaches a "survival of the fittest" concept that makes nature "red in tooth and claw" so that the strong subjugates the weak, might makes right, and "selfish genes" ensure that it is "every man for himself." Truth be told, whom would you rather have for **your** neighbor—the believer, or the unbeliever?

Unbelief

When you see the above section heading of "Unbelief" listed as a **cause** of unbelief, you might think that surely I have erred. How, pray tell, could **unbelief** be a cause of **unbelief**? Please allow me to explain.

It is my contention that unbelief engenders **more** unbelief. In his book, *Therefore Stand*, Wilbur M. Smith compared unchecked unbelief to

> ...a contagious disease. Unless it is restrained it grows in intensity, and will infect an increasingly large number of people. It is difficult to determine whether this is an age of unbelief because so many men do not believe, or many men do not believe because it is an age of unbelief. I suppose that some would say you cannot have an age of unbelief unless it is caused by the unbelief of men. Well, I am not so sure. There are certain intellectual and moral characteristics that mark each age of human history, and it would seem that the outstanding mark of our particular age is Unbelief (1974, p. 173).

Dr. Smith made these comments in the original printing of his book in 1945. If he was correct in his assessment that **his** was an "age of unbelief" (and the documentation he provided incontrovertibly proved his point), then what may be said about **our** age?

Smith wrote at a time when America had just emerged from the shadows and ravages of World War II. It was a time in our nation's history when people had sacrificed—first, their finances at home and, second, their sons and daughters on foreign battle fields—to bring an end to tyranny. It also was a time when people actually realized that they **needed** God.

Compare that set of circumstances to those of today. The economy is booming. America has not been involved in a war in over thirty years. Unemployment is at an all-time low. Simply put, people do not feel the "need" for God that they did in post-war America. And there are other factors to be considered. As Smith explained:

> Great thinkers, leaders of thought, men of achievement, men with great gifts of expression, inevitably must influence vast multitudes of people who look up to them as their leaders, as their guide, and when the outstanding men of the great segments of thought in our generation are atheistic, and antagonistic to the Christian Faith, what can one expect the younger generation to be, willingly following in their steps? (1974, p. 174).

We are living in an age where some of the most visible, most respected, and most prolific intellectuals on the world stage are outspoken proponents of unbelief. We view the late Carl Sagan's lavish television extravaganza, *Cosmos*, and are informed that evolution is a "scientific fact" from which no reasonable person dissents. Our children go to their school libraries to select a book for a required reading assignment and are able to choose from over 500 volumes authored by the late evolutionist and humanist, Isaac Asimov, whose vitriolic diatribes against God were his stock-in-trade.

Those same children then go off to college and receive class handouts that are reprints from *Natural History* magazine of the monthly column, "This View of Life," authored by Harvard's renowned Marxist and evolutionist, Stephen Jay Gould. The editors of *National Geographic* send their full-color, slick-paper, professionally produced, eye-catching magazine into our homes each and every month so that we, our children, and our grandchildren can read articles by such world-famous evolutionists as Donald C. Johanson (discoverer of our alleged hominid ancestor, "Lucy") or the late Louis and Mary Leakey (both of whom spent their entire professional careers on the African continent searching for the ever-elusive "missing link" between humans and ape-like ancestors).

Our children sit at the feet of evolutionary professors who strive daily to convince them that they have evolved from some sort of primordial slime on the primeval Earth. They view television shows (produced by amoral unbelievers who have become Hollywood's financial darlings) intended to help rid them of their archaic "Bible-belt mentality." They are required to read and digest articles by atheistic wordsmiths whose purpose it is to convince them that God is no more real than the Man in the Moon or the Easter Bunny. They digest books by prolific, infidelic authors who revel in every facet of human immorality—and who beckon them to do likewise.

Then one day our precious 19- or 20-year-old son or daughter unexpectedly announces, "Mom, Dad, I don't think I believe in God any more." And we stand in shocked amazement—wondering how in the world this could have happened. This is the point I am trying to make when I say that unbelief causes unbelief.

Conclusion

Every person familiar with the Bible is aware of one of its central themes—the evil results of unbelief. Throughout the Bible, Heaven's warning was that belief (and its accompanying faithfulness) would bring spiritual life and God's blessings, while unbelief (and its accompanying unfaithfulness) would bring God's wrath and spiritual death. The prophet Ezekiel spoke of the man who "turneth away from righteousness and comitteth iniquity, and dieth therein" as being one who "in his iniquity...shall die" (18:26). The apostle Paul observed that the Old Testament was a "schoolmaster" (Galatians

3:24), and as such had been penned "for our learning" (Romans 15:4). It should come as no surprise, then, to see Paul catalog in 1 Corinthians 10 a number of instances of apostasy— as a warning to those who might be thinking about following in the footsteps of their unbelieving predecessors.

All too often man's "wisdom" has replaced God's (see 1 Corinthians 1:18-25), causing many to lose their way in what has become one of the most horrible, and yet one of the most common, tragedies of our day. The price humans have paid for being intellectually learned but spiritually ignorant—the loss of their own souls—has been far higher than we ever could have imagined.

In the New Testament book of Mark, there is an intriguing comment about the Lord. The text states simply: "And he could there do no mighty work,...and he marvelled because of their unbelief" (6:5-6). What is the meaning of this statement? Certainly, it cannot mean that Jesus was **incapable** of performing miracles on this particular occasion. As a member of the Godhead, He was all-powerful (cf. Genesis 17:1, 1 Timothy 6:16), and could not be restrained (cf. Job 42:2). Thus, He could do anything not contradictory to His nature (Habakkuk 1:13; Hebrews 6:18; James 1:13). Performing a miracle certainly was not contradictory to that nature. In fact, on numerous other occasions He had cured those who were blind (Matthew 9:27ff.), deaf and dumb (Mark 7:31ff.), leprous (Luke 17:11ff.), or had crippled limbs (Matthew 9:2; 12:10). He even raised the dead (Luke 7:11ff.). Why, then, does the text specifically record that "he could do there no mighty work"?

When Matthew discussed this event in his Gospel, he wrote: "And he **did not** many mighty works there **because of their unbelief**" (13:58, emp. added). Why, then, did Mark say that the Lord **could not** do mighty works? The Greek employed in Mark's expression is *ouk edunato*. Wayne Jackson has pointed out:

> These words are idiomatically used in the New Testament occasionally to denote what one **deliberately purposed not to do**. Perhaps some examples will be helpful. In one

> of the Lord's parables, he has a man, who is rejecting the invitation to a great supper, say, "I have married a wife, and therefore I cannot [*ou dunami*] come" (Luke 14:20). It was not that the man was literally unable to attend; rather, for other reasons he **chose not to do so**. Again, John writes: "Whosoever is begotten of God doeth no sin, because his [God's] seed abideth in him: and he cannot [*ou dunatai*] sin, because he is begotten of God" (I Jn. 3:9). This passage teaches that the child of God, because of the seed [the Word of God —Luke 8:11] that abides in him, **chooses** to refrain from practicing a life of habitual sin. So, similarly, the Lord determined not to perform many mighty works in his own country because of the quality of unbelief that was characteristic of them.
>
> This latter observation needs a little amplification. In both Matthew 13:58 and Mark 6:6, the term "unbelief" is preceded by the definite article (*ten*), literally, therefore, "the unbelief of them." Now the Greek article is sort of like an index finger, it points to, draws attention to, an object. Here, it calls attention to the fact that the unbelief of these people was so strong, so downright rebellious, that Jesus would not perform many miracles in their presence in an attempt to coerce them into accepting him (1981, 1:13, emp. and brackets in orig.).

These people had heard the testimony of the many "mighty works" Christ had done throughout the region, and even had witnessed some of His miracles themselves. [The text in Mark indicates that while He did not perform "many" miracles among them, He did heal some of their illnesses (Mark 6:5).] They had the miracle-working Son of God in their midst, and yet their attitude was one of such staunch stubbornness that—in spite of the evidence before them—they steadfastly refused to believe. Today, unbelief often is seen as a "badge of courage" to be displayed openly and worn proudly. Modern spiritual descendants of those first-century unbelievers exhibit what the Hebrew writer termed "an evil heart of unbelief" that has driven them "away from the living God" (Hebrews 10:12).

The Lord was happy to help those of His day whose unbelief resulted from a genuine ignorance of God's teachings. In Mark 9:20-24, the story is told of a father who brought his son to Christ with the request that the Son of God remove the demon that had possessed the youngster from the time he was a small child. The pleading-but-not-quite-able-to-believe father implored the Lord with these words: "If thou canst do anything, have compassion on us, and help us" (9:22). Christ's response to the man's doubt was, "If thou canst! All things are possible to him that believeth" (9:23). Then, "straightway the father of the child cried out, and said, 'I believe; help thou mine unbelief'" (9:24). And the Lord did just that!

The Lord also is happy to help those today who live in honest unbelief, and has provided ample evidence that they might believe. Speaking through the apostle John, God addressed those who, having seen and accepted that evidence, spent a lifetime building their faith upon it. "I am the Alpha and the Omega, the beginning and the end. I will give unto him that is athirst of the fountain of the water of life freely. He that overcometh shall inherit these things; and I will be his God, and he shall be my son" (Revelation 21:6-7).

But what of those who resolutely reject God's message? Their fate, too, was discussed by John: "But for the fearful, and **unbelieving**, and abominable, and murderers, and fornicators, and sorcerers, and idolaters, and all liars, their part shall be in the lake that burneth with fire and brimstone; which is the second death" (Revelation 21:8). Paul, writing to the first-century Christians in Rome, said:

> For the wrath of God is revealed from heaven against all ungodliness and unrighteousness of men, who hinder the truth in unrighteousness; because that which is known of God is manifest in them; for God manifested it unto them. For the invisible things of him since the creation of the world are clearly seen, being perceived through the things that are made, even his everlasting power and divinity; that they may be without excuse: because that, knowing God, they glorified him not as God, neither gave thanks; but became vain in their reasonings, and their senseless heart was darkened. Professing themselves to be wise, they became fools (Romans 1:18-22).

Surely, the words of poet John Greenleaf Whittier are appropriate here: "For all sad words of tongue or pen, the saddest are these: 'It might have been'."

CHAPTER 5

THE CASE FOR THE EXISTENCE OF GOD [PART I]

One of the most basic, and most fundamental, issues that can be considered by the human mind is the question, "Does God exist?" In the field of logic, there are principles—or as they are called more often, laws—that govern human thought processes and that are accepted as analytically true. One of these is the Law of the Excluded Middle. When applied to objects, this law states that an object cannot both possess and not possess a certain trait or characteristic at the same time and in the same fashion. When applied to propositions, this law states that all precisely stated propositions are either true or false; they cannot be both true and false at the same time and in the same fashion.

The statement, "God exists," is a precisely stated proposition. Thus, it is either true or false. The simple fact is, either God exists or He does not. There is no middle ground. One cannot affirm logically both the existence and nonexistence of God. The atheist boldly states that God does not exist; the theist affirms just as boldly that God does exist; the agnostic laments that there is not enough evidence to make a decision on the matter; and the skeptic doubts that God's existence can be proven with certainty. Who is correct? Does God exist or not?

The only way to answer this question, of course, is to seek out and examine the evidence. It certainly is reasonable to suggest that if there is a God, He would make available to us evidence adequate to the task of proving His existence. But does such evidence exist? And if it does, what is the nature of that evidence?

The theist advocates the view that evidence is available to prove conclusively that God does exist and that this evidence is adequate to establish beyond reasonable doubt the existence of God. However, when we employ the word "prove," we do not mean that God's existence can be demonstrated scientifically in the same fashion that one might prove that a sack of potatoes weighs ten pounds or that a human heart has four distinct chambers within it. Such matters as the weight of a sack of vegetables, or the divisions within a muscle, are matters that may be verified empirically using the five senses. And while empirical evidence often is quite useful in establishing the validity of a case, it is not the sole means of arriving at proof. For example, legal authorities recognize the validity of a *prima facie* case, which is acknowledged to exist when adequate evidence is available to establish the presumption of a fact that, unless such fact can be refuted, legally stands proven (see Jackson, 1974, p. 13). It is the contention of the theist that there is a vast body of evidence that makes an impregnable *prima facie* case for the existence of God—a case that simply cannot be refuted. I would like to present here the *prima facie* case for the existence of God, along with a small portion of the evidence upon which that case is based.

Cause and Effect—The Cosmological Argument

Throughout human history, one of the most effective arguments for the existence of God has been the cosmological argument, which addresses the fact that the Universe (Cosmos) is here and therefore must be explained in some fashion. In his book, *Not A Chance*, R.C. Sproul observed:

> Traditional philosophy argued for the existence of God on the foundation of the law of causality. The cosmological argument went from the presence of a cosmos back to a creator of the cosmos. It sought a rational answer to the question, "**Why** is there something rather than nothing?" It sought a sufficient reason for a real world (1994, p. 169, emp. in orig.).

The Universe exists and is real. Atheists and agnostics not only acknowledge its existence, but admit that it is a grand effect (e.g., see Jastrow, 1977, pp. 19-21). If an entity cannot account for its own being (i.e., it is not sufficient to have caused itself), then it is said to be "contingent" because it is dependent upon something outside of itself to explain its existence. The Universe is a contingent entity since it is inadequate to cause, or explain, its own existence. Sproul has noted: "Logic requires that if something exists contingently, it must have a cause. That is merely to say, if it is an effect it must have an antecedent cause" (1994, p. 172). Thus, since the Universe is a contingent effect, the obvious question becomes, "What **caused** the Universe?"

It is here that the Law of Cause and Effect (also known as the Law of Causality) is tied firmly to the cosmological argument. Scientists, and philosophers of science, recognize laws as "reflecting actual regularities in nature" (Hull, 1974, p. 3). So far as scientific knowledge can attest, laws know no exceptions. This certainly is true of the Law of Cause and Effect. It is, indisputably, the most universal, and most certain, of all scientific laws. Simply put, the Law of Causality states that every material effect must have an adequate antecedent cause. Just as the Law of the Excluded Middle is true analytically, so the Law of Cause and Effect is true analytically as well. Sproul addressed this when he wrote:

> The statement "Every effect has an antecedent cause" is **analytically true**. To say that it is analytically or formally true is to say that it is true by definition or analysis. There is nothing in the predicate that is not already contained by resistless logic in the subject. It is like the statement, "A bachelor is an unmarried man" or "A triangle has three sides" or "Two plus two are four...." Cause and effect, though distinct ideas, are inseparably bound together in rational discourse. It is meaningless to say that something is a **cause** if it yields no **effect**. It is likewise meaningless to say that something is an **effect** if it has no **cause**. A cause, by definition, must have an effect, or it is not a cause. An effect, by definition, must have a cause, or it is not an effect (1994, pp. 172,171 emp. in orig.).

Effects without adequate causes are unknown. Further, causes never occur subsequent to the effect. It is meaningless to speak of a cause following an effect, or an effect preceding a cause. In addition, the effect never is qualitatively superior to, or quantitatively greater than, the cause. This knowledge is responsible for our formulation of the Law of Causality in these words: Every material effect must have an **adequate** antecedent cause. The river did not turn muddy because the frog jumped in; the book did not fall from the table because the fly lighted on it. These are not adequate causes. For whatever effects we observe, we must postulate adequate antecedent causes—which brings us back to the original question: What **caused** the Universe?

There are but three possible answers to this question: (1) the Universe is eternal; it always has existed and always will exist; (2) the Universe is not eternal; rather, it created itself out of nothing; (3) the Universe is not eternal, and did not create itself out of nothing; rather, it was created by something (or Someone) anterior, and superior, to itself. These three options merit serious consideration.

Is the Universe Eternal?

The most comfortable position for the person who does not believe in God is the idea that the Universe is eternal, because it avoids the problem of a beginning or ending and thus the need for any "first cause" such as God. In fact, it was to avoid just such a problem that evolutionists Thomas Gold, Hermann Bondi, and Sir Fred Hoyle developed the Steady State Theory. Information had come to light that indicated the Universe was expanding. Dr. Hoyle suggested that the best way to try to explain both an expanding and eternal Universe was to suggest that at points in space called "irtrons" hydrogen was coming into existence **from nothing**. As hydrogen atoms arrived, they had to "go" somewhere, and as they did, they displaced matter already in existence, causing the Universe to expand. Hoyle suggested that the atoms of gaseous hydrogen gradually condensed into clouds of virgin matter, that within these clouds new stars and galaxies formed, etc.

In his book, *Until the Sun Dies*, astronomer Robert Jastrow noted that "the proposal for the creation of matter out of nothing possesses a strong appeal to the scientist, since it permits him to contemplate a Universe without beginning and without end" (1977, p. 32). Even after evidence began to appear that showed the Steady State theory to be incorrect, Jastrow suggested that "some astronomers still favored it because the notion of a world with a beginning and an end made them feel so uncomfortable" (1977, p. 33). Dr. Jastrow went on to say:

> The Universe is the totality of all matter, animate and inanimate, throughout space and time. If there was a beginning, what came before? If there is an end, what will come after? On both scientific and philosophical grounds, the concept of an eternal Universe seems more acceptable than the concept of a transient Universe that springs into being suddenly, and then fades slowly into darkness.
>
> Astronomers try not to be influenced by philosophical considerations. However, the idea of a Universe that has both a beginning and an end is distasteful to the scientific mind. In a desperate effort to avoid it, some astronomers have searched for another interpretation of the measurements that indicate the retreating motion of the galaxies, an interpretation that would not require the Universe to expand. If the evidence for the expanding Universe could be explained

> away, the need for a moment of creation would be eliminated, and the concept of time without end would return to science. But these attempts have not succeeded, and most astronomers have come to the conclusion that they live in an exploding world (1977, p. 31).

What does Jastrow mean when he says that "these attempts have not succeeded"? In a comment that was an obvious reference to the fact that Hoyle's "creation of hydrogen out of nothing in irtrons" violates the First Law of Thermodynamics, Jastrow noted:

> But the creation of matter out of nothing would violate a cherished concept in science—the principle of the conservation of matter and energy—which states that matter and energy can be neither created nor destroyed. Matter can be converted into energy, and vice versa, but the total amount of all matter and energy in the Universe must remain unchanged forever. It is difficult to accept a theory that violates such a firmly established scientific fact (1977, p. 32).

In his book, *God and the Astronomers*, Dr. Jastrow explained why attempts to prove an eternal Universe failed. "Now three lines of evidence—the motions of the galaxies, the laws of thermodynamics, and the life story of the stars—pointed to one conclusion; all indicated that the Universe had a beginning" (1978, p. 111). Jastrow—who is considered by many to be one of the greatest science writers of our time—certainly is no creationist. But as a scientist who is an astrophysicist, he has written often on the inescapable conclusion that the Universe had a beginning. Consider, for example, these statements from his pen:

> Now both theory and observation pointed to an expanding Universe and a beginning in time.... About thirty years ago science solved the mystery of the birth and death of stars, and acquired new evidence that the Universe had a beginning (1978, pp. 47,105).

> And concurrently there was a great deal of discussion about the fact that the second law of thermodynamics, applied to the Cosmos, indicates the Universe is running down like a clock. If it is running down, there must have been a time when it was fully wound up. Arthur Eddington, the most distin-

> guished British astronomer of his day, wrote, "If our views are right, somewhere between the beginning of time and the present day we must place the winding up of the universe." When that occurred, and Who or what wound up the Universe, were questions that bemused theologians, physicists and astronomers, particularly in the 1920's and 1930's (1978, pp. 48-49).
>
> Most remarkable of all is the fact that in science, as in the Bible, the World begins with an act of creation. That view has not always been held by scientists. Only as a result of the most recent discoveries can we say with a fair degree of confidence that the world has not existed forever; that it began abruptly, without apparent cause, in a blinding event that defies scientific explanation (1977, p. 19).

The conclusion to be drawn from the scientific data was inescapable, as Dr. Jastrow himself remarked:

> The lingering decline predicted by astronomers for the end of the world differs from the explosive conditions they have calculated for its birth, but the impact is the same: **modern science denies an eternal existence to the Universe, either in the past or in the future** (1977, p. 30, emp. added).

The evidence states that the Universe had a beginning. The Second Law of Thermodynamics, as Dr. Jastrow has indicated, shows this to be true. Henry Morris correctly commented: "The Second Law requires the universe to have had a beginning" (1974b, p. 26). Indeed, it does. The Universe is not eternal.

Did the Universe Create Itself Out of Nothing?

In the past, it would have been practically impossible to find any reputable scientist who would be willing to advocate a self-created Universe. George Davis, a prominent physicist of the past generation, explained why when he wrote: "No material thing can create itself." Further, Dr. Davis affirmed that this statement "cannot be logically attacked on the basis of any knowledge available to us" (1958, p. 71). The Universe is the created, not the creator. And until very recently, it seemed there could be no disagreement about that fact.

However, so strong is the evidence that the Universe had a beginning, and therefore a cause anterior and superior to itself, some evolutionists are suggesting, in order to avoid the implications, that **something came from nothing**—that is, **the Universe literally created itself from nothing**! Anthony Kenny, a British evolutionist, suggested in his book, *Five Ways of Thomas Aquinas*, that something actually came from nothing. Edward P. Tryon, professor of physics at the City University of New York, agreed when he wrote: "In 1973, I proposed that our Universe had been created spontaneously from nothing, as a result of established principles of physics. This proposal variously struck people as preposterous, enchanting, or both" (1984, 101:14). This is the same Edward P. Tryon who is on record as stating that "Our universe is simply one of those things which happen from time to time" (as quoted in Trefil, 1984, 92[6]:100).

In the May 1984 issue of *Scientific American*, evolutionists Alan Guth and Paul Steinhardt authored an article on "The Inflationary Universe" in which they suggested:

> From a historical point of view probably the most revolutionary aspect of the inflationary model is the notion that all the matter and energy in the observable universe may have emerged from almost nothing.... The inflationary model of the universe provides a possible mechanism by which the observed universe could have evolved from an infinitesimal region. It is then tempting to go one step further and speculate that **the entire universe evolved from literally nothing** (1984, 250:128, emp. added).

Therefore, even though principles of physics that "cannot be logically attacked on the basis of any knowledge available to us" preclude the creation of something out of nothing, suddenly, in a last-ditch effort to avoid the implications of the Universe having a cause, it is being suggested that indeed, the Universe simply "created itself out of nothing."

Naturally, such a proposal would seem—to use Dr. Tryon's words—"preposterous." Be that as it may, some in the evolutionary camp have been willing to defend it. One such scientist is Victor J. Stenger, professor of physics at the University of Hawaii. In 1987, Dr. Stenger authored an article titled, "Was the Universe Created?," in which he said:

> ...the universe is probably the result of a random quantum fluctuation in a spaceless, timeless void.... So what had to happen to start the universe was the formation of an empty bubble of highly curved space-time. How did this bubble form? What **caused** it? Not everything requires a cause. It could have just happened spontaneously as one of the many linear combinations of universes that has the quantum numbers of the void.... Much is still in the speculative stage, and **I must admit that there are yet no empirical or observational tests that can be used to test the idea of an accidental origin** (1987, 7[3]:26-30, first emp. in orig., second emp. added).

Such a concept, however, has met with serious opposition from within the scientific establishment. For example, in the summer 1994 edition of the *Skeptical Inquirer*, Ralph Estling wrote a stinging rebuke of the idea that the Universe created itself out of nothing. In his article, curiously titled "The Scalp-Tinglin', Mind-Blowin', Eye-Poppin', Heart-Wrenchin', Stomach-Churnin', Foot-Stumpin', Great Big Doodley Science Show!!!," Estling wrote:

> The problem emerges in science when scientists leave the realm of science and enter that of philosophy and metaphysics, too often grandiose names for mere personal opinion, untrammeled by empirical evidence or logical analysis, and wearing the mask of deep wisdom.
>
> And so they conjure us an entire Cosmos, or myriads of cosmoses, suddenly, inexplicably, causelessly leaping into being out of—out of Nothing Whatsoever, for no reason at all, and thereafter expanding faster than light into more Nothing Whatsoever. And so cosmologists have given us Creation *ex nihilo*.... And at the instant of this Creation, they inform us, almost parenthetically, the universe possessed the

> interesting attributes of Infinite Temperature, Infinite Density, and Infinitesimal Volume, a rather gripping state of affairs, as well as something of a sudden and dramatic change from Nothing Whatsoever. They then intone equations and other ritual mathematical formulae and look upon it and pronounce it good.
>
> I do not think that what these cosmologists, these quantum theorists, these universe-makers, are doing is science. I can't help feeling that universes are notoriously disinclined to spring into being, ready-made, out of nothing. Even if Edward Tryon (ah, a name at last!) has written that "our universe is simply one of those things which happen from time to time." ...Perhaps, although we have the word of many famous scientists for it, our universe is **not** simply one of those things that happen from time to time (1994, 18[4]: 430, emp. added, parenthetical comment in orig.).

Estling's statements set off a wave of controversy, as was evident from subsequent letters to the *Skeptical Inquirer*. In the January/February 1995 edition of that journal, numerous letters were published, discussing Estling's article. Estling's response to his critics was published as well, and included the following observations:

> All things begin with speculation, science not excluded. But if no empirical evidence is eventually forthcoming, or can be forthcoming, all speculation is barren.... **There is no evidence, so far, that the entire universe, observable and unobservable, emerged from a state of absolute Nothingness**. Quantum cosmologists insist both on this absolute Nothingness and on endowing it with various qualities and characteristics: this particular Nothingness possesses virtual quanta seething in a false vacuum. Quanta, virtual or actual, false or true, are not Nothing, they are definitely Something, although we may argue over what exactly. For one thing, quanta are entities having energy, a vacuum has energy and moreover, extension, i.e., it is something into which other things, such as universes, can be put, i.e., we cannot have our absolute Nothingness and eat it too. If we have quanta and a vacuum as given, we in fact have a pre-existent state of existence that either pre-existed timelessly or brought itself into existence from absolute Nothingness (no quanta, no vacuum, no pre-existing initial conditions) at some

> precise moment in time; it creates this time, along with the space, matter, and energy, which we call the universe.... I've had correspondence with Paul Davies [a British astronomer who has championed the idea that the Universe created itself from nothing—BT] on cosmological theory, in the course of which I asked him what he meant by "Nothing." He wrote back that he had asked Alexander Vilenkin what he meant by it and that Vilenkin had replied, "By Nothing I mean Nothing," which seemed pretty straightforward at the time, but these quantum cosmologists go on from there to tell us what their particular breed of Nothing consists of. I pointed this out to Davies, who replied that these things are very complicated. I'm willing to admit the truth of that statement, but I think **it does not solve the problem** (1995, 19[1]:69-70, emp. added).

This is an interesting turn of events. Evolutionists like Tryon, Stenger, Guth, and Steinhardt insist that this marvelously intricate Universe is "simply one of those things which happen from time to time" as the result of a "random quantum fluctuation in a spaceless, timeless void" that caused matter to evolve from "literally nothing." This suggestion, of course, is in clear violation of the First Law of Thermodynamics, which states that neither matter nor energy may be created or destroyed in nature. Further, science is based on observation, reproducibility, and empirical data. But when pressed for the empirical data that document the claim that the Universe created itself from nothing, evolutionists are forced to admit, as Dr. Stenger did, that "there are yet no empirical or observational tests that can be used to test the idea...." Estling summarized the problem quite well when he stated: "There is no evidence, so far, that the entire universe, observable and unobservable, emerged from a state of absolute Nothingness."

Ultimately, the Guth/Steinhardt inflationary model was shown to be incorrect, and a newer version was suggested. Working independently, Russian physicist Andrei Linde, and American physicists Andreas Albrecht and Paul Steinhardt, developed the "new inflationary model" (see Hawking, 1988, pp. 131-132). However, this model also was shown to be incorrect and was discarded. Renowned British astrophysicist Stephen W. Hawking put the matter in proper perspective when he wrote:

> The new inflationary model was a good attempt to explain why the universe is the way it is.... In my personal opinion, **the new inflationary model is now dead as a scientific theory**, although a lot of people do not seem to have heard of its demise and are still writing papers on it as if it were viable (1988, p. 132, emp. added).

Later, Linde himself suggested numerous modifications and is credited with producing what now is known as the "chaotic inflationary model" (see Hawking, 1988, pp. 132ff.). Dr. Hawking himself performed additional work on this particular model. But in an interview on June 8, 1994 dealing specifically with inflationary models, Alan Guth conceded:

> First of all, I will say that at the purely technical level, inflation itself does not explain how the universe arose from nothing.... Inflation itself takes a very small universe and produces from it a very big universe. But inflation by itself does not explain where that very small universe came from (as quoted in Heeren, 1995, p. 148).

Science is based on observation and reproducibility. But when pressed for the reproducible, empirical data that document their claim of a self-created Universe, scientists and philosophers are at a loss to produce those data. Perhaps this is why Alan Guth lamented: "In the end, I must admit that questions of plausibility are not logically determinable and depend somewhat on intuition" (1988, 11[2]:76)—which is little more than a fancy way of saying, "I certainly **wish** this were true, but I could not **prove** it to you if my life depended on it." To suggest that the Universe created itself is to posit a self-contradictory position. Sproul addressed this when he wrote that what an atheist or agnostic

> ...deems possible for the world to do—come into being without a cause—is something no judicious philosopher would grant that even God could do. It is as formally and rationally

> impossible for God to come into being without a cause as it is for the world to do so.... For something to bring itself into being it must have the power of being within itself. It must at least have enough causal power to cause its own being. If it derives its being from some other source, then it clearly would not be either self-existent or self-created. It would be, plainly and simply, an effect. Of course, the problem is complicated by the other necessity we've labored so painstakingly to establish: It would have to have the causal power of being before it was. It would have to have the power of being before it had any being with which to exercise that power (1994, pp. 179,180).

The Universe did not create itself. Such an idea is absurd, both philosophically and scientifically.

Was the Universe Created?

Either the Universe had a beginning, or it did not. But all available evidence indicates that the Universe did, in fact, have a beginning. If the Universe had a beginning, it either had a cause or it did not. One thing we know assuredly, however: it is correct—logically and scientifically—to acknowledge that the Universe had a cause, because the Universe is an effect and requires an adequate antecedent cause. Henry Morris was correct when he suggested that the Law of Cause and Effect is "universally accepted and followed in every field of science" (1974b, p. 19). The cause/effect principle states that wherever there is a material effect, there must be an adequate antecedent cause. Further indicated, however, is the fact that no effect can be qualitatively superior to, or quantitatively greater than, its cause.

Since it is apparent that the Universe it not eternal, and since likewise it is apparent that the Universe could not have created itself, the only remaining alternative is that the Universe **was created** by something, or Someone, that: (a) existed before it, i.e., some eternal, uncaused First Cause; (b) is superior to it—since the created cannot be superior to the creator; and (c) is of a different nature, since the finite, contingent Universe of matter is unable to explain itself (see Jackson and Carroll, n.d., 2:98-154). As Hoyle and Wickramasinghe have observed: "To be consistent logically, we have to say that the intelligence which assembled the enzymes did not itself contain them" (1981, p. 139).

In connection with this, another fact should be considered. If there ever had been a time when absolutely **nothing** existed, then there would be nothing now. It is a self-evident truth that nothing produces nothing. In view of this, **since something does exist, it must follow logically that something has existed forever**! As Sproul observed:

> Indeed, reason demands that if something exists, either the world or God (or anything else), then **something** must be self-existent.... There must be a self-existent being of some sort somewhere, or nothing would or could exist (1994, pp. 179,185 emp. in orig.).

Everything that humans known to exist can be classified as either **matter** or **mind**. There is no third alternative. The argument then, is this:

1. Everything that exists is either matter or mind.
2. Something exists now, so something eternal exists.
3. Therefore, either matter or mind is eternal.

A. Either matter or mind is eternal.
B. Matter is not eternal, as per evidence cited above.
C. Thus, it is mind that is eternal.

Or, to reason somewhat differently:

1. Everything that is, is either dependent (i.e., contingent) or independent (non-contingent).
2. If the Universe is not eternal, it is dependent (contingent).
3. The Universe is not eternal.
4. Therefore, the Universe is dependent (contingent).

A. If the Universe is dependent, it must have been caused by something that is independent.
B. But the Universe is dependent (contingent).
C. Therefore, the Universe was produced by some eternal, independent (non-contingent) force.

In the past, atheistic evolutionists suggested that the mind is nothing more than a function of the brain, which is matter; thus the mind and the brain are the same, and matter is all that exists. As the late evolutionist of Cornell University, Carl Sagan, said in the opening sentence of his television extravaganza (and book by the same name), *Cosmos*, "The Cosmos is all that is or ever was or ever will be" (1980, p. 4). However, that viewpoint no longer is credible scientifically, due in large part to the experiments of Australian physiologist Sir John Eccles. Dr. Eccles, who won the Nobel Prize for his discoveries relating to the neural synapses within the brain, documented that the mind is more than merely physical. He showed that the supplementary motor area of the brain may be fired by mere **intention** to do something, without the motor cortex (which controls muscle movements) operating. In effect, the mind is to the brain what a librarian is to a library. The former is not reducible to the latter. Eccles explained his methodology and conclusions in *The Self and Its Brain*, co-authored with the renowned philosopher of science, Sir Karl Popper (see Popper and Eccles, 1977).

In an article—"Scientists in Search of the Soul"—that examined the groundbreaking work of Dr. Eccles (and other scientists like him who have been studying the mind/brain relationship), science writer John Gliedman wrote:

> At age 79, Sir John Eccles is not going "gentle into the night." Still trim and vigorous, the great physiologist has declared war on the past 300 years of scientific speculation about man's nature.
>
> Winner of the 1963 Nobel Prize in Physiology or Medicine for his pioneering research on the synapse—the point at which nerve cells communicate with the brain—Eccles strongly

> defends the ancient religious belief that human beings consist of a mysterious compound of physical and intangible spirit.
>
> Each of us embodies a nonmaterial thinking and perceiving self that "entered" our physical brain sometime during embryological development or very early childhood, says the man who helped lay the cornerstones of modern neurophysiology. This "ghost in the machine" is responsible for everything that makes us distinctly human: conscious self-awareness, free will, personal identity, creativity and even emotions such as love, fear, and hate. Our nonmaterial self controls its "liaison brain" the way a driver steers a car or a programmer directs a computer. Man's ghostly spiritual presence, says Eccles, exerts just the whisper of a physical influence on the computerlike brain, enough to encourage some neurons to fire and others to remain silent. Boldly advancing what for most scientists is the greatest heresy of all, Eccles also asserts that our nonmaterial self survives the death of the physical brain (1982, p. 77).

While discussing the same type of conclusions reached by Dr. Eccles, philosopher Norman Geisler explored the concept of an eternal, all-knowing Mind.

> Further, this infinite cause of all that is must be all-knowing. It must be knowing because knowing beings exist. I am a knowing being, and I know it. I cannot meaningfully deny that I can know without engaging in an act of knowledge.... But a cause can communicate to its effect only what it has to communicate. If the effect actually possesses some characteristic, then this characteristic is properly attributed to its cause. The cause cannot give what it does not have to give. If my mind or ability to know is received, then there must be Mind or Knower who gave it to me. The intellectual does not arise from the nonintellectual; something cannot arise from nothing. The cause of knowing, however, is infinite. Therefore it must know infinitely. It is also simple, eternal, and unchanging. Hence, whatever it knows—and it knows anything it is possible to know—it must know simply, eternally, and in an unchanging way (1976, p. 247).

From such evidence, Robert Jastrow concluded: "That there are what I or anyone would call supernatural forces at work is now, I think, a scientifically proven fact..." (1982, p. 18). Apparently Dr. Jastrow is not alone. As Gliedman put it:

> Eccles is not the only world-famous scientist taking a controversial new look at the ancient mind-body conundrum. From Berkeley to Paris and from London to Princeton, prominent scientists from fields as diverse as neurophysiology and quantum physics are coming out of the closet and admitting they believe in the possibility, at least, of such unscientific entities as the immortal human spirit and divine creation (1982, p. 77).

In an article titled "Modern Biology and the Turn to Belief in God" that he wrote for the book, *The Intellectuals Speak Out About God* (for which former United States president Ronald Reagan wrote the preface), Dr. Eccles concluded:

> Science and religion are very much alike. Both are imaginative and creative aspects of the human mind. The appearance of a conflict is a result of ignorance. We come to exist through a divine act. That divine guidance is a theme throughout our life; at our death the brain goes, but that divine guidance and love continues. Each of us is a unique, conscious being, a divine creation. It is the religious view. It is the only view consistent with all the evidence (1984, p. 50, emp. added).

Scientifically, the choice is between matter only and more than matter as the fundamental explanation for the existence and orderliness of the Universe. The difference, therefore, between the two models is the difference between: (a) time, chance, and the inherent properties of matter; or (b) design, creation, and the irreducible properties of organization. In fact, when it comes to any particular case, there are again only two scientific explanations for the origin of the order that characterizes the Universe and life in the Universe: either the order was imposed on matter, or it resides within matter.

However, if it is suggested that the order resides within matter, we respond by saying that we certainly have not seen the evidence of such. The evidence that we do possess speaks clearly to the existence of a non-contingent, eternal, self-existent Mind that created this Universe and everything within it.

Conclusion

The Law of Cause and Effect, and the cosmological argument based upon that law, have implications in every field of human endeavor. The Universe is here and must have an adequate antecedent cause. In addressing this matter, R.L. Wysong commented:

> Everyone concludes naturally and comfortably that highly ordered and designed items (machines, houses, etc.) owe existence to a designer. It is unnatural to conclude otherwise. But evolution asks us to break stride from what is natural to believe and then believe in that which is unnatural, unreasonable, and...unbelievable.... The basis for this departure from what is natural and reasonable to believe is not fact, observation, or experience but rather unreasonable extrapolations from abstract probabilities, mathematics, and philosophy (1976, p. 412, first ellipsis in orig.).

Dr. Wysong then presented an interesting historical case to illustrate his point. Some years ago, scientists were called to Great Britain to study orderly patterns of concentric rocks and holes—a find designated as Stonehenge. As studies progressed, it became apparent that these patterns had been designed specifically to allow certain astronomical predictions. Many questions (e.g., how ancient peoples were able to construct an astronomical observatory, how the data derived from their studies were used, etc.) remain unsolved. But one thing we do know—the **cause** of Stonehenge was intelligent design.

Now, suggested Dr. Wysong, compare Stonehenge to the situation paralleling the origin of the Universe, and of life itself. We study life, observe its functions, contemplate its complexity (which defies duplication even by intelligent men with the most advanced methodology and technology), and what are we to conclude? Stonehenge **might** have been produced by the erosion of a mountain, or by catastrophic natural forces working in conjunction with meteorites to produce rock formations and concentric holes. But what scientist or philosopher would ever suggest such an idea?

No one ever could be convinced that Stonehenge "just happened" by accident, yet atheists and agnostics expect us to believe that this highly ordered, well-designed Universe (and the complicated life it contains) "just happened." To accept such an idea is, to use Dr. Wysong's words, "to break stride from what is natural to believe" because the conclusion is unreasonable, unwarranted, and unsupported by the facts at hand. The cause simply is not adequate to produce the effect.

The central message of the cosmological argument, and the Law of Cause and Effect upon which it is based, is this: Every material effect must have an adequate antecedent cause. The Universe is here; intelligent life is here; morality is here; love is here. What is their adequate antecedent cause? Since the effect never can precede, or be greater than the cause, it then stands to reason that the Cause of life must be a living Intelligence which Itself is both moral and loving. When the Bible records, "In the beginning, God," it makes known to us just such a First Cause.

CHAPTER 6

THE CASE FOR THE EXISTENCE OF GOD [PART II]

One of the laws of thought employed in the field of logic is the Law of Rationality, which states that one should accept as true only those conclusions for which there is adequate evidence. This is sensible, for accepting as true a conclusion for which there is no evidence, or inadequate evidence, would be irrational. In discussing the *prima facie* case for God's existence, theists present—through logic, clear reasoning, and factual data—arguments that are adequate to justify the acceptance of the conclusion that God exists. The approach is intended to be positive in nature, and to establish a proposition for which adequate evidence is available.

The evidence used to substantiate the theist's proposition concerning God's existence may take many forms. This should not be surprising since, if He does exist, God would be the greatest of all realities. His existence, therefore, could be extrapolated not from just a single line of reasoning, but from numerous avenues. As one writer of the past suggested:

> The reality of such a Being can be firmly established only by concurrent reasons coming from various realms of existence, and approved by various powers of the human spirit. It is a conclusion that cannot be reached without the aid of arguments inadequate by themselves to so great a result, yet valid in their place, proving each some part of the great truth; proofs cumulative and complementary, each requiring others for its completion (Clarke, 1912, p. 104).

The various arguments presented by theists, all combined, make an ironclad case for God's existence. Where one particular argument fails to impress or convince an inquirer, another will avail. Considered cumulatively, the evidence is adequate to justify the intended conclusion. It is my purpose here to present and discuss additional evidence substantiating the proposition: God exists.

Design in Nature—The Teleological Argument

In contending for the existence of God, theists often employ the Teleological Argument. "Teleology" has reference to purpose or design. Thus, this approach suggests that where there is purposeful design, there must be a designer. The deduction being made, of course, is that order, planning, and design in a system are indicative of intelligence, purpose, and specific intent on the part of the originating cause. In logical form, the theist's argument may be presented as follows:

1. If the Universe evinces purposeful design, there must have been a designer.
2. The Universe does evince purposeful design.
3. Thus, the Universe must have had a designer.

This correct form of logical reasoning, and the implications that flow from it, have not escaped the attention of those who do not believe in God. Paul Ricci, an atheistic philosopher and university professor, has written that "...it's true that everything designed has a designer..." (1986, p. 190). In fact, Mr. Ricci even conceded that the statement, " 'Everything designed has a designer,' is an analytically true statement" and thus requires no formal proof (p. 190). Apparently Mr. Ricci understands that one does not get a poem without a poet, a law without a lawgiver, a painting without a painter, or design without a designer.

He is in good company among his disbelieving counterparts. For example, atheistic evolutionist Richard Lewontin made the following admission in an article he authored for *Scientific American*:

> Life forms are more than simply multiple and diverse, however. Organisms fit remarkably well into the external world in which they live. They have morphologies, physiologies and behaviors that **appear to have been carefully and artfully designed** to enable each organism to appropriate the world around it for its own life. It was the marvelous fit of organisms to the environment, much more than the great diversity of forms, that was **the chief evidence of a Supreme Designer** (1978, 239[3]:213, emp. added).

To be fair to both of these authors, and others like them, let me quickly point out that while they agree with the thrust of the theist's argument (i.e., that design leads inevitably to a designer), they do not believe that there is evidence warranting the conclusion that a Supreme Designer exists, and they therefore reject any belief in God. Their disagreement with the theist, therefore, would center on statement number two (the minor premise) in the above syllogism. While admitting that design demands a designer, they would deny that there is design in nature providing proof of the existence of a Great Designer.

A good example of such a denial can be found in a book written by British evolutionist, Richard Dawkins. During the 1800s, William Paley employed his now-famous "watch argument." Paley argued that if one were to discover a watch lying upon the ground and were to examine it closely, the design inherent in the watch would be enough to force the conclusion that there must have been a watchmaker. Paley continued his line of argumentation to suggest that the design inherent in the Universe should be enough to force the conclusion that there must have been a Great Designer. In 1986, Dawkins published *The Blind Watchmaker*, which was intended to put to rest once and for all Paley's argument. The dust jacket of Dawkins' book made that point clear:

> There may be good reasons for belief in God, but the argument from design is not one of them. ...despite all appearances to the contrary, there is no watchmaker in nature beyond the blind forces of physics.... Natural selection, the unconscious, automatic, blind yet essentially nonrandom process that Darwin discovered, and that we now understand to be the explanation for the existence and form of all life, has no purpose in mind. It has no mind and no mind's eye. It does not plan for the future. It has no vision, no foresight, no sight at all. If it can be said to play the role of watchmaker in nature, it is the **blind** watchmaker (1986, emp. in orig.).

The disagreement between the theist and atheist is not whether design demands a designer. Rather, the point of contention is whether or not there **is** design in nature adequate to substantiate the conclusion that a Designer does, in fact, exist. This is where the Teleological Argument is of benefit.

Design of the Universe

Our Universe operates in accordance with exact scientific laws. The precision of the Universe, and the exactness of these laws, allow scientists to launch rockets to the Moon, with the full knowledge that, upon their arrival, they can land within a few feet of their intended target. Such precision and exactness also allow astronomers to predict solar/lunar eclipses years in advance or to determine when Halley's Comet can be seen once again from the Earth. Science writer Lincoln Barnett once observed:

> This functional harmony of nature Berkeley, Descartes, and Spinoza attributed to God. Modern physicists who prefer to solve their problems without recourse to God (although this seems to be more difficult all the time) emphasize that nature mysteriously operates on mathematical principles. It is the mathematical orthodoxy of the Universe that enables theorists like Einstein to predict and discover natural laws, simply by the solution of equations (1959, p. 22).

The precision, complexity, and orderliness within the Universe are not in dispute; writers such as Ricci, Dawkins, and Lewontin acknowledge as much. But while atheists willingly concede complexity, and even order, they are not prepared to concede design because the implication of such a concession would demand a Designer. Is there evidence of **design**? The atheist claims no such evidence exists. The theist, however, affirms that it does, and offers the following information in support of that affirmation.

We live in a tremendously large Universe. While its outer limits have not been measured, it is estimated to be as much as 20 billion light years in diameter (i.e., the distance it would take light to travel across the Universe at a speed of over 186,000 miles per second; see Lawton, 1981, 89[1]:105). There are an estimated one billion galaxies in the Universe (Lawton, 1981, 89[1]:98), and an estimated 25 sextillion stars. The Milky Way galaxy in which we live contains over 100 billion stars, and is so large that even traveling at the speed of light would require 100,000 years to cross its diameter. Light travels approximately 5.87×10^{12} miles in a single year; in 100,000 years, that would be 5.87×10^{17} miles, or 587 quadrillion miles just to cross the diameter of a single galaxy. If we drew a map of the Milky Way galaxy, and represented the Earth and Sun as two dots one inch apart (thus a scale of one inch equals 93 million miles—the distance between the Earth and the Sun), we would need a map at least four miles wide to locate the next nearest star, and a map 25,000 miles wide to reach the center of our galaxy. Without doubt, this is a rather impressive Universe.

Yet while the size itself is impressive, the inherent design is even more so. The Sun's interior temperature is estimated to be over 20 million degrees Celsius (Lawton, 1981, 89[1]:102). The Earth, however, is located at exactly the correct distance from the Sun to receive the proper amount of heat and radiation to sustain life as we know it. If the Earth were moved just 10% closer to the Sun (about 10 million miles), far too much heat and radiation would be absorbed. If the Earth were moved just 10% further from the Sun, too little heat would be absorbed. Either scenario would spell doom for life on the Earth.

The Earth is rotating on its axis at 1,000 miles per hour at the equator, and moving around the Sun at 70,000 miles per hour (approximately 19 miles per second), while the Sun and its solar system are moving through space at 600,000 miles per hour in an orbit so large it would take over 220 million years just to complete a single orbit. Interestingly, however, as the Earth moves in its orbit around the Sun, it departs from a straight line by only one-ninth of an inch every eighteen miles. If it departed by one-eighth of an inch, we would come so close to the Sun that we would be incinerated; if it departed by one-tenth of an inch, we would find ourselves so far from the Sun that we would all freeze to death (*Science Digest*, 1981, 89[1]:124). The Earth is poised some 240,000 miles from the Moon, whose gravitational pull produces ocean tides. If the Moon were moved closer to the Earth by just a fifth, the tides would be so enormous that twice a day they would reach 35-50 feet high over most of the Earth's surface.

What would happen if the rotation rate of the Earth were cut in half, or doubled? If it were halved, the seasons would be doubled in their length, which would cause such harsh heat and cold over much of the Earth that it would be difficult, if not impossible, to grow enough food to feed the Earth's population. If the rotation rate were doubled, the length of each season would be halved, and it would be difficult or impossible to grow enough food to feed the Earth's population. The Earth is tilted on its axis at exactly 23.5 degrees. Were that tilt to be reduced to zero, much of the Earth's water would accumulate around the two poles, leaving vast deserts in their place. If the atmosphere surrounding the Earth were much thinner, meteorites could strike our planet with greater force and frequency, causing worldwide devastation.

The oceans provide a huge reservoir of moisture that is constantly evaporating and condensing, thus falling upon the land as refreshing rain. It is a well-known fact that water heats and cools at a much slower rate than a solid land mass, which explains why desert regions can be blistering hot in the daytime and freezing cold at night. Water, however, holds its temperature longer, and provides a sort of natural heating/air-conditioning system for the land areas of the Earth. Temperature extremes would be much more erratic than they are, were it not for the fact that approximately four-fifths of the Earth is covered with water. In addition, humans and animals inhale oxygen and exhale carbon dioxide. On the other hand, plants take in carbon dioxide and give off oxygen. We depend upon the world of botany for our oxygen supply, yet we often fail to realize that approximately 90% of our oxygen comes from microscopic plants in the seas (see Asimov, 1975, 2: 116). If our oceans were appreciably smaller, we would soon be out of air to breathe.

Can a person reasonably be expected to believe that these exacting requirements for life as we know it have been met "just by accident"? The Earth is exactly the right distance from the Sun; it is exactly the right distance from the Moon; it has exactly the right diameter; it has exactly the right atmospheric pressure; it has exactly the right tilt; it has exactly the right amount of oceanic water; it has exactly the right weight and mass; and so on. Were this many requirements to be met in any other essential area of life, the idea that they had been provided "just by accident" would be dismissed immediately as ludicrous. Yet atheists and agnostics suggest that the Universe, the Earth, and life on the Earth are all here as a result of fortuitous accidents. Physicist John Gribbin (1983), writing on the numerous specific requirements necessary for life on our planet, emphasized in great detail both the nature and essentiality of those requirements, yet curiously chose to title his article, "Earth's Lucky Break"—as if all of the precision, orderliness, and intricate design in the Universe could be explained by postulating that the Earth simply received, in a roll of the cosmic dice, a "lucky break."

For more than a decade-and-a-half, British evolutionist Sir Fred Hoyle has stressed the insurmountable problems with such thinking and has addressed specifically the many problems faced by those who defend the idea of a naturalistic origin of life on Earth.

In fact, Dr. Hoyle described the atheistic concept that disorder gives rise to order in a rather picturesque manner when he observed that "the chance that higher forms have emerged in this way is comparable with the chance that a tornado sweeping through a junkyard might assemble a Boeing 747 from the materials therein" (1981b, p. 105). Dr. Hoyle, even went so far as to draw the following conclusion:

> Once we see, however, that the probability of life originating at random is so utterly minuscule as to make the random concept absurd, it becomes sensible to think that the favourable properties of physics on which life depends, are in every respect deliberate.... It is therefore almost inevitable that our own measure of intelligence must reflect in a valid way the higher intelligences...even to the extreme idealized limit of **God** (Hoyle and Wickramasinghe, 1981, pp. 141, 144, emp. in orig.).

Atheist Richard Dawkins was forced to admit: "The more statistically improbable a thing is, the less we can believe that it just happened by blind chance. Superficially, **the obvious alternative to chance is an intelligent Designer**" (1982, 94:130, emp. added). That is the very conclusion theists have drawn from the available evidence—in keeping with the Law of Rationality. The statistical improbability of the Universe "just happening by blind chance" is staggering. The only alternative is an Intelligent Designer—God.

Design of the Human Body

Many years ago, the ancient scholar Augustine observed that "Men go abroad to wonder at the height of mountains, at the huge waves of the sea, at the long course of the rivers, at the vast compass of the ocean, at the circular motion of the stars; and they pass by themselves without wondering." Indeed, while we stand in amazement at so many stunning scenes from our unique Universe, we often fail to stand equally amazed at the marvelous creation of man. According to those who do not believe in God, the human body is little more than the result of a set of fortuitous circumstances credited to that mythical lady, "Mother Nature." Yet such a suggestion does not fit the actual facts of the case, as even evolutionists have been forced to recognize from time to time. The late George Gaylord Simpson of Harvard once suggested that in man one finds "the most highly endowed organization of matter that has yet appeared on the earth..." (1949, p. 293). Another evolutionist observed:

> When you come right down to it, the most incredible creation in the universe is you—with your fantastic senses and strengths, your ingenious defense systems, and mental capabilities so great you can never use them to the fullest. Your body is a structural masterpiece more amazing than science fiction (Guinness, 1987, p. 5).

Can one reasonably be expected to conclude that the "structural masterpiece" of the human body—with its "ingenious" systems and "highly endowed organization"—is the result of blind chance operating over eons of time in nature as atheism suggests? Or would it be more in keeping with the facts of the matter to suggest that the human body is the result of purposeful design by a Master Designer?

For organizational purposes, the human body may be considered at four different levels (see Jackson, 1993, pp. 5-6). First, there are cells, representing the smallest unit of life. Second, there are tissues (muscle tissue, nerve tissue, etc.), which are groups of the same kind of cells carrying on the same kind of activity. Third, there are organs (heart, liver, etc.), which are groups of tissues working together in unison. Fourth, there are systems (reproductive system, circulatory system, etc.), which are composed of groups of organs carrying out specific bodily functions. While I will not have the space in this chapter to examine each of them, an investigation of these various levels of organization, and of the human body as a whole, leads inescapably to the conclusion that there is intelligent design at work. As Wayne Jackson noted: "It is therefore quite clear...that the physical body has been marvelously designed and intricately organized, for the purpose of facilitating human existence upon the planet Earth" (1993, p. 6). In light of the following facts, such a statement is certainly justified.

A human body is composed of over 30 different kinds of cells (red blood cells, white blood cells, nerve cells, etc.), totaling approximately 100 trillion cells in an average adult (Beck, 1971, p. 189). These cells come in a variety of sizes and shapes with different functions and life expectancies. For example, some cells (e.g., male spermatozoa) are so small that 20,000 would fit inside a capital "O" from a standard typewriter, each being only 0.05 mm long. Some cells, placed end-to-end, would make only one inch if 6,000 were assembled together. Yet all the cells of the human body, if set end-to-end, would encircle the Earth over 200 times. Even the largest cell of the human body, the female ovum, is unbelievably small, being only 0.01 of an inch in diameter. Cells have three major components. First, each cell is composed of a cell membrane that encloses the organism. Second, inside the cell is a three-dimensional cytoplasm—a watery matrix containing specialized organelles. Third, within the cytoplasm is the nucleus, which contains most of the genetic material, and which serves as the control center of the cell.

The lipoprotein cell membrane (lipids/proteins/lipids) is approximately 0.06-0.08 of a micrometer thick, yet allows selective transport into, and out of, the cell. Evolutionist Ernest Borek observed: "The membrane recognizes with its uncanny molecular memory the hundreds of compounds swimming around it and permits or denies passage according to the cell's requirements" (1973, p. 5).

Inside the cytoplasm, there are over 20 different chemical re actions occurring at any one time, with each cell containing five major components for: (1) communication; (2) waste disposal; (3) nutrition; (4) repair; and (5) reproduction. Within this watery matrix there are such organelles as the mitochondria (over 1,000 per cell in many instances) that provide the cell with its energy. The endoplasmic reticulum is "believed to be a transport system designed to carry materials from one part of the cell to the other" (Pfeiffer, 1964, p. 13). Ribosomes are miniature protein-producing factories. Golgi bodies store the proteins manufactured by the ribosomes. Lysozomes within the cytoplasm function as garbage disposal units.

The nucleus is the control center of the cell, and is separated from the cytoplasm by a nuclear membrane. Within the nucleus is the genetic machinery of the cell (chromosomes and genes containing deoxyribonucleic acid—DNA). The DNA is a supermolecule that carries the coded information for the replication of the cell. If the DNA from a single human cell were removed from the nucleus and unraveled (it is found in the cell in a spiral configuration), it would be approximately six feet long, and would contain over a billion biochemical steps. It has been estimated that if all the DNA in an adult human were placed end-to-end, it would reach to the Sun and back (186 million miles) 400 times.

It also should be noted that the DNA molecule does something that we as humans have yet to accomplish: it stores coded information in a chemical format and then uses a biologic agent (RNA) to decode and activate it. As Darrel Kautz stated: "Human technology has not yet advanced to the point of storing information **chemically** as it is in the DNA molecule" (1988, p. 45, emp. in orig.; see also Jackson, 1993, pp. 11-12). If transcribed into English, the DNA in a single human cell would fill a 1,000 volume set of encyclopedias approximately 600 pages each (Gore, 1976, p. 357). Yet just as amazing is the fact that all the genetic information needed to reproduce the entire human population (about five billion people) could be placed into a space of about one-eighth of a square inch. In comparing the amount of information contained in the DNA molecule with a much larger computer microchip, evolutionist Irvin Block remarked: "We marvel at the feats of memory and transcription accomplished by computer microchips, but these are gargantuan compared to the protein granules of deoxyribonucleic acid, DNA" (1980, p. 52). In an article he authored for *Encyclopaedia Britannica*, Carl Sagan observed that "The information content of a simple cell has been estimated as around 10^{12} bits [i.e., one trillion—BT]..." (1974, 10:894). To emphasize to the reader the enormity of this figure, Dr. Sagan then noted that if one were to count every letter in every word of every book in the world's largest library (over ten million volumes), the final tally would be approximately a trillion letters. Thus, a single cell contains the equivalent information content of all the books in the world's largest library of more than ten million volumes! Every rational person recognizes that not one of the books in such a library "just happened." Rather, each and every one is the result of intelligence and painstaking **design**.

What, then, may we say about the infinitely more complex genetic code found within the DNA in each cell? Sir Fred Hoyle concluded that the notion that the code's complexity could be arrived at by chance is "nonsense of a high order" (1981a, p. 527). In their classic text on the origin of life, Thaxton, Bradley, and Olsen addressed the implications of the genetic code found within the DNA molecule.

> We know that in numerous cases certain effects always have intelligent causes, such as dictionaries, sculptures, machines and paintings. We reason by analogy that similar effects have intelligent causes. For example, after looking up to see "BUY FORD" spelled out in smoke across the sky we infer the presence of a skywriter even if we heard or saw no airplane. We would similarly conclude the presence of intelligent activity were we to come upon an elephant-shaped topiary in a cedar forest.
>
> In like manner an intelligible communication via radio signal from some distant galaxy would be widely hailed as evidence of an intelligent source. Why then doesn't the message sequence on the DNA molecule also constitute *prima facie* evidence for an intelligent source? After all, DNA information is not just analogous to a message sequence such as Morse code, it **is** such a message sequence....

> We believe that if this question is considered, it will be seen that most often it is answered in the negative simply because it is thought to be inappropriate to bring a Creator into science (1984, pp. 211-212, emp. in orig.).

The complexity and intricacy of the DNA molecule—combined with the staggering amount of chemically coded information it contains—speak unerringly to the fact that this "supermolecule" simply could not have happened by blind chance. As Andrews has observed:

> It is not possible for a code, of any kind, to arise by chance or accident.... A code is the work of an intelligent mind. Even the cleverest dog or chimpanzee could not work out a code of any kind. It is obvious then that chance cannot do it.... This could no more have been the work of chance or accident than could the "Moonlight Sonata" be played by mice running up and down the keyboard of my piano! Codes do not arise from chaos (1978, pp. 28-29).

Indeed, codes do not arise from chaos. As Dawkins correctly remarked: "The more statistically improbable a thing is, the less we can believe that it just happened by blind chance. Superficially, **the obvious alternative to chance is an intelligent Designer**" (1982, p. 130, emp. added). That is the exact point the theist is making: an intelligent Designer is demanded by the evidence.

Conclusion

Atheistic philosopher Paul Ricci has suggested that "Although many have difficulty understanding the tremendous **order and complexity** of functions of the human body (the eye, for example), **there is no obvious designer**" (1986, p. 191, emp. added). The only people who "have difficulty understanding the tremendous order and complexity" found in the Universe are those who have "refused to have God in their knowledge" (Romans 1:28). Such people can parrot the phrase that "there is no obvious designer," but their arguments are not convincing. One does not get a poem without a poet, or a law without a lawgiver. One does not get a painting without a painter, or a musical score without a composer. And just as surely, one does not get purposeful design without a designer. The design inherent in the Universe is evident—from the macrocosm to the microcosm—and is sufficient to draw the conclusion demanded by the evidence, in keeping with the Law of Rationality. God does exist.

CHAPTER 7

THE CASE FOR THE EXISTENCE OF GOD [PART III]

It is a well-known and widely admitted fact that actions have consequences. But no less true is the fact that beliefs have implications—a fact that atheists and theists alike acknowledge. Earlier in this book, I mentioned that atheist Martin Gardner devoted a chapter in one of his books to "The Relevance of Belief Systems," in an attempt to explain that **what a person believes** profoundly influences **how a person acts** (1988, pp. 57-64). In his book, *An Introduction to Christian Apologetics*, the late theist Edward John Carnell remarked:

> It is evident that we must act, if we are to remain alive, but we find ourselves in such multifarious circumstances that it is difficult to know at times whether it is better to turn to the right or better to turn to the left, or better not to turn at all. And, before one can choose a direction in which to turn, he must answer the question, better in relation to **what or to whom**? In other words, if a man is going to act **meaningfully** and not haphazardly, he must rationally count the cost; he must think before he acts. Right judgment, then, and proper actions always go together.... If it has not been evident to men before that we must be guided in our social life by universal and necessary ethical rules, it certainly is clear today (1948, pp. 316,315, emp. in orig.).

The points made by these two authors—one an atheist, the other a theist—are well taken. What a person believes **does** influence how a person acts. Yet we **must** act in our daily lives. Furthermore, right judgments and proper actions **do** go together. How, then, shall we choose to do one thing while choosing not to do another? As A.E. Taylor wrote:

> But it is an undeniable fact that men not merely love and procreate, they also hold that there is a difference between right and wrong; there are things which they **ought** to do and other things which they **ought not** to do. Different groups of men, living under different conditions and in different ages, may disagree widely on the question whether a certain thing belongs to the first or the second of these classes. They may draw the line between right and wrong in a different place, but at least they all agree that there is such a line to be drawn (1945, p 83, emp. in orig.).

But where do we "draw the line"? By what standard (or standards) are our choices to be measured and judged?

One thing is for certain. The choices that we are being required to make today (and the judgments that those actions require on our part) are becoming increasingly complex and far-reaching in their implications. A slew of problems now sits at our proverbial doorstep—each of which requires rational, reasonable answers on how we ought to act in any given situation. Shall we encourage surrogate motherhood? Shall we countenance abortion? Shall we recommend euthanasia? We will not answer these types of questions, or even discuss them meaningfully, by relying merely on our own intuition or emotions. Furthermore, in many instances looking to the past provides little (if any) aid or comfort. In many ways, the set of problems now facing us is entirely different than the set of problems that once faced generations long since gone.

The simple fact is that morals and ethics **are** important. Even those who eschew any belief in God, and consequently any absolute standard of morality/ethics, concede that morality and ethics play a critical role in man's everyday life. In his book, *Ethics With-*

out God, atheist Kai Nielsen admitted that to ask, "Is murder evil?," is to ask a self-answering question (1973, p. 16). The late evolutionist of Harvard University, George Gaylord Simpson, stated that although "man is the result of a purposeless and materialistic process that did not have him in mind," nonetheless "**good and evil, right and wrong, concepts irrelevant in nature except from the human viewpoint, become real and pressing features** of the whole cosmos as viewed morally because morals arise only in man" (1967, p. 346, emp. added). Wayne Jackson correctly observed:

> All rational people are concerned, to a greater or lesser degree, about human moral and ethical conduct. How we act, and are acted upon, with respect to our fellow man determines the progress and happiness of mankind and, ultimately, contributes in one form or another to human destiny. The existence of, and need for, morality and ethics are self-evident. No sane person will argue that absolutely anything goes. The expressions "ought" and "ought not" are as much a part of the atheist's vocabulary as anyone else's. While it is true that one may become so insensitive that he abandons virtually all of his personal ethical obligations, but he will never ignore the lack of such in those who would abuse him (1995, 15:56).

Thomas C. Mayberry summarized this point well when he wrote: "There is broad agreement that lying, promise breaking, killing, and so on are generally wrong" (1970, 54:113). C.S. Lewis used the somewhat common concept of quarreling to make the same point when he observed that men who quarrel appeal

> to some kind of standard of behavior which he expects the other man to know about.... Quarreling means trying to show that the other man is in the wrong. And there would be no sense in trying to do that unless you and he had some sort of agreement as to what Right and Wrong are (1952, pp. 17,18).

If: (a) every living person must act from day to day in one way or another—and he must; (b) during the course of our actions, choices must be made—and they must; (c) the range of those choices is broadening every single day—and it is; (d) the scope of both the choices in front of us and the implications of those choices is widening—and it is; and (e) morality and ethics are important—and they are (even to those who believe in no objective, unchanging standard), then by what set of rules, decision-making process, or knowledge system shall human beings determine what they **ought** or **ought not** to do? How shall we come to grips with, and evaluate, these "real and pressing features" of "good and evil, right and wrong"? Stated simply, by what ethical/moral system(s) shall we live and thereby justify our actions and choices?

Morality and Ethics

As I begin this study into the importance and origin of morality and ethics, a brief definition of terms is in order. The English word "morality" derives from the Latin word *mores*, meaning habits or customs. Morality, therefore, is "the character of being in accord with the principles or standards of right conduct" (Jackson, 1995, 15:50). "Ethics" is from a Greek word meaning "character." The standard dictionary definition of ethics is "the discipline dealing with what is good and bad or right and wrong; a group of moral principles or a set of values." Ethics, then, "is generally viewed as the system or code by which attitudes and actions are determined to be either right or wrong" (Jackson, 1995, 15:50). Or, as Carnell put it: "Ethics is the science of conduct, and the fundamental problem of ethics is determining what constitutes proper conduct" (1948, p. 315). Moral or ethical philosophy, then, deals with right conduct, ethical duty, and virtue—i.e., how we ought to behave. The question now is: How **ought** we to behave?

If such concepts as "good and evil, right and wrong" are, in fact, "real and pressing features," how, then, should moral and ethical systems be determined? Morals and ethics are universally accepted traits among the human family. Their origin, therefore, must be explained. Simply put, there are but two options. Either morality and ethics are **theocentric**—that is, they originate from the mind of God as an external source of infinite goodness, or they are **anthropocentric**—that is, they originate from man himself (see Geisler and Corduan, 1988, pp. 109-122). Carnell asked in this regard:

> But where shall we locate these rules of duty? **That** is the question. In answering the question, however, one has little latitude of choice. Since duty is proper meaning, and since meaning is a property of either mind or of law, we can expect to locate our rule of duty either in a mind or in a law. **Either the law that rules the mind is supreme, or the mind which makes the law is paramount**. These fairly well exhaust the possibilities, for, if mind does not make the law, it is law that makes the mind. The Christian will defend the primacy of the lawgiver; non-Christianity will defend the primacy of the law... (1948, pp. 320-321, first emp. in orig., last emp. added).

The person who refuses to acknowledge the existence of God does indeed have "little latitude of choice." Simpson was forced to conclude: "Discovery that the universe apart from man or before his coming lacks and lacked any purpose or plan has the inevitable corollary that the workings of the universe cannot provide any automatic, universal, eternal, or absolute ethical criteria of right and wrong" (1967, p. 346). Since man is viewed as little more than the last animal among many to be produced by the long, meandering process of organic evolution, this becomes problematic. In their book, *Origins*, Richard Leakey and Roger Lewin wrote: "There is now a critical need for a deep awareness that, no matter how special we are **as an animal**, we are still part of the greater balance of nature..." (1977, p. 256, emp. added). Charles Darwin declared: "There is no fundamental difference between man and the higher mammals in their mental faculties" (as quoted in Francis Darwin, 1898, 1:64). A lion is not plagued by guilt after killing a gazelle's infant offspring for its noon meal. A dog does not experience remorse after stealing a bone from one of its peers.

In 1986, British evolutionist Richard Dawkins [who has described himself as "a fairly militant atheist, with a fair degree of hostility toward religion" (see Bass, 1990, p. 86)] authored a book titled *The Selfish Gene* in which he set forth his theory of genetic determinism. In summarizing the basic thesis of the book, Dawkins said: "You are for nothing. You are here to propagate your selfish genes. There is no higher purpose in life" (Bass, 1990, p. 60). Dawkins then explained:

> I am not advocating a morality based on evolution. I am saying how things have evolved. I am not saying how we humans morally ought to behave.... My own feeling is that **a human society based simply on the gene's law of universal ruthless selfishness would be a very nasty society in which to live**. But unfortunately, however much we may deplore something, it does not stop it being true (1989b, pp. 2,3, emp. added).

Dawkins is correct in his assessment—a society based on the concept of godless evolution would be "a very nasty" place to live. Since no other animal throughout evolutionary history has been able to locate and live by moral standards, should we somehow trust a "naked ape" (to use zoologist Desmond Morris' colorful expression) to do any better? Darwin himself complained: "Can the mind of man, which has, as I fully believe, been developed from a mind as low as that possessed by the lowest animals, be trusted when it draws such grand conclusions?" (as quoted in Francis Darwin, 1898, 1:282).

Matter—by itself—is completely impotent to "evolve" any sense of moral consciousness. If there is no purpose in the Universe, as Simpson and others have asserted, then there is no purpose to morality or ethics. But the concept of a "purposeless morality," or a "purposeless ethic," is irrational. Unbelief therefore must contend, and does contend, that there is no ultimate standard of moral/ethical truth, and that morality and ethics, at best, are relative and situational. That being the case, who could ever suggest, correctly, that someone else's conduct was "wrong," or that a man "ought" or "ought not" to do thus and so? The simple fact of the matter is that infidelity cannot explain the origin of morality and ethics.

Whether the unbeliever is willing to admit it or not, if there is no God man exists in an environment where "anything goes." Russian novelist Fyodor Dostoyevsky, in *The Brothers Karamazov* (1880), had one of his characters (Ivan) remark that in the absence of God, everything is allowed. French existential philosopher, Jean Paul Sartre, wrote:

> Everything is indeed permitted if God does not exist, and man is in consequence forlorn, for he cannot find anything to depend upon either within or outside himself.... Nor, on the other hand, if God does not exist, are we provided with any values or commands that could legitimize our behavior (1961, p. 485).

Sartre contended that **whatever** one chooses to do is right; value is attached to the choice itself so that "...we can never choose evil" (1966, p. 279). These men are correct about one thing. If evolution is true and there is no God, "anything goes" is the name of the game. Thus, it is impossible to formulate a system of ethics by which one objectively can differentiate "right" from "wrong." Agnostic philosopher Bertrand Russell observed:

> We feel that the man who brings widespread happiness at the expense of misery to himself is a better man than the man who brings unhappiness to others and happiness to himself. I do not know of any rational ground for this view, or, perhaps, for the somewhat more rational view that whatever the majority desires (called utilitarian hedonism) is preferable to what the minority desires. These are truly ethical problems but I do not know of any way in which they can be solved except by politics or war. All that I can find to say on this subject is that **an ethical opinion can only be defended by an ethical axiom, but, if the axiom is not accepted, there is no way of reaching a rational conclusion** (1969, 3:29, emp. added).

With no way to reach a rational conclusion on what is ethical, man finds himself adrift in a chaotic sea of despair where "might makes right," where "the strong subjugates the weak," and where each man does what is right in his own eyes. The late atheistic philosopher Ayn Rand even went so far as to title one of her books, *The Virtue of Selfishness—A New Concept of Egoism*. This is not a system based on morals and ethics but a society of anarchy.

In his book, *Options in Contemporary Christian Ethics* (1981), Norman Geisler discussed various ethical systems that have been proposed by those who have abandoned belief in God. These systems range from no option at all (relativism) to an option no human can resist (determinism)—and, of course, everything in between. Morals and ethics without God is not a pretty picture, as the following investigation of these various systems documents all too well.

Relativism, for example, suggests that there are no universal, objective criteria for determining morals and ethics. Since all value systems are considered to be "culturally derived," all such systems are equally valid; no one system has the right to claim that it is the "correct" system by which men should determine their actions and judge their choices based on those actions. But, as Wayne Jackson has noted,

> ...relativism falls of its own weaknesses, and its proponents will not stay with it. What if a particular culture, e.g., that of the "Bible Belt," believes that ethics is absolute? Would the relativists yield to that? Perish the thought! In some cultures, infanticide has been (or is being) deemed a proper form of population control. Is that then "right"? What about slavery, or the abuse of women? Where is the relativist that will declare openly and publicly the morality of such practices? (1995, 15:53).

Hedonism is the philosophy which argues that the aim of "moral" conduct is the attainment of the greatest possible pleasure with the greatest possible avoidance of pain. In an article titled, "Confessions of a Professed Atheist," Aldous Huxley wrote eloquently about why he, and others of his generation, purposely chose to flout both convention and established moral/ethical principles to "do their own thing":

> I had motives for not wanting the world to have meaning; consequently, assumed it had none, and was able without any difficulty to find satisfying reasons for this assumption.... The philosopher who finds no meaning in the world is not concerned exclusively with a problem in pure metaphysics; he is also concerned to prove there is no valid reason why he personally should not do as he wants to do.... For myself, as no doubt for most of my contemporaries, the philosophy of meaninglessness was essentially an instrument of liberation. The liberation we desired was simultaneously liberation from a certain political and economic system and liberation from a certain system of morality. **We objected to the morality because it interfered with our sexual freedom** (1966, 3:19, emp. added).

Such statements do not leave a whole lot to the imagination. Huxley's goal was to be ready for any sexual pleasure. Humanists of our day have made it clear that they share that goal. One of the tenets of humanism, as expressed in the *Humanist Manifesto of 1973, suggested:*

> [W]e believe that intolerant attitudes, often cultivated by orthodox religions and puritanical cultures, unduly repress sexual conduct. The right to birth control, abortion, and divorce should be recognized. While we do not approve of exploitive, denigrating forms of sexual expression, neither do we wish to prohibit, by law or social sanction, sexual behavior between consenting adults. The many varieties of sexual exploration should not in themselves be considered "evil." Without countenancing mindless permissiveness or unbridled promiscuity, a civilized society should be a **tolerant** one. Short of harming others or compelling them to do likewise, individuals should be permitted to express their sexual proclivities and pursue their lifestyles as they desire (1973, pp. 18-19, emp. in orig.).

What have been the consequences of this kind of thinking? Sexually transmitted diseases are occurring in epidemic proportions. Teenage pregnancies are rampant. Babies are born already infected with deadly diseases such as AIDS because their mothers contracted the diseases during their pregnancies and passed them on to their unborn offspring. In many places divorces are so common that they equal or outnumber marriages. Jails are filled to overflowing with rapists, stalkers, and child molesters. What else, pray tell, will have to go wrong before it becomes apparent that attempts to live without God are futile?

Utilitarianism is the edifice that stands upon the foundation of hedonism. As advocated by J.S. Mill, Jeremy Bentham, and others, it suggests that "good" is that which ultimately gives the greatest amount of pleasure to the greatest number of people. But, as Jackson has noted:

> ...the theory is seriously flawed for several reasons. First, it cannot answer the vital query: If pleasure to the greatest number of people prevents a man from achieving his own personal pleasure, what is there to motivate him toward the pleasure of the many? Second, utilitarianism provides no guideline to determine what the "pleasure" (genuine happiness) of the many actually is. Third, it is the philosophy that stands behind, and is perfectly consistent with, numerous atrocities perpetrated in the alleged interest of humanity. When Hitler slaughtered countless millions, and bred people like animals in behalf of evolving his master race, he felt he was operating in the genuine interest of mankind as a whole. The principle is: If some have to suffer in order for the ultimate good to be accomplished, so what? Of course, the leaders of such movements are always willing to step forward with their definition of what that "ultimate good" is! Finally, however, this idea cannot provide any rational reason as to why it would be "wrong" to ignore what is in the interest of the many and, instead, simply pursue one's personal pleasure (1995, 15:51).

The proof of such a point, oddly enough, comes from an intriguing book written by Katherine Tait, the only daughter of renowned British agnostic, Bertrand Russell. In *My Father, Bertrand Russell*, Mrs. Tait described what it was like to live in the Russell household with her brothers. She commented, for example, that her father firmly believed that parents should teach a child "with its very first breath that it has entered into a moral world" (1975, p. 59). But as any evolutionist would, her father had great difficulty in defending such a position. Mrs. Tait recounted in her book the fact that as a child she would say "I don't want to; why should I?" when her father told her that she "ought" to do something. She noted that a normal parent might say, "Because I say so," or "because your father says so," or "because God says so." Admittedly, however, Bertrand Russell was not your "normal" parent. He would say to young Katherine, "Because more people will be happy if you do than if you don't." "So what!" she would scream. "I don't care about other people!" "Oh, but you should," her father would reply. In her youthful naïveté, Katherine would ask, "But why?" To which her father would respond: "Because more people will be happy if you do than if you don't." In the end, however, Mrs. Tait wrote: "We felt the heavy pressure of his rectitude and obeyed, but the reason was not convincing—neither to us nor to him" (1975, pp. 184-185). Would it be convincing—for any rational human being with a smattering of common sense?

Situationism teaches that something is "right" because the **individual** determines it is right on a case-by-case basis, thus invalidating the concept of common moral law applied consistently. The atheistic authors of *Humanist Manifesto II* bluntly affirmed that "moral values derive their source from human experience. Ethics is autonomous and situational, needing no theological or ideological sanction. Ethics stems from human need and interest" (1973, p. 17). Writing in *Science* magazine, one author summarized the matter as follows: "An ethical system that bases its premises on absolute pronouncements will not usually be acceptable to those who view human nature by evolutionary criteria" (Motulsky, 1974, 185:654). Thus, Simpson wrote:

> The point is that an evolutionary ethic for man (which is of course the one we, as men, seek, if not the only possible kind) should be based on man's own nature, on his evolutionary position and significance.... It cannot be expected to be absolute, but must be subject to evolution itself and must be the result of responsible and rational choice in the full light of such knowledge of man and of life as we have (1967, p. 309, parenthetical comment in orig.).

In his influential book, *Situation Ethics: The New Morality*, Joseph Fletcher argued against the "legalistic" approach to making ethical decisions in which "one enters into every decision-making situation encumbered with a whole apparatus of prefabricated rules and regulations" (1966, p. 18). Thus, for Fletcher (and those who think like him) biblical injunctions are regarded as inconvenient encumbrances. Fletcher went on to argue that if the demands of "love" are better fulfilled by "breaking the rules" in a given set of circumstances, then actions like lying, stealing, and yes, even murder, are justifiable under those circumstances. Simply put, Fletcher argued that there are no absolute "rights" or "wrongs"; instead each moral decision must be made in light of the specific situation in view.

If a sane man therefore decided it was "right" to kill his business competitors, upon what basis could we (justifiably) ask someone (e.g., the police) to stop him without denying his autonomy and thus violating (and ultimately invalidating) the very principle upon which this ethic is supposed to work? If humans are merely "matter in motion," if no one piece of matter is worth more than any other piece of matter, if we are autonomous, if the situation warrants it, and if we can further our own selfish interests by doing so, could we not lie, steal, maim, or murder at will? Yes indeed. But who would want to live in such a society? As Carnell wrote:

> When Christianity is scrapped, man becomes one minor gear in a mechanical universe; he contributes his little part, just as do mud, hair, and filth. Each is a gear, and each in its own way makes for the smoother movement of the whole. But it is not at all clear that humanity is worthy of any more honor than the other gears in the machine. Why should man be more laudable than, for example, the elephant? Both are doomed to die without hope in a universe which is under the decrees of the second law of thermodynamics, and the animal is bigger than the human. Without God to tell us otherwise, humanity appears to be a huddling mass of groveling protoplasm, crowded together in a nervous wait for death, not unlike a group of helpless children that aggregate to-

> gether in a burning building, pledging to love each other till the end comes. But, since we are **all** going to die, and since "the wages of virtue is dust," as Sidgwick expresses it, what possible incentive for heroic personal living can humanism proffer? Shall **I** give up **my** own desires to follow some abstractly conceived theory of justice, prudence, and benevolence, when, as a result of **my** lifetime sacrifice, all I receive is a dash of dirt? Inasmuch as I can be assured of my happiness here and now if I do my own, rather than the will of the whole, what reason is there for me **not** to follow my own desires? After all, it is just one gear against another, and may the best gear win (1948, pp. 327-328, emp. in orig.).

Determinism is the idea that ultimately man is not responsible for his actions. In its early stages, the concept flowed from the teachings of John Watson (1878-1958), a psychologist who taught at Johns Hopkins University. He believed that the long evolutionary process had imbued mankind with certain habits, from which flowed both personality and conduct. Later, psychologist B.F. Skinner of Harvard would inherit the mantle of Watson and become the primary proponent of what was known as "behavioral determinism." Ultimately, said Skinner, the concept of "human responsi bility" was so much nonsense since no one was "responsible" in the true sense of the word. Renowned criminal defense lawyer, Clarence Darrow, strongly defended the same position. Once, during a tour of the Cook County jail in Chicago, Illinois, Darrow told the inmates:

> There is no such thing as crime as the word is generally understood. I do not believe there is any sort of distinction between the real moral condition of the people in and out of jail. One is just as good as the other. The people here can no more help being here than the people outside can avoid being outside. I do not believe that people are in jail because they deserve to be. They are in jail simply because they can not avoid it on account of circumstances which are entirely beyond their control and for which they are in no way responsible (1988, p. 58).

In his best-selling book, *Attorney for the Damned*, Arthur Weinberg recounted the story of how Darrow (of Scopes trial fame) used the idea of people ultimately possessing no personal responsibility as a defense ploy for his two rich, young clients, Nathan Leopold and Richard Loeb, who viciously murdered 14-year-old Robert (Bobbie) Franks in cold blood just to see what it was like to kill another human being. Darrow's plea to the judge in a bench hearing on their behalf was that they were in no way responsible for their conduct since their destinies had been shaped for them years earlier by evolutionary forces over which they had absolutely no control (Weinberg, 1957, pp. 16-88). Fortunately, the judge was not swayed by such a specious argument. He found Darrow's two clients guilty and sentenced them both to life in prison.

In more recent times, Harvard entomologist E.O. Wilson, in his book, *Sociobiology: The New Synthesis*, has suggested that determinism can be documented and studied via the concept known as "sociobiology." This attempted amalgamation between certain of the social sciences and biology propagates the view that man has been "programmed" by his genetics to act as he does. Instead of the refrain made popular in the 1970s by talented comedian Flip Wilson (in character as the hilarious, loud-mouthed "Geraldine"), "The devil made me do it," the mantra for the 1990s became "My genes made me do it!" In assessing such an idea, Wayne Jackson wrote:

> First, if determinism is true, there is no such thing as human responsibility. This is a necessary corollary of the theory. In spite of this, determinists frequently speak, write, and act as though human accountability existed. Consistency is a rare jewel among them. Second, if man is not responsible for his actions, such terms as "good" and "evil" are meaningless. Third, if man is not accountable, no one should ever be punished for robbery, rape, child abuse, murder, etc. Do we punish a machine that maims or kills a person? Fourth, how can we be expected to be persuaded by the doctrine of determinism, since the determinists were "programmed" to teach their ideas, and thus these ideas may not be true at all.

> Fifth, determinists won't abide by their own doctrine. If I re-copied Edward *Sociobiology: The New Synthesis*, and had it published in **my** name, I would quickly find out whether Wilson thought I was responsible for the action or if only my genetic background was! (1995, 15:54, emp. in orig.).

The Practical Impact of Morals and Ethics Without God

When Martin Gardner wrote on "The Relevance of Belief Systems" in his book, *The New Age: Notes of a Fringe Watcher*, and observed that **what a person believes profoundly influences how a person acts**, he could not have been more right (1988, pp. 57-64). Nowhere has this been more true than in regard to the effect of incorrect beliefs concerning morality and ethics. And what a price we as humans have paid! One example (and there are many!) comes to mind immediately in regard to the value (or lack thereof) that we have placed on human life.

Having grown up under a father who was a veterinarian, and personally having served as a professor in the College of Veterinary Medicine at Texas A&M University for a number of years, I have seen firsthand the fate of animals that have suffered irreparable injuries, have become riddled with incurable diseases, or have become too old and decrepit to control their bodily functions. I have had to stand by helplessly and watch my father, or my colleagues, discharge a firearm to end the life of a horse because of a broken leg that could not be healed. I have had to draw into a syringe the life-ending drug to be inserted into the veins of someone's pet dog to "put it to sleep" because the combination of senility and disease had taken a toll that not even the ablest practitioner of the healing arts could reverse. It is neither a pleasant task nor a pretty sight. But while a pet dog or champion 4-H gelding may have held a place of esteem in a child's heart, the simple fact of the matter is that the dog is not someone's father or mother and the horse is not someone's brother or sister. These are animals—which is why they shoot horses.

In the evolutionary scheme of things, however, man occupies the same status. He may be more knowledgeable, more intellectual, and more scheming than his counterparts in the animal kingdom. But he is still an animal. And so the question is bound to arise: Why should man be treated any differently when his life no longer is deemed worth living? Truth be told, there is no logical reason that he should. From cradle to grave, life—from an evolutionary vantage point—is completely expendable. And so it should be—at least if Charles Darwin is to be taken at face value. In his book, *The Descent of Man*, he wrote:

> With savages, the weak in body or mind are soon eliminated; and those that survive commonly exhibit a vigorous state of health. We civilised men, on the other hand, do our utmost to check the process of elimination; we build asylums for the imbecile, the maimed, and the sick; we institute poor-laws; and our medical men exert their utmost skills to save the life of everyone to the last moment. There is reason to believe that vaccination has preserved thousands, who from a weak constitution would formerly have succumbed to small-pox. Thus the weak members of civilised societies propagate their kind. No one who has attended to the breeding of domestic animals will doubt that this must be highly injurious to the race of man. It is surprising how soon a want of care, or care wrongly directed, leads to the degeneration of a domestic race; but excepting in the case of man himself, hardly any one is so ignorant as to allow his worst animals to breed (1870, p. 501).

In Darwin's day (and even in the early parts of this century), some applied this view to the human race via the concept of eugenics. By January 22, 1973, the United States Supreme Court, in a 7-to-2 vote, decided that the human embryo growing within the human womb no longer is "human." Rather, it is a "thing" that may be ripped out, slaughtered, and tossed into the nearest garbage dump. And the lengths to which some will go in order to justify such a position defy description. As an example, consider the position of the late atheist Carl Sagan and his wife, Ann Druyan. In an article on

"The Question of Abortion" that they co-authored for *Parade* magazine, these two humanists contended for the ethical permissibility of human abortion on the grounds that the fetus, growing within a woman's body for several months following conception, is not a human being. Their conclusion, therefore, was this: the killing of this tiny creature is not murder.

And what was the basis for this assertion? Sagan and Druyan argued their case by subtly employing the concept known as "embryonic recapitulation," which suggests that as the human embryo develops, it repeats its evolutionary history, going through ancestral stages such as an amoeba-like blob, a fish, an amphibian, a reptile, etc. So, watching the human embryo grow is like watching a "silent moving picture" of evolution. They stated that the embryo first is "a kind of parasite" that eventually looks like a "segmented worm." Further alterations, they wrote, reveal "gill arches" like that of a "fish or amphibian." Supposedly, "reptilian" features emerge, and later give rise to "mammalian...pig-like" traits. By the end of two months, according to these two authors, the creature resembles a "primate but is still not quite human" (1990, p. 6).

The concept of embryonic recapitulation, which first was set forth in the mid-1860s by German scientist Ernst Haeckel, long since has been discredited and shown to be without any basis in scientific fact (see Simpson et al., 1957, p. 352). But so desperate were Sagan and Druyan to find something—anything—in science to justify their belief that abortion is not murder, they resurrected the ancient concept, dusted it off, and attempted to give it some credibility as an appropriate reason why abortion is not murder. Surely this demonstrates the lengths to which evolutionists will go to substantiate their theory, as well as the inordinate practices that the theory generates when followed to its logical ends.

According to Darwin, "weaker" members of society are unfit and, by the laws of nature, normally would not survive. Who is weaker than a tiny baby growing in the womb? The baby cannot defend himself, cannot feed himself, and cannot even speak for himself. He (or she) is completely and totally dependent upon the mother for life. Since nature "selects against" the weaker animal, and since man is an animal, why should man expect any deferential treatment?

Once those who are helpless, weak, and young become expendable, who will be next? Will it be the helpless, weak, and old? Will it be those whose infirmities make them "unfit" to survive in a society that values the beautiful and the strong? Will it be those who are lame, blind, maimed? Will it be those whose IQ falls below a certain point or whose skin is a different color? Some in our so ciety already are calling for such "cleansing" processes to be made legal, using euphemisms such as "euthanasia" or "mercy killing." After all, they shoot horses, don't they?

Morality, Ethics, and the Existence of God

When George Gaylord Simpson commented that "morals arise only in man" (1967, p. 346), he acknowledged (whether or not he intended to) the fact that morality is something unique to humankind. No two apes ever sat down and said, "Hey, I've got a good idea. Today let's talk about morals and ethics." On the same page of his book, Simpson thus was forced to admit that "the workings of the universe cannot provide any automatic, universal, eternal, or absolute ethical criteria of right and wrong" (1967, p. 346). In their book, *Why Believe? God Exists!*, Miethe and Habermas observed:

> At every turn in the discussion of moral values, the naturalistic position is weighted down with difficulties. It has the appearance of a drowning swimmer trying to keep its head above water. If it concedes something on the one hand, it is condemned on the other. But if it fails to admit the point, it appears to be in even more trouble. It is an understatement to say, at the very least, that naturalism is not even close to being the **best** explanation for the existence of our moral conscience (1993, p. 219, emp. in orig.).

What, then, is the "best explanation for the existence of our moral conscience"? John Henry Newman assessed the situation like this:

> Inanimate things cannot stir our affections; these are correlative with persons. If, as is the case, we feel responsibility, are ashamed, are frightened, at transgressing the voice of conscience, this implies that there is One to whom we are responsible, before whom we are ashamed, whose claims upon us we fear...we are not affectionate towards a stone, nor do we feel shame before a horse or a dog; we have no remorse or compunction on breaking mere human law...and thus the phenomena of Conscience, as a dictate, avail to impress the imagination with the picture of a Supreme Governor, a Judge, holy, just, powerful, all-seeing, retributive (1887, pp. 105,106).

Theistic philosopher David Lipe wrote:

> In conflicts of moral judgments, some judgments are recognized as better than others... If it is not the case that one moral judgment is any better than any other moral judgment, then it is nonsensical to prefer one over the other. However, every person finds himself preferring one judgment over another, and in this admission (that one is better than the other), it is claimed that one is responding to a law which, in effect, measures the judgments...I am convinced that all men have the moral experience of feeling "obligated" in a certain way, and that this sense of "moral obligation" is connected with God. This idea is consistent with the meaning of religion itself. The word "religion" is a compound of the Latin *re* and *ligare*, meaning "to bind back." Thus, for the religionist, there is a bond existing between man and God. This bond is the feeling of being morally obligated to live up to a specific moral law or standard which is the expression of the commands of God and which presses down on everyone (1987b, 7:40,37).

In the long run, morality simply cannot survive if its ties to religion are cut. W.T. Stace, who was neither a theist nor a friend of religion, nevertheless agreed wholeheartedly with such an assessment when he wrote:

> The Catholic bishops of America once issued a statement in which they said that the chaotic and bewildered state of the modern world is due to man's loss of faith, his abandonment of God and religion. **I agree** with this statement.... Along with the ruin of the religious vision there went the ruin of moral principles and indeed of all values (1967, pp. 3,9, emp. in orig.).

This "ruin of moral principles" is what Glenn C. Graber referred to in his doctoral dissertation on "The Relationship of Morality and Religion" as the "cut-flowers thesis"—a concept that explains what happens to morals and ethics when they are divorced from their religious moorings based on the existence of the "Supreme Governor"—God (1972, pp. 1-5). Perhaps Leo Tolstoy provided an early statement of this thesis when he suggested:

> The attempts to found a morality apart from religion are like the attempts of children who, wishing to transplant a flower that pleases them, pluck it from the roots that seem to them unpleasing and superfluous, and stick it rootless into the ground. Without religion there can be no real, sincere morality, just as without roots there can be no real flower (1964, pp. 31,32).

In discussing the cut-flowers thesis, Lipe remarked:

> Tolstoy's conclusion is a matter of grave importance to those who take religion seriously. Thus, on the cut-flowers thesis, those who believe morality is a valuable human institution, and those who wish to avoid moral disaster, will make every effort to preserve its connection with religion and the religious belief which forms its roots. The apologetic force of the cut-flowers thesis becomes even stronger if the religionist makes the additional claim that morality **is presently** in a withering stage. This claim takes on a sense of **urgency** when the decline in morality is identified with the muddle in which civilization now finds itself (1987a, 7:27, emp. in orig.).

And civilization is indeed in a "muddle" identified by a definite "decline in morality." With guns blasting, children (some as young as 10 or 11 years old) bearing a grudge or desiring to settle a score walk into school hallways, classrooms, and libraries, shoot until they have emptied every round from all chambers, and watch gleefully as shell casings, teachers, and classmates alike fall silently at their feet. Then parents, administrators, and friends congregate amidst the bloody aftermath and wonder what went wrong. Yet why are we shocked or enraged by such conduct? Our children have been taught they are nothing more than "naked apes"—and they are intelligent enough to figure out exactly what that means. As Guy N. Woods lamented, "Convince a man that he came from a monkey, and he'll act like one!" (1976, 118[33]:514). They have been taught that religion is an outward sign of inner weakness—a crutch used by people too weak and cowardly to "pull themselves up by their own boot straps." Why, then, should we be at all surprised when they react accordingly (even violently!)? After all, "nature," said Lord Tennyson, "is red in tooth and claw."

The truth of the matter is that only the theocentric approach to this problem is consistent logically and internally; only the theocentric approach can provide an objective, absolute set of morals and ethics. But why is this the case?

True morality is based on the fact of the unchanging nature of Almighty God. He is eternal (Psalm 90:2; 1 Timothy 1:17), holy (Isaiah 6:3; Revelation 4:8), just and righteous (Psalm 89:14), and forever consistent (Malachi 3:6). In the ultimate sense, only He is good (Mark 10:18). Furthermore, since He is perfect (Matthew 5:48), the morality that issues from such a God is good, unchanging, just, and consistent—i.e., exactly the opposite of the relativistic, deterministic, or situational ethics of the world.

When Newman suggested in the above quotation that we as humans "feel responsibility," it was a recognition on his part that there is indeed within each man, woman, and child a sense of moral responsibility which derives from the fact that God is our Creator (Psalm 100:3) and that we have been fashioned in His spiritual image (Genesis 1:26-27). As the potter has sovereign right over the clay with which he works (Romans 9:21), so our Maker has the sovereign right over His creation since in His hand "is the soul of every living thing" (Job 12:10). As the patriarch Job learned much too late, God is not a man with whom one can argue (Job 9:32).

Whatever God does, commands, and approves is good (Psalm 119:39,68; cf. Genesis 18:25). What He has commanded results from the essence of His being—Who He is—and therefore also is good. In the Old Testament, the prophet Micah declared of God: "He showed thee, O man, what is good; and what doth Jehovah require of thee, but to do justly, and to love kindness, and walk humbly with thy God" (Micah 6:8). In the New Testament, the apostle Peter admonished: "As he who called you is holy, be ye yourselves also holy in all manner of living; because it is written, 'Ye shall be holy: for I am holy'" (1 Peter 1:15).

The basic thrust of God-based ethics concerns the relationship of man to the One Who created and sustains him. God Himself is the unchanging standard of moral law. His perfectly holy nature is the ground or basis upon which "right" and "wrong," "good" and "evil" are determined. The Divine will—expressive of the very nature of God—constitutes the ultimate ground of moral obligation. Why are we to pursue holiness? Because God is holy (Leviticus 19:1; 1 Peter 1:16). Why are we not to lie, cheat, or steal (Colossians 3:9)? Because God's nature is such that He cannot lie (Titus 1:2; Hebrews 6:18). Since God's nature is unchanging, it follows that moral law, which reflects the divine nature, is equally immutable.

While there have been times in human history when each man "did that which was right in his own eyes" (Judges 17:6), that never was God's plan. He has not left us to our own devices to determine what is right and wrong because He knew that through sin man's heart would become "exceedingly corrupt" (Jeremiah 17:9). Therefore, God "has spoken" (Hebrews 1:1), and in so doing He has made known to man His laws and precepts through the revelation He has provided in written form within the Bible (1 Corinthians 2:11ff.; 2 Timothy 3:16-17; 2 Peter 1:20-21). Thus, mankind is expected to act in a morally responsible manner (Matthew

19:9; Acts 14:15-16; 17:30; Hebrews 10:28ff.) in accordance with biblical laws and precepts. In addressing this point, Wayne Jackson commented that the Bible "contains many rich **principles** which challenge us to develop a greater sense of spiritual maturity and to soar to heights that are God-honoring.... Our Creator has placed us 'on our honor' to grow to greater heights.... [Biblical] morality runs deep into the soul; it challenges us to get our hearts under control" (1984, 4:23, emp. in orig.).

Herbert Lockyer discussed this concept in vividly expressive terms when he wrote:

> Being made righteous before God, it is imperative for us to live righteously before men. God, however, has not only a standard for us, He intends Christians **to be standards** (I Timothy 4:12; James 1:22). Think of these manifold requirements. We are told to be different from the world (II Corinthians 5:17; Romans 6:4; 12:1,2). We are to shine as lights amidst the world's darkness (Matthew 5:14-16). We are to walk worthy of God, as His ambassadors (II Corinthians 5:20; Ephesians 5:8). We are to live pleasing to God (I Thessalonians 4:1; II Thessalonians 1:11-2:17; Colossians 1:10). We are to be examples to others in all things (I Corinthians 4:13; I Timothy 4:12). We are to be victorious in temptation and tribulation (Romans 12:12; Colossians 1:11, James 1:2-4). We are to be conspicuous for our humility (Ephesians 4:12; Colossians 3:13; I Peter 3:3,4). We must appropriate divine power for the accomplishment of all God wants to make us, and desires us to be (Philippians 3:13; 3:21; II Peter 1:3)....
>
> Throughout all of the **epistles** are scattered rules and directions, covering the whole ground of private and social life. The apostles taught that as a man **believes**, so must he **behave**. Creed should be reflected in conduct. **Virtues** must be acquired (Galatians 5:22,23; Colossians 3:12-17; II Peter 1:5-7; Titus 2:12), and **vices** shunned (Galatians 5:19, 20,21; Colossians 3:5-9). Love, as the parent of all virtue must be fostered (Romans 5:1,2,7,8; I Corinthians 13; II Corinthians 5:19; Hebrews 11). Christ's image must be reflected in the lives of those He saves (Romans 8:37-39; 1 Corinthians 15:49-58; 11 Corinthians 5:8; Philippians 3: 8-14).

> Truly, ours is a high and holy calling. Belonging to Christ, we must behave accordingly. Having accepted Christ we must **live** Christ, which is not a mere fleshly imitation of Him but the outworking of His own life within. If His law is written upon our heart (Hebrews 8:10), and His Spirit enlightens our conscience (John 16:13); then, with a will harmonized to the Lord's will (Psalm 143:10), and affections set on heavenly things (Colossians 3:1), there will be no contradiction between profession and practice. What we believe will influence behavior, and creed will harmonize with conduct and character (1964, pp. 221-223, emp. in orig.).

Lockyer's last point is one that I have tried to make over and over within this discussion: "What we believe will influence behavior, and creed will harmonize with conduct and character." If a man believes he came from an animal, if he is consistent with his belief his conduct will match accordingly. If a man believes he was "created in the image and likeness of God," if he is consistent with his belief his conduct will match accordingly.

David Lipe, speaking as both a philosopher and a theist, has suggested that for quite some time certain philosophers and theologians generally have "turned away from" standard textbook arguments for the existence of God, not because the doctrines were weak or had been disproved, but because "morality has furnished the main support" (1987a, 7:26). Indeed it has.

Miethe and Habermas were correct when they suggested that "naturalism is not even close to being the best explanation for the existence of our moral conscience" (1993, p. 219). Man's moral and ethical nature, as Newman proclaimed, "implies that there is One to whom we are responsible...a Supreme Governor, a Judge, holy, just, powerful" (1887, pp. 105,106).

Eventually, each of us will meet "the righteous judgment of God, who will render to every man according to his works" (Romans 2:5-6). It therefore behooves us to "live soberly, righteously, and godly in this present age" (Titus 2:12) for, as Carnell put it:

Death is the one sure arch under which all men must pass. But if death ends all—and it very well may unless we have inerrant revelation to assure us to the contrary—what virtue is there in present striving? Job...expressed [that] man lives as if there is a sense to life, but in the end, his mortal remains provide but a banquet for the worms, for man dies and "The worm shall feed sweetly on him" (Job 24:20).... The only full relief man can find from the clutches of these "tiny cannibals" is to locate some point of reference outside of the flux of time and space which can serve as an elevated place of rest. In Christianity, and in it alone, we find the necessary help, the help of the Almighty, He who rules eternity (1948, pp. 332,333).

CHAPTER 8

IN DEFENSE OF THE BIBLE'S INSPIRATION [PART I]

Knowledge and truth are precious commodities. As a body of factual information and legitimate principles, knowledge is indispensable in human relationships. Truth, as knowledge justifiably believed, represents a fundamental reality that transcends both the provincial and the temporal. Most people are desirous of obtaining a certain amount of knowledge that they then can put to good use in their everyday lives. And, undoubtedly, most people prefer not be deceived, but instead prefer to be dealt with honestly and truthfully. One of the Ten Commandments, in fact, was based upon just such a concept: "Thou shalt not bear false witness against thy neighbor" (Exodus 20:16).

Truthfulness always has been the basis for the moral, legal, and ethical codes of nations. And, an abiding respect for truth has undergirded the legitimacy of those codes. "Buy the truth, and sell it not," said the Proverbs writer (23:23). He who possesses correct knowledge has within him the potential to discern, and then act upon, truth. Knowledge frees from the shackles of ignorance; truth frees from the shackles of error. Indeed, knowledge and truth **are** precious commodities.

While almost anyone you ask will admit, **in theory**, that knowledge and truth are indispensable attributes of a sensible, everyday existence, **in practice** many people live out that daily existence as if knowledge and truth ultimately do not matter. Much of mankind lives according to an abstract, confusing, and largely inconsistent system of personal behavior. This is a bit odd, to say the least. In most matters, a man likely will insist upon complete **objectivity**. For example, in regard to his eating habits he might say, "I will not eat this food; it contains bacterial toxins that will kill me." In regard to matters of civil law, he might suggest, "That action is illegal; it violates my rights."

Yet when it comes to religion in general, and Christianity in particular, **subjectivity** rules the day. People can be so certain about their beliefs in the physical realm, but so nebulous about their beliefs in the spiritual realm. For example, on occasion when a person who believes in God is asked if God does, in fact, exist, he may opine: "I **believe** He exists," or "I **hope** He exists," or "I **think** He exists." But rarely do you hear him say boldly, "I **know** He exists." Or, if a Christian is asked the question, "Do you know you are saved?," the response may go something like this: "I believe that I am," or "I hope that I am," or "I think that I am." But rarely do you hear someone confidently assert, "Yes, I **know** that I am saved."

This is indeed a sad state of affairs. We now have progressed to the point where in matters as mundane as food choices or legal wrangling, objectivity is an absolute requirement. Meanwhile, in the much more important area of spiritual matters, we not only expect, but in many cases insist upon, a subjectivity that we would not tolerate in any other sphere of our lives. It is as if the pluralistic postmodernism that has affected secular society (the "I'm OK, you're OK" or "Who am I to judge?" concept) finally has made its way into the spiritual community as well. Apparently, some among us either once knew but long since have forgotten, or never really understood in the first place, the proper concept of truth. Similarly, we either have forgotten, or no longer care, about the damage that an improper concept of truth can cause.

The time has come for Christians to embolden themselves once again with the same high regard for truth that Jesus expressed when He stated: "And ye shall know the truth, and the truth shall make you free" (John 8:32). Christianity is not an "I-hope-so/pie-in-the-sky-by-and-by" kind of religion based upon some esoteric, fairy-tale-like concept. Rather, it is rooted and grounded in the provable existence of the one true God and the verifiable nature of the historical facts surrounding the life, death, and resurrection of His Son. When the apostle John wrote to comfort and reassure first-century Christians who found themselves in the midst of numerous trials and persecutions, he said: "These things have I written unto you, that ye may **know** that ye have eternal life, even unto you that believe on the name of the Son of God" (1 John 5:13, emp. added). Thus, according to both Jesus and John, a person not only can know something, but he can know that he knows it.

There are certain undeniable, critically important implications standing behind this kind of firm and confident declaration. Consider the following. If a person cannot **know** (with certainty) that God exists, then he cannot know (with certainty) that the Bible is His inspired Word. If a person cannot know that the Bible is the inspired Word of God, then he cannot know that Jesus is God's Son, for the Bible provides the evidentiary basis for such a claim. If a person cannot know that Christ is God's Son, then he cannot know that he is saved. Yet John specifically stated: "These things have I written unto you, that ye may **know** that ye have eternal life."

The simple fact is—Christians are not agnostics! The agnostic suggests, "I **cannot know** whether God exists." Christians, on the other hand, **know** that God exists (cf. Psalm 46:10). Consider the alternative. Do Christians serve a God Who "may" or "may not" exist? Do Christians believe, and ask others to believe, the testimony of a Bible that "may" or "may not" be inspired? Do Christians trust, obey, and place their faith in a Christ Who "may" or "may not" be the Son of God? Hardly!

Even the casual reader will discern the close relationship among these vital issues. Knowledge of God's existence is foundational, which is why I have marshaled the evidence for it (Thompson, 1995a, 1995b). Knowledge of Christ's Sonship is pivotal, which is why I have documented the facts that attend it (Thompson, 1997). Knowledge of salvation is essential, which is why I have assembled the testimony of Scripture that attests to it (Thompson, 1998a; 1998b). But no less important is the evidence that establishes the inspiration of God's Word—the topic to which I now direct your attention.

The Need for Revelation from God

With the existence of God established, it becomes reasonable to think that such a Creator-God would wish to communicate with His creation. Mankind shows evidence of high intelligence, kindness, goodness, justice, and many other unique characteristics. Since it is inconceivable that the Creator could be inferior to His creation in any fashion, and since the effect never is greater than the cause, it is inevitable that God would exhibit infinite intelligence, kindness, goodness, justice, etc. Therefore, some form of personal communication between the intelligent Creator and His intelligent creature would be expected. Else, how could mankind ever come to know, or appreciate, certain aspects of the Creator, or understand what the Creator might possibly require of the beings He had created? Furthermore, some form of revelation from the Creator would be needed in order to instruct mankind in certain areas, such as the following.

The Character of God. While something of God's essence, power, and wisdom can be gleaned vaguely from the vastness and marvelous intricacies of the creation itself, a more concrete communication is needed to establish the exact nature of His character.

The Origin of Evil. As mankind found itself adrift in a sea of evil, pain, and suffering, the question eventually would arise: Why? Man thus needed to be educated concerning the exact reason(s) for his predicament.

Mankind's Origin. Without revelation to the contrary, men might come to the conclusion that they owe their ultimate origin to "accidental forces of nature," rather than to the omnipotence of a divine Creator. The confusion of modern-day evolutionary theories is evidence aplenty of this.

Mankind's Purpose. Man—left to his own devices—never could understand completely the ultimate purpose for his creation at the hand of an Almighty God. With no adequately defined role, and no immediate or future goals, he would wander aimlessly—from cradle to grave—in a sea of uncertainty.

Mankind's Destiny. In the absence of divine revelation, man never would know with certainty anything about the existence of life beyond this one. He therefore might conclude incorrectly—as many have in every generation—that this life is all there is. The urgency of mankind having access to this knowledge is evinced by the general despair of those who reject the concept of supernatural revelation.

A revelation from God might take almost any form. God could choose to communicate with His creation directly via word of mouth, through messengers (e.g., angels), or through dreams and visions. For that matter, He could choose any means that suited the occasion. Seemingly, however, the most appropriate medium for long-term results would be one that ensured permanence. That is to say, it would withstand the test of time and could be passed faithfully from generation to generation throughout human history. One possible way to accomplish such a goal would be to produce the revelation in a written form that could be duplicated and distributed as needed, thus benefitting the whole of mankind across the ages.

The question then becomes: Is there any evidence that mankind possesses such a revelation? And the answer to that question is: Yes, evidence does exist to establish the claim that God has given mankind His revelation in the written form known as the Bible. The late B.C. Goodpasture, distinguished editor of the *Gospel Advocate* for almost forty years, wrote:

> The nature and contents of the Bible are such that the rank and file of its readers in all generations have recognized God as its author. Man would not have written such a book, if he could; and could not, if he would. It moves on a superhuman plane in design, in nature, and in teaching. It caters not to worldly desire and ambition. It condemns much which men in the flesh highly prize, and commends much which they despise. Its thoughts are not the thoughts of men (1970, p. 54).

Harold Lindsell, former editor of *Christianity Today*, remarked:

> Had God chosen not to reveal Himself, man could never have known Him. And man can never know more about God than God chooses to disclose.... Whatever knowledge of God is available exists solely because God has chosen to make it known. This is His self-revelation (1976, p. 28).

God's written revelation makes it clear that in the past He provided that "self-revelation" in a variety of ways. The Maker of the Universe manifested His presence in the works of His creative genius (Psalm 19:1; Romans 1:20-21). He spoke to various men and women in a direct, word-of-mouth fashion (Genesis 3:9-16; Numbers 12:8). He revealed Himself through visions and dreams (Genesis 20:3; Numbers 12:6; Isaiah 29:10-11; Ezekiel 1:3-4; Daniel 2:19; Amos 1:1). He addressed His creation through angels (Genesis 16:10-12; 18:13-14; 22:11ff.; 32:1-2; Acts 7:38). On unique occasions, He even made known His presence through such media as "a still, small voice" (1 Kings 19:12), the mouth of a donkey (Numbers 22:28), and a bright cloud (Matthew 17:5). God's greatest revelation of Himself, however, was in the person of His Son, Jesus Christ (John 3:16; 14:9; Colossians 2:9).

Lacking adequate revelation from God, we would have no accurate way of understanding what we needed to know regarding God, His Son, our place in the creation, and many other topics of ultimate importance to humanity. We would have no objective standard upon which to base ethics and morals. We would know little of the ministry and message of Jesus of Nazareth. We would have no information regarding the theological purpose of His crucifixion and resurrection—namely, that they were essential ingredients in God's plan to offer ruined man a way of escape from the devastating consequences of his sin (Matthew 20:28; 26:28). We would know nothing of how to enter that sacred body of saved souls, the church (Ephesians 5:23; 1 Corinthians 12:13), or how, once we had entered, to worship God correctly. Without God's revelation, we would know utterly nothing about these important spiritual matters that impact our eternal destiny. Perhaps it was with such things in mind that Arthur W. Pink wrote these beautiful words:

> If it were announced upon reliable authority that on a certain date in the near future an angel from heaven would visit New York and would deliver a sermon upon the invisible world, the future destiny of man, or the secret deliverance from the power of sin, what an audience he would command! There is no building in that city large enough to accommodate the crowd which would throng to hear him. If upon the next day, the newspapers were to give a verbatim report of his discourse, how eagerly it would be read! And yet, we have between the covers of the Bible not merely an angelic communication, but a Divine revelation. How great then is our wick edness if we undervalue and despise it! And yet we do (1976, p. 103).

Truly, we should be grateful to God for providing us with a revelation that could be retained in a permanent form, studied faithfully, and used profitably by all of mankind.

What Does The Bible Contain?

The fact that the Bible exists in the first place brings to mind the question: What does the Bible contain? It contains two things: (1) known facts; and (2) revelation. What is the difference between the two?

When we say that the Bible contains "known facts," we mean that it contains information known to the people of that time and place. For example, if the Bible mentions people known as Hittites (Exodus 23:28), then historical records could verify their existence. If the Bible mentions that the Roman Emperor, Caesar Augustus, commanded that a census be taken at a certain time (Luke 2:1), then we could set about corroborating the truthfulness of such a statement.

But to say that the Bible "contains" known facts implies that it also contains something else. That "something else" is revelation. By definition, revelation designates the unveiling of facts and truths to man by God—facts and truths that man, on his own, otherwise could not have known. Revelation has reference to the communication of information.

Compare and contrast the following. When Moses wrote in the book of Numbers about Israel's wilderness wanderings subsequent to the Exodus from Egypt, he did not need revelation from God to do so. He was their leader during that period and simply wrote what he had observed as an eyewitness. When Luke penned the book in the New Testament that bears his name, he did not need revelation from God to do so. He acknowledged as much when he said: "It seemed good to me also, **having traced the course of all things accurately from the first**, to write unto thee in order, most excellent Theophilus" (Luke 1:3, emp. added). Luke had been on certain of the missionary journeys, and thus was able to write from firsthand experience.

On the other hand, notice Moses' statement in Deuteronomy 29:29: "The secret things belong unto Jehovah our God; but **the things that are revealed** belong unto us and to our children forever, that we may do all the words of this law" (emp. added). As an illustration of this fact, we may observe that Moses would have had absolutely no way to know either generic or specific details of the activities of the creation week (Genesis 1:1ff.), unless God Himself had revealed those details to Moses. Nor could the apostle John have described in such a beautiful panorama the splendors of heaven (as he did within the book of Revelation), unless God first described to John the splendors of heaven.

On occasion, the various Bible writers could, and did, place into print what they had seen or what they had been told by credible witnesses. When they penned such matters, they had no need whatsoever of revelation from God since they wrote from firsthand experience. At times, however, they wrote about things they neither had experienced themselves nor had been told by others. When they did so, it was God's revelation that provided the information they needed (Amos 3:7; Daniel 2:28; Ephesians 3:3-5).

The Two Types Of Revelation

There are two different types of revelation. **General** (or natural) revelation designates the revelation that God has provided of Himself in nature (cf. Romans 1:20-21, Acts 14:17, Psalm 19:1, et al.). **Special** (or supernatural) revelation is the name that designates the revelation that God has provided within the Bible.

General Revelation

General revelation comes to man through nature. The first six verses of Psalm 19 declare that God has given a revelation of Himself in nature that constantly testifies of the Creator. In Romans 1: 20, Paul stated that "the invisible things of him since the creation of the world are clearly seen, being perceived **through the things that are made**, even his everlasting power and divinity; that they may be without excuse" (emp. added).

The Scriptures teach that general revelation is universal. At no time in history has God left Himself without a witness of Himself (Acts 14:17). General revelation is universal in both scope and territory. God's glory can be seen whenever and wherever a heavenly body is observed. It can be seen in the glistening of a gorgeous afternoon rainbow, or in the still, sweet waters of a gently flowing brook through a rainforest. Though men often refuse to recognize and accept God's revelation of Himself in nature, it abides nevertheless.

Just as general revelation was present before man sinned in the Garden of Eden, so it is present after his fall. But truth be told, general revelation is not always understood as it should be due to the fact that man's mind has become corrupt. The reason for man's apostasy and mental depravity is due to his initial fall from Heaven's favor (a sad story, the details of which are recorded in Genesis 3). Man was created in the image of God, yet became a rebel, subject to evil passions and subsequently blinded to the spiritual values that are so important (2 Corinthians 4:3-4). His heart also became subject to corruption (Romans 3:10-18; Ephesians 2:1ff.).

With the fall of man, not an **evolution** but a **devolution** began. As a result of his disobedience to God's laws, man has become afflicted with a blindness that sometimes prevents him from understanding properly God's revelation in nature. The noetic effects of sin have darkened his mind so that he often does not grasp the message of the revelation of God that appears all around him on a daily basis.

As great as general revelation is, however, it is deficient in and of itself. For many people, nature has ceased to be a perspicuous revelation of God. It may have been so before sin entered the world, but even if it were, man's nature now has become so polluted that he no longer can read the divine script around him. General revelation simply is not enough. It never was intended to be. It does not afford man the reliable knowledge of God (or other important spiritual matters) that he needs for salvation. By itself, therefore, it is inadequate as the sole foundation of a person's faith. From nature alone, man never would be able to infer the need for a personal Savior. Therefore, God has seen fit to give man a second type of revelation.

Special Revelation

God has revealed Himself in the sixty-six books of the Bible in a most specific fashion. Speaking in general terms, there has been only one permanent revelation, i.e., the supernatural revelation found within the Scriptures. Actually, however, throughout human history God has disclosed Himself and His will in at least three different ways: theophanies, direct communications, and miracles.

Theophanies are appearances of God Himself. He is spoken of as dwelling between the cherubim (Psalm 80:1; 99:1). He appeared in fire and clouds and smoke (cf. Genesis 15:17, Exodus 3:2, 19:9, 16ff., 33:9, Psalms 78:14, 99:7). He appeared in stormy winds (Job 38:1; 40:6; Psalm 18:10-16). Theophany reached its highest point in the incarnation, in which Jesus Christ became flesh and dwelt among men (Colossians 1:19; 2:9).

God disclosed Himself in a second way through **direct communications**. In doing so, He made His thoughts and will known to men. Sometimes it was through an audible voice (Genesis 2:16; 3:8-19; 4:6-15; 9:1,8,12; 32:26; Exodus 19:9; Deuteronomy 5:4-5; 1 Samuel 3:4). He worked through dreams (Numbers 12:6; Deuteronomy 13:1-6; 1 Samuel 28:6; Joel 2:28). He communicated through visions (Isaiah 6; 21:6ff.; Ezekiel 1-3; 8-11; Daniel 1:17; 2:19; 7-10). And lastly, God has communicated His thoughts and will to men via the Holy Spirit (Mark 13:11; Luke 12:12; John 14:17; 15:26; 16:13; 20:22; Acts 6:10; 8:29; 2 Peter 1:20-21).

God also chose to reveal Himself through **miracles** that not only showcased His power and presence but emphasized great truths as well. They confirmed the words of prophecy and stood as evidence of God's omnipotence among the people that He had created. The greatest of these miracles was the incarnation.

Revelation is of word and fact; as such, it is historical in nature. Its purposes are many, but among those purposes are justification, sanctification, and redemption. God's revelation was progressive and unfolding in character—dim at first, then gradually increasing in light until its fullness finally arrived. As Harold Lindsell observed:

> This revelation of God of which I have been speaking has become inscripturated. It has come down to us in written form. Thus, there are two Words: the Word of God incarnate, Jesus Christ, and the Word of God written, the Bible. It is the Word of God written that reveals the Word of God incarnate to man. The Bible, then, is **the** Word of God and it is of this Word we now speak. When we say the Bible is the Word of God, it makes no difference whether the writers of Scripture gained their information by direct revelation from God as in the case of the Book of Revelation, or whether they researched matters as Luke did, or whether they got their knowledge from extant sources, court records, or even by word of mouth. The question we must now ask is whether what they wrote, wherever they may have secured their knowledge, can be trusted. This brings us to the doctrine of inspiration, which is clearly taught in the Bible itself (1976, p. 30, emp. in orig.).

The Bible's Claims for Its Own Inspiration

Imagine, if you can, that somehow you could have access to every religious book that has ever been written. Imagine, also, that you could run those books through some sort of a sieve to winnow out only those volumes that claimed to be a creed book, by which you should pattern and live your life. That, admittedly, would be a tough test and one that, likely, very few books could pass. Then, imagine further that you could take the books that passed this test and run them through the same sieve in order to winnow out only those books that claimed to be both a creed book for regulating your life **and inspired of God**. The number remaining after such a winnowing process would be so small that you could count it on the fingers of both hands!

The claim of inspiration at the hand of God is rare indeed. Sadly, misguided devotees of various religions clamor about, defending this book or that book as allegedly being "inspired of God" when, in fact, the books themselves do not even make such a claim. So, the first question that should be asked of any volume for which inspiration is touted is this: Does the **book itself** claim to be inspired?

When it comes to the Bible, that question can be answered in the affirmative. In his first letter to his coworker, Timothy, Paul stated: "All scripture is given by inspiration of God, and is profitable for doctrine, for reproof, for correction, for instruction in righteousness: That the man of God may be perfect, throughly furnished unto all good works" (2 Timothy 3:16-17). Peter wrote: "Knowing this first, that no prophecy of scripture is of private interpretation. For no prophecy ever came by the will of man: but men spake from God, being moved by the Holy Spirit" (2 Peter 1:20-21). When he wrote his first epistle to the Christians at Corinth, Paul reminded them:

> But we received, not the spirit of the world, but the spirit which is from God; that we might know the things that were freely given to us of God. Which things also we speak, not in words which man's wisdom teacheth, but which the Spirit teacheth; combining spiritual things with spiritual words (1 Corinthians 2:12-13).

Furthermore, statements such as "God said..." or "these are the words of the Lord..." appear thousands of times in both the Old and New Testaments. Moses wrote in Exodus 20:1: "And God spake all these words...." The psalmist wrote in 119:89: "For ever, O Jehovah, Thy word is settled in heaven." In Matthew 22:31, the Lord asked: "Have ye not read that which was spoken unto you by God?" In fact, "[t]here are 2,700 such statements in the Old Testament alone, all of which make direct claim that the Bible is the Word of God" (Ridenour, 1967, p. 2).

When we say that the Bible claims to be inspired, what do we mean by the word "inspired"? Our English term "inspiration" derives from the Latin *inspirare*, which means "to breathe upon or into" something. The five English words, "given by inspiration of God," in the King James Version of 1611 actually are translated from the single Greek adjective, *theopneustos*, which is derived from two Greek root words (*theos*—God, *pneo*—to blow or breathe). *Pneuma*, meaning "spirit," comes from the verb *pneo*. *Pneustos*, then, might mean "spirited," and *theopneustos* would mean God -spirited, God-breathed, filled with the breath of God, the product of the divine breath (or Spirit), or given by God through the Spirit. The word implies an influence from without that has the ability to produce effects that are beyond natural powers. "The book that is in this sense inspired is one into which something of another spirit or mind has been breathed; in other words, its author has been overshadowed by a power **outside** himself" (Goodpasture, 1970, p. 57, emp. in orig.). In his book, *The Battle for the Bible*, Lindsell stated unequivocally:

> Inspiration may be defined as the inward work of the Holy Spirit in the hearts and minds of chosen men who then wrote the Scriptures so that God got written what He wanted. The Bible in all of its parts constitutes the written Word of God to man. This word is free from all error in the original autographs. It is wholly trustworthy in matters of history and doctrine. However limited may have been their knowledge, and however much they may have erred when they were not writing sacred Scripture, the authors of Scripture, under the guidance of the Holy Spirit, were preserved from making factual, historical, scientific, or other errors. The Bible does not purport to be a textbook of history, science, or mathematics; yet when the writers of Scripture spoke of matters embraced in these disciples, they did not indite error; they wrote what was true.
>
> The very nature of inspiration renders the Bible infallible, which means that it cannot deceive us. It is inerrant in that it is not false, mistaken, or defective. Inspiration extends to all parts or the written Word of God and it includes the guiding hand of the Holy Spirit even in the selection of the words of Scripture.
>
> Inspiration involved infallibility from start to finish. God the Holy Spirit by nature cannot lie or be the author of untruth. If the Scripture is inspired at all it must be infallible. If any part of it is not infallible, then that part cannot be inspired. If inspiration allows for the possibility of error then inspiration ceases to be inspiration (1976, pp. 30-31).

Theologically, then, "inspiration" is used for the condition of **being directly under divine influence**. Paul's point was that every scripture is "God breathed." [The word "scripture" in 2 Timothy 3:16 refers primarily to the Old Testament Scriptures. However, as the New Testament was written, it, too, was referred to as "scripture." Peter, for example, referred to Paul's epistles as authoritative "scripture" (2 Peter 3:15-16). Thus, "all scripture" refers to the content of both testaments.]

One will search in vain throughout the Bible for an explicit statement containing the details of exactly **how** God related to the apostles and others in the production of the words they spoke or wrote. We know that the Spirit spoke by men and that His word was on their tongues (2 Samuel 23:2). We know the Holy Spirit spoke by the mouth of men (Acts 1:16). We know the things spoken were in words taught by the Holy Spirit (1 Corinthians 2:12-13). But no one knows the exact details of how the Spirit guided and superintended the writers to produce the end result. There are hidden details here that we may not presume to know. Holy men of God spoke as they were moved by the Spirit (2 Peter 1:20-21), guaranteeing that all Scripture is inspired of God (2 Timothy 3:16-17). But one must be content with these and similar statements. God simply has not seen fit to spell out the intricate details of how His Spirit entered into the minds of the writers and how He worked with their hands as they wrote. The point is that the work produced was God's Word, not man's. As such, it bears His divine stamp.

When Peter wrote in 2 Peter 1:20-21 that "men spake from God, being **moved** by the Holy Spirit," he employed the Greek word *pheromenoi*, which literally means "borne along." His point was that the Bible writers did not speak for themselves but were "borne along" by God's Holy Spirit to write what they did. The Bible writers never credited their words to mere human reason. Both Old and New Testament passages bear this out. In 2 Samuel 23:2 it is written: "The Spirit of Jehovah spake by me, And his word was upon my tongue." In Acts 1:16, Luke observed that "the Holy Spirit spake before by the mouth of David." Likely, however, the best explanatory passage regarding inspiration is Paul's commentary in 1 Corinthians 2:12-13, wherein he affirmed that the information the Bible writers received came not from human wisdom, but instead directly from God. Further, that wisdom was not expressed in man's choice of words, but via words guided by the Holy Spirit.

There are several different ideas concerning the inspiration of the Bible. "Perhaps it would be more accurate to say that different men believe in different levels of inspiration" (Baxter, 1971, p. 171). Let us now turn our attention to some of the various theories regarding inspiration.

Universal (Naturalistic) Inspiration. This theory holds that the Bible is inspired only in the sense that writers and artists are "inspired" when they produce great works of literature, music, or art. Actually this is the theory that certain men are inspired in the sense that they are exceptionally talented. In this sense, Shakespeare, Milton, Beethoven, Browning, Frost, and Van Gogh all were "inspired." This theory of inspiration holds that, in essence, the Bible is just like any other book. Although God may have given the authors an unusual ability to convey thoughts, the Bible is, after all, a human production without supernatural guidance. But, of course, this is not really inspiration at all. It might be called "natural genius," but not inspiration. As Wayne Jackson pointed out in his text, *Fortify Your Faith*:

> This theory is to be rejected for the following reasons. (a) It makes liars out of the N.T. writers who claimed the Holy Spirit as the source of their works. (b) The biblical documents are vastly superior to the ablest production of men. (c) It leaves the marvelous unity of the Bible as an inexplicable mystery. (d) If the Scriptures were the result of natural genius, modern genius could make them obsolete; instead, the Bible remains the world's best-seller (1974, p. 52).

Thought (Dynamic or Concept) Inspiration. This view asserts that the "thoughts" of the men are inspired, but not the words. According to this idea, the important thing is that spiritual truths be conveyed to the reader; it really does not matter what words are used or even whether the words described events that actually occurred. This concept may sound spiritual and pious, but it has grave problems. The human authors may have understood only partially what God was revealing to them and, as they restated it in their own words, they may have interjected considerable error. It is possible to convey precise thoughts and ideas only by using precise words! If the words are unimportant, then the thoughts that come from the words are entirely subjective. In other words:

> But what good are "infallible ideas" if channeled through "fallible" words? The truth is, one can no more have ideas without words than he can have a tune without notes or a sum without figures. The very idea is absurd! And I tell you honestly, it never ceases to puzzle me how some modernists can do such marvelous "word studies" from the text of the Bible, at the same time denying the "verbal" inspiration thereof. If the words of the sacred volume are uninspired, why the interest in them? Do scholars produce volumes of "word studies" on Shakespeare? (Jackson, 1974, p. 52).

Neo-Orthodox Inspiration. During the twentieth century another view of inspiration was advanced by such men as Karl Barth. L.S. Chafer, in his book, *Major Bible Themes*, explained.

> While not necessarily denying that supernatural elements exist in the writing of Scripture, this view acknowledges that there are errors in the Bible and thus the Bible cannot be taken literally as true. Neo-orthodoxy holds that God speaks through the Scriptures and uses them as a means by which to communicate truth to us. Accordingly, the Bible becomes a channel of divine revelation much as a beautiful flower or a lovely sunset communicates the concept that God is the Creator. The Bible under this theory becomes true only as it is comprehended and truth is realized by the individual reader. The history of this view demonstrates that no two of its advocates exactly agree as to what the Bible actually teaches,

> and like the view of partial inspiration, leaves the individual as the final authority concerning what is true and what is false (1926, p. 19).

Speaking in support of this theory, Emil Brunner once said that those "conservatives" who consider the Bible objectively and propositionally to be the Word of God are setting up a "paper pope" and thereby commit "bibliolatry" (see Merideth, 1972, pp. 377-378). Such an erroneous view of inspiration obviously contradicts the Bible's claims for its own inspiration and leaves people with little more than ethical subjectivism as their standard.

Encounter Inspiration. This theory holds that the Bible is a **vehicle** of revelation but **is not itself** a divine revelation. It becomes "inspired" when, and only when, it "inspires" the reader. It may well be the medium through which a person encounters God in an act of faith, but it is a human document nevertheless and as such is subject to human error throughout. According to this particular theory, then, inspiration becomes entirely subjective. One must have as much faith in his "encounter" session as the Christian has in Scripture. A passage that may be "inspired"to one reader may be utterly "uninspired" to someone else who reads the very same passage. Scripture therefore loses all of its evangelistic power.

Dictation (Mechanical) Inspiration. Some Bible critics claim that God dictated the Scriptures (every word, every punctuation mark, etc.) to men who were little more than mechanical stenographers that dutifully copied it all down. If God dictated the Bible, however, the style of writing and the vocabulary of the Bible would be the same throughout. Yet a simple reading of the Scriptures proves that the mechanical dictation viewpoint is without any basis in fact. The personality and style of each author are evident in every book of the Bible. In many instances the writers displayed their own fears and feelings, expressed their private prayers for God's deliverance, or in a host of other ways interjected their own personalities into the Divine Record. God allowed each man his own individuality and creativity, but worked through them all to inspire His Word. While inspiration extends to every word of Scripture, it does not rule out human personality and human personal interest. Direct dictation was not God's plan for inspiration.

Verbal, Plenary Inspiration. This is the correct view of inspiration. It holds that men wrote exactly what God wanted them to write, without errors or mistakes, yet with their own personalities in evidence in their writings. By "verbal," we mean that every word in the Bible is there because God permitted it by the direction of the Holy Spirit. By "plenary" (from the Latin, *plenus*—full), we mean that **each and every part** of the Bible is inspired, with nothing having been omitted.

In other words, by employing what we today call verbal (word-for-word), plenary (full) inspiration, God ensured that the writings were correct and consistent with His will. This view holds that men wrote exactly what God wanted them to write, without errors or mistakes, yet with their own individual characteristics in evidence. While the various books of the Bible reflect the writers' personalities as expressed in the human element that often is so evident (type of language used, fears expressed, prayers offered, etc.), it was only by verbal, plenary inspiration that God could convey—objectively and accurately—His Word to mankind.

There is compelling evidence from within the Bible itself about the nature of its inspiration. Immediately after His baptism, Christ went into the wilderness for a crucial confrontation with Satan. When the devil suggested that He convert stones into bread to stay His hunger after a lengthy fast, the Savior replied by quoting Deuteronomy 8:3: "It is written, 'Man shall not live by bread alone, but by every word that proceedeth out of the mouth of God'" (Matthew 4:4). Twice more He stopped the devil's mouth with "It is written...," citing Deuteronomy 6:13,16. In declaring, "It is written," Jesus employed the Greek perfect tense, denoting completed action with abiding results. He thus declared that God's words were written—and remain so.

Jesus endorsed the whole Old Testament at least a dozen times, using such designations as: the Scriptures (John 5:39); the law (John 10:34); the law and the prophets (Matthew 5:17); the law, the prophets, and the psalms (Luke 24:44); or Moses and the prophets (Luke 16:29). In addition, the Son of God quoted, cited from, or alluded to incidents in at least eighteen different Old Testament books. But to what degree did Christ believe in inspiration? The following references document beyond doubt that the Lord affirmed **verbal, plenary** inspiration: In Matthew 5:17-18, Christ exclaimed:

> Think not that I came to destroy the law and the prophets: I came not to destroy, but to fulfill. For verily I say unto you, Till heaven and earth pass away, one jot or one tittle shall in no wise pass from the law, till all things be accomplished.

The "jot" was the smallest Hebrew letter and the "tittle" was the tiny projection extending from certain Hebrew letters. When He employed these specific terms as examples, the Lord affirmed the minutest accuracy for the whole of the Old Testament.

In the midst of His discussion with the Sadducees about their denial of the resurrection of the dead (Matthew 22:23-33), Jesus referred to Exodus 3:6 wherein God said to Moses: "I am the God of Abraham, and the God of Isaac, and the God of Jacob." When God spoke these words, Abraham had been dead almost 400 years, yet He still said, "I **am** the God of Abraham." As Jesus correctly pointed out to the Sadducees, "God is not the God of the dead, but of the living" (Matthew 22:32). Thus, Abraham, Isaac, and Jacob must have been living. The only way they could be living was if their spirits continued to survive the death of their bodies. That kind of conscious existence implies a future resurrection of the body —the very point Christ was attempting to make. Of interest is the fact that His entire argument rested on the **tense** of the verb!

In addition to these examples from Christ, there are other clear indications of the recognition of verbal inspiration. David once said: "The Spirit of Jehovah spake by me, and His word was upon my tongue" (2 Samuel 23:2). Observe that the king did not say God's "thoughts" or "concepts" were upon his tongue, but that Jehovah's **word** was upon his tongue. If that is not verbal inspiration, one would be hard pressed to know how verbal inspiration would be expressed.

In the first letter of Paul to the Corinthians, the apostle declared that the things of God were revealed to men by the Spirit. Then, concerning the divine messages, he said, "which things we speak, not in words which man's wisdom teacheth, but which the Spirit teacheth; combining spiritual things with spiritual words" (1 Corinthians 2:13). The words of divine revelation are Spirit-directed words and not words of mere human wisdom. That is **verbal, plenary** inspiration.

The same kind of reliance on a single word was expressed by Paul (as he referred to Genesis 22:18) in Galatians 3:16: "Now to Abraham were the promises spoken, and to his seed. He saith not, 'And to seeds,' as of many; but as of one, 'And to thy **seed**, which is Christ'" (emp. added). The force of his argument rested on the number of the noun (singular, as opposed to plural). In John 8:58, Jesus said: "I say unto you, Before Abraham was born, I **am.**" He was attempting to impress upon the Jews His eternal nature, and to do so, He once again based His entire argument on the tense of the verb.

We should note, however, that this inspiration process applied only to the original autographs of the sacred writings (i.e., the actual document as penned by the writer). While Bible writers were inspired, the scribes, translators, and others who followed were not. This does not mean, as some have suggested, that we do not have God's Word in an accurate form today. The text of the Bible we possess can be trusted and counted as reliable. The modernistic idea which suggests that the copying process through the ages has destroyed the essence of inspiration is a "theological scarecrow to frighten those who are not knowledgeable of the art of transmission of the Bible" (Dickson, 1997, p. 319).

Whenever duplicates of the Scriptures were needed, copies had to be made by hand—a painstaking, time-consuming task that required extreme concentration and special working conditions. Eventually, an elite group of scribes arose just for this purpose. Geisler and Nix discussed these scribes—the Masoretes—in their book, *A General Introduction to the Bible*.

> The Masoretic period (flourished c. A.D. 500-1000) of Old Testament copying indicates a complete review of established rules, a deep reverence for the Scriptures, and a systematic renovation of transmission techniques.... Copies were made by an official class of sacred scribes who labored under strict rules (1986, pp. 354,467, cf. also pp. 371,374, 380).

Anyone who has studied the exacting conditions under which the Masoretes worked, and the lengths to which they went to ensure fidelity in their reproductions, could attest to the fact that their singular goal was accuracy. They were, nevertheless, still human. And humans are prone to mistakes, regardless of the care they take or the strictness of the rules under which they labor. The copyists' task was made all the more difficult by the sheer complexity of the languages involved, and by the various ways in which potential errors could be introduced (even if inadvertently) into the copying process.

Yet that process through the centuries was so meticulous, and the number of extant manuscripts available for comparison is so large, that the minute variations which do occur are detected quite easily. Furthermore, these variations are insignificant in nature and do not affect points of doctrine. Timothy, from his early years, had known the Old Testament "sacred writings" that were able to make him "wise unto salvation" (2 Timothy 3:15). Interestingly, those "sacred writings" were mere copies of the original Old Testament manuscripts, but had been preserved so faithfully through the centuries that the apostle Paul could affirm that their original design—to make mankind "wise unto salvation"—remained intact.

Several other points should be clarified as well. First, there is an important difference between revelation and inspiration. Revelation represents the revealing of facts and truths by God to humans. Inspiration is the process by which God guided the writing down of those facts and truths. "Revelation is the body of truth which God desired men to possess; inspiration is the way in which He gave this body of truth to men" (Woods, n.d., p. 6). The whole Bible is the result of inspiration, but not all inspired material was revelatory in nature. Paul could quote pagan poets in Acts 17:28 and Titus 1:12 because he already had access to this information and did not need revelation to employ it. But God inspired him to record these sayings—and to record them accurately. Thus, whether the Bible writer used information already available to him, his own eyewitness accounts, or revelation from God, inspiration guaranteed that it was placed in print in the form that God desired.

Second, uninspired people frequently received revelation in Bible times. The children of Israel, assembled under the burning crags of Sinai, heard God speak in awful majesty (Exodus 20:18-21; Hebrews 12:19), but no one would say that they were inspired. When the martyr Stephen was being stoned, he said: "Behold, I see the heavens opened, and the Son of Man standing on the right hand of God" (Acts 7:56). This was indeed revelation—but not inspiration. Thus, it is correct to say that the Bible **contains** revelation from God, because such a statement implies that it likewise contains items that are not revelatory in nature—which it does (e.g., historical facts already known to the writers). But it is improper to say that the Bible **contains** inspired writings, because such a statement implies that it likewise contains items that are not inspired. Such a position is false, because **all** of the books that comprise the Bible are inspired by the Spirit of God. As Goodpasture rightly remarked: "What he [Paul—BT] said is quite different from the modernistic statement: 'The Bible contains the word of God.' According to Paul, the Bible **is** the word of God; it is all given by inspiration" (1970, p. 55, emp. in orig.).

Revelation assures men that they possess all the information that God decided to make available to them; inspiration certifies that the revelation given to men in written form is truthful and correct. With the death of John, the last New Testament writer, all revelation ceased (simultaneously, inspiration likewise ceased). Since John's death, no new revelation has been given. We have God's word that the Scriptures were "**once for all delivered**" (Jude 3, emp. added).

Third, the fact that a person wrote by inspiration does not mean that he was free from personal sin in his life. Israel's King David penned several Old Testament psalms. The apostle Peter acknowledged that "the Holy Spirit spake before by the mouth of David" (Acts 1:16). Yet this was the very same king who committed adultery with Bathsheba and had her husband, Uriah the Hittite, slain to cover his sin. Peter himself presented some extremely powerful sermons (e.g., Acts 2:14ff.) and penned two New Testament epistles. Yet he played the hypocrite when he separated himself from the Gentiles to seek favor with the Jews (and received a public rebuke from Paul for it—Galatians 2:11ff.). Thus, while inspiration preserved the integrity of the writer's words as he was "moved by the Holy Spirit," that process did not diminish his freedom of choice or compel him to live a sinless life.

Fourth, inspiration was not a twenty-four-hour-a-day process. A few months prior to His death, the Lord informed His disciples that shortly He would enter Jerusalem, where He would suffer and eventually die. Peter, however, rebuked the Lord and said: "Be it far from thee, Lord: this shall never be unto thee" (Matthew 16:22). Obviously, that impetuous utterance was not inspired. In Luke, the story is told of a group of Samaritans who refused aid and comfort to the Lord (9:51ff.). James and John bitterly suggested that the Lord enjoin a "heavenly barbecue" to consume these ill-tempered Samaritans. Their attempt at vengeance—for which they drew the Lord's ire—hardly was inspired. The truth of the matter is that inspiration guided the writers in what they wrote and spoke from God as they were "borne along" by God's Spirit—a process that was not active every minute of every day.

Fifth, inspiration extended to a variety of disparate subjects. Today, it is not uncommon to hear liberal theologians, and those sympathetic with them, suggest that the "spiritual" sections of Scripture are inspired, but that all other portions dealing with matters of history, science, geography, medicine, and the like are not. This concept, known as the doctrine of "partial inspiration," is false. Were it true, everyone who reads the text would have the personal responsibility of wading through the biblical documents to decide which matters are "spiritual" (thus, inspired) and which are not (thus, uninspired). On some occasions, therefore, apparently God would have "breathed" truth while on others He would have "breathed" error. But the question must be asked: If God cannot handle correctly trivial matters (such as geographical directions, or the name of an individual), why would anyone think that they could trust Him with something as critically important as the safety of their eternal soul and expect Him to handle it in a more appropriate fashion? The psalmist stated: "The **sum** of thy word is truth; And **every one** of thy righteous ordinances endureth for ever" (119:160; emp. added). The concept of partial inspiration impugns the integrity and nature of God, conflicts with the evidence for inspiration, and should be rejected.

Sixth, not only did the Bible writers view each others' works as inspired, but no Bible writer ever criticized another. Today, it is not at all unusual for one religious writer to take issue with another, even when they share the same religious views, or are members of the same religious group. But the Bible writers do not fall into that category—even when one might expect them to do so. For example, as mentioned above, Paul rebuked Peter publicly for his dissimulation (Galatians 2:11ff.). Yet Peter never avenged himself by denigrating Paul's writings. In fact, Peter wrote:

> And account that the longsuffering of our Lord is salvation; even as our beloved brother Paul also, according to the wisdom given to him, wrote unto you; as also in all his epistles, speaking in them of these things; wherein are some things hard to be understood, which the ignorant and unstedfast wrest, as they do also the **other scriptures**, unto their own destruction (2 Peter 3:15-16, emp. added).

Note especially that Peter referred to Paul's writings as being classified by the same kind of inspiration as the "other scriptures." Additionally, in defending the right of elders to receive remuneration from the church treasury for their work, Paul quoted Deuteronomy 25:4 and Luke 10:7, classifying them both as "scripture" (1 Timothy 5:18). It is clear that the Bible writers considered each others' works to be inspired—a view we today would do well to entertain.

CHAPTER 9

IN DEFENSE OF THE BIBLE'S INSPIRATION [PART II]

Evidence to substantiate the Bible's claims of its own inspiration can be drawn from two general sources. **External** evidences for inspiration include such things as historical documentation of biblical people, places, and events, or archaeological artifacts that corroborate biblical statements or circumstances. **Internal** evidences are part of the warp and woof of the actual biblical fabric itself. These are self-authenticating phenomena from within the Sacred Volume that bear singular testimony to the fact that the very existence of the Holy Scriptures cannot be explained in any other way except to acknowledge that they are the result of an overriding, superintending, guiding Mind. Critics, of course, have objected to the use of the Bible as a witness to its own inspiration. Dickson has pointed out correctly, however, that

> ...this contention is really unjust. One does not have a right to deny the authenticity of a document without considering the document itself. We would not deny Shakespeare's authorship of the Shakespearean plays without first considering their text. The Bible should at least be treated as just another book. Nevertheless, even this right is rejected by the prejudiced minds of some (1997, p. 328).

Clark H. Pinnock once observed:

> While insisting on their right to treat the Bible "like any other book" (vs. a book produced by man alone), some critics proceed to treat it like no other book, by bathing it in the acid solution of their skepticism and historical pessimism" (1972, pp. 22-23, parenthetical comment in orig.).

When the evidences for the Bible's inspiration are allowed to speak for themselves, however, the story they tell is totally in accord with the Bible's claims for its own inspiration. Consider, for example, the following.

The Unity of the Bible

The Bible exhibits a unity that—on purely human terms—is quite simply inexplicable. In order to appreciate that unity, one first must come to terms with how The Book was put together. The Bible was written by more than forty different men from practically every walk of life. Nehemiah was a royal cupbearer. Peter was a fisherman. Luke was a physician. Matthew was a tax collector. Solomon was a king. Moses was a shepherd. Paul was a tentmaker. Furthermore, these men wrote from almost every conceivable human condition. David wrote from heights of joy on the rolling, grassy hills of Judea. Paul wrote from pits of despair caused by Roman incarceration. They wrote in three languages (Hebrew, Aramaic, and Greek), from at least two continents (Europe and Asia), over a period of time that spanned approximately sixteen centuries (1500 B.C. to A.D. 100). And they covered topics as diverse as eschatology, soteriology, theology, psychology, geography, history, medicine, and many others.

All this being true, one might expect that so diverse a group of men, writing on so varied a group of subjects, over such a lengthy span of time, would have produced a book that would be a tangled mishmash of subjects more often than not marred by an incredible number of inconsistencies, errors, and incongruities. Yet this hardly is the case. In fact, quite the opposite is true. The Bible exhibits such astounding harmony, such consistent flow, and such unparalleled unity that it defies any purely naturalistic explanation. It is as if the Bible were a magnificent symphony orchestrated by a single Conductor. The "musicians" each may have played a different instrument, in a different place, at a different time. But when the talented Maestro combined the individual efforts, the end result was a striking masterpiece.

Consider this analogy. Suppose you assembled forty contemporary scholars with the highest academic training possible in a single field of study (e.g., forty academicians with terminal Ph.D. degrees in world history). Suppose, further, that you placed them in a room and asked them to write a twenty-page paper on a single topic—the causes of World War I. What kind of consensus would be exhibited when all of their treatises were completed? Likely, the forty scholars would be unable to agree on all but a few points; their compositions would be recognized more for the **dis**agreements they contained than for the agreements. The Bible writers, by contrast, generally were not contemporaries. They worked independently, and the majority never even met another biblical writer. Most were not highly trained, and what training they did have certainly was not in the same field of study. Nor were they allowed to write on a single topic in which they already had an interest. Yet they produced a book that is unified from beginning to end. The books of 1 and 2 Chronicles and 1 and 2 Kings corroborate one another in numerous historical events. Joshua 1 verifies Deuteronomy 34. Judges 1:1 verifies Joshua 24:27-33. Jeremiah 52:31-34 verifies 2 Kings 25:25,27-30. Ezra 1 verifies 2 Chronicles 36:22-23. Daniel refers to Jeremiah (Daniel 9:2). Ezekiel refers to Daniel (Ezekiel 28:3). And so on. This kind of unity, which is in evidence throughout the Sacred Volume, attests to the fact that there was a Superintending Intelligence behind it. So many writers, over so many years, covering so many themes, simply could not have been so harmonious by mere coincidence.

Each book of the Bible complements the others in a single unified **theme**. From Genesis to Revelation there is a marvelous unfolding of the general theme of man's fall from his holy estate, God's plan for his redemption (as carefully worked out across the centuries), the sinless life and atoning death of Jesus Christ, and the ultimate victory of the Christian system. In essence, the Bible is the story of one problem—sin—with one solution, Jesus Christ. In commenting on the Bible's remarkable unity of theme, Wayne Jackson has noted:

> The redemptive thread that runs through the Scriptures is wonderfully illustrated by a comparison between Genesis and Revelation, the first and last books of the holy canon. In Genesis the origin of the heavens and Earth is revealed (1:1), while in Revelation the consummation of earthly affairs is effected, and the old order is replaced by a "new heaven and earth" (i.e., heaven itself), spiritual in nature.... Man, who was originally perfect, but who fell into sin (Genesis 3:6), is, by virtue of his obedience, granted the opportunity to become perfect again (Revelation 7:14; 22:14). All of this is made possible, of course, by the seed of woman (Genesis 3:15), the offspring of David (Revelation 22:16), who, as a consequence of his sacrifice (Genesis 4:4), became an enthroned Lamb (Revelation 21:4). Thus, the sorrow of Eden (Genesis 3:16) will be transformed into the joy of heaven (Revelation 21:4), and that tree of life, from which our early parents were separated (Genesis 3:22-24), will be our glad possession once more (Revelation 22:14) [1991a, 11:1].

James Orr wrote:

> But the impartial mind cannot ignore the fact that in the writings which constitute our Bible there is a unity and progression, a guiding purpose, culminating in Jesus Christ and His redemption, a fullness and power of religious truth, which place them in a category, and compel the acknowledgement, of a unique origin answering to their unique character (1969, pp. 12-12).

Each book of the Bible complements the others in a single, unified **plan**. In Genesis, there is the record of humanity's pristine origin and covenant relationship with God, followed by its tragic fall into a sinful state. But, a specific family line (the Hebrew nation) was selected to provide a remedy for this disaster (Genesis 12:1ff.; 22:18). Man needed to learn precisely what sin is, thus the books of Exodus through Deuteronomy document the giving of the law of God to Moses. Via a set of ordinances, sin would be defined and humanity would be illuminated regarding the price of rebellion against God (Romans 7:7,13; Galatians 3:19). The historical books of the Old Testament revealed mankind's inability to keep perfectly God's law system (Galatians 3:10), and therefore underscored the need for a Justifier—Someone to do for man what he could not do for himself. The prophets of the Old Testament heralded the arrival of that Savior (Luke 24:44); more than 300 prophecies focus on the promised Messiah.

After four silent centuries (referred to as the "inter-biblical era"), four Gospel writers described in great detail the arrival, and life's work, of the Justifier—Jesus of Nazareth. The books of Matthew, Mark, Luke, and John are carefully crafted accounts of the birth, life, death, and ultimate resurrection of the Son of God (John 20: 30-31). Each emphasized different parts of Christ's ministry in order to relate the "good news" to Jews or Gentiles. Matthew directed his record primarily to the Jewish nation. Mark stressed the works of Jesus. Luke, being the only Gentile writer of a Bible book (except possibly the author of Job), wrote to Gentiles. John's primary purpose in writing was to produce faith.

The book of Acts was written to convey the means by which mankind was to appropriate God's saving grace. It is a historical record that instructs a person on how to become a Christian. It also teaches about how the church of Christ was established in Jerusalem, and how that same church flourished throughout the Roman Empire of the first century. The various epistles that follow the book of Acts in the English Bible were directions to individuals and churches on how to obtain, and maintain, spiritual maturity. Finally, the book of Revelation predicted (in symbolic fashion) the ultimate triumph of good over evil—acknowledging that Christians would win, and Satan would lose. To the careful reader, the unity of both theme and plan in the Bible are apparent.

The Factual Accuracy of the Bible

The Bible claims to be the inspired Word of God. Therefore, it should be accurate in whatever subject(s) it discusses, since God is not the Author of confusion and contradiction (1 Corinthians 14: 33), but of truth (John 17:17). The factual accuracy of the Bible proves that it **is** accurate. Time and again the Bible's facts have withstood the test. Examples abound.

Numerous passages indicate that Moses wrote the Pentateuch (2 Chronicles 34:14; Ezra 6:18; Nehemiah 13:1; Exodus 17:14; John 5:46; Mark 12:26). Having been adopted by the royal family of Egypt, he would have had access to the finest schools, best tutors, and greatest libraries that country had to offer, thus securing for himself an impressive education (see Acts 7:22). Yet Bible critics suggested that Moses could not have written the Pentateuch because the art of writing was not developed until well after his death. This criticism, however, has been blunted by a veritable plethora of archaeological discoveries. In 1933, J.L. Starkey, who had studied under famed archaeologist W.M.F. Petrie, excavated the city of Lachish, which had figured prominently in Joshua's conquest of Canaan (Joshua 10). Among other things, he unearthed a pottery water pitcher "inscribed with a dedication in eleven archaic letters, the earliest 'Hebrew' inscription known" (Cheyne, 1899, 2: 1055). Pfeiffer has noted: "The Old, or palaeo-Hebrew script is the form of writing which is similar to that used by the Phoenicians. A royal inscription of King Shaphatball of Gebal (Byblos) in this alphabet dates from about 1600 B.C." (1966, p. 33). In 1949, C.F.A. Schaeffer "found a table at Ras Shamra containing the thirty letters of the Ugaritic alphabet in their proper order. It was discovered that the sequence of the Ugaritic alphabet was the same as modern Hebrew, revealing that the Hebrew alphabet goes back at least 3,500 years" (Jackson, 1982, p. 32).

The Code of Hammurabi, (c. 2000-1700 B.C.) was discovered by a French archaeological expedition under the direction of Jacques de Morgan in 1901-1902 at the ancient site of Susa in what is now Iran. It was written on a piece of black diorite nearly eight feet high, and contained 282 sections. Free and Vos stated:

> The Code of Hammurabi was written several hundred years before the time of Moses (c. 1500-1400 B.C.).... This code, from the period 2000-1700 B.C., contains advanced laws similar to those in the Mosaic laws.... In view of this archaeological evidence, the destructive critic can no longer insist that the laws of Moses are too advanced for his time (1992, pp. 103,55).

The Code of Hammurabi established beyond doubt that writing was known hundreds of years before Moses. In fact, the renowned Jewish historian, Josephus, confirmed that Moses authored the Pentateuch (*Against Apion*, 1,8), and various non-Christian writers (Hecataeus, Manetha, Lysimachus, Eupolemus, Tacitus, Juvenal, and Longinus, to name only a few), credited Moses as having authored the first five books of the English Bible (see Rawlinson, 1877, pp. 254ff.).

In days of yore, detractors accused Isaiah of having made a historical mistake when he wrote of Sargon as king of Assyria (Isaiah 20:1). For years, this remained the sole historical reference—secular or biblical—to Sargon having been linked with the Assyrian nation. Thus, critics assumed Isaiah had erred. But in 1843, Paul Emile Botta, the French consular agent at Mosul, working with Austen Layard, unearthed historical evidence that established Sargon as having been exactly what Isaiah said he was—king of the Assyrians. At Khorsabad, Botta discovered Sargon's palace. Pictures of the find may be found in *Halley's Bible Handbook* (1962, p. 289). Apparently, from what scholars have been able to piece together from archaeological and historical records, Sargon made his capital successively at Ashur, Calah, Nineveh, and finally at Khorsabad, where his palace was constructed in the closing years of his reign (c. 706 B.C.). The walls of the palace were adorned quite intricately with ornate text that described the events of his reign. Today, an artifact from the palace—a forty-ton stone bull (slab)—is on display at the University of Chicago's Oriental Institute (rather "weighty" evidence of Sargon's existence). Isaiah had been correct all along. And the critics had been wrong—all along.

One of the most famous archaeologists of the last century was Sir William Ramsay, who disputed the accuracy of events recorded by Luke in the book of Acts. Ramsay believed those events to be little more than second-century, fictitious accounts. Yet after years of literally digging through the evidence in Asia Minor, Ramsay concluded that Luke was an exemplary historian. In the decades since Ramsay, other scholars have suggested that Luke's historical background of the New Testament is among the best ever produced. As Wayne Jackson has noted:

> In Acts, Luke mentions thirty-two countries, fifty-four cities, and nine Mediterranean islands. He also mentions ninety-five persons, sixty-two of which are not named elsewhere in the New Testament. And his references, where checkable, are always correct. This is truly remarkable, in view of the fact that the political/territorial situation of his day was in a state of almost constant change. Only inspiration can account for Luke's precision (1991b, 27[1]:2).

Other Bible critics have suggested that Luke misspoke when he designated Sergius Paulus as proconsul of Cyprus (Acts 13:7). Their claim was that Cyprus was governed by a propraetor (also known as a consular legate), not a proconsul. Upon further examination, such a charge can be seen to be completely vacuous, as Thomas Eaves has documented.

> As we turn to the writers of history for that period, Dia Cassius (*Roman History*) and Strabo (*The Geography of Strabo*), we learn that there were two periods of Cyprus' history: first, it was an imperial province governed by a propraetor,

> and later in 22 B.C., it was made a senatorial province governed by a proconsul. Therefore, the historians support Luke in his statement that Cyprus was ruled by a proconsul, for it was between 40-50 A.D. when Paul made his first missionary journey. If we accept secular history as being true we must also accept Biblical history for they are in agreement (1980, p. 234).

The science of archaeology seems to have outdone itself in verifying the Scriptures. Famed archaeologist William F. Albright wrote: "There can be no doubt that archaeology has confirmed the substantial historicity of the Old Testament tradition" (1953, p. 176). Nelson Glueck, himself a pillar within the archaeological community, said: "It may be stated categorically that no archaeological discovery has ever controverted a Biblical reference. Scores of archaeological findings have been made which conform in clear outline or exact detail historical statements in the Bible" (1959, p. 31). Such statements, offered 30+ years ago, are as true today as the day they were made. Jerry Moffitt observed:

> Over thirty names (emperors, high priests, Roman governors, princes, etc.) are mentioned in the New Testament, and all but a handful have been verified. In every way the Bible accounts have been found accurate (though vigorously challenged). In no single case does the Bible let us down in geographical accuracy. Without one mistake, the Bible lists around forty-five countries. Each is accurately placed and named. About the same number of cities are named and no one mistake can be listed. Further, about thirty-six towns are mentioned, and most have been identified. Wherever accuracy can be checked, minute detail has been found correct—every time! (1993, p. 129).

The Hittites are mentioned over forty times in Scripture (Exodus 23:28; Joshua 1:4; et al.), and were so feared that on one occasion they caused the Syrians to flee from Israel (2 Kings 7:6). Yet critics suggested that Hittites were a figment of the Bible writers' imaginations, since no evidence of their existence had been located. But in the late 1800s, A.H. Sayce discovered inscriptions in Syria that he designated as Hittite. Then, in 1906, Hugh Winckler excavated Boghazkoy, Turkey and discovered that the Hittite capital had been located on that very site. His find was all the more powerful because of the more than 10,000 clay tablets that were found in the ancient city's library and that contained the society's law system—which eventually came to be known as the Hittite Code. Thus, Ira Price wrote of the Hittites:

> The lack of extra-biblical testimony to their existence led some scholars about a half-century ago to deny their historicity. They scoffed at the idea of Israel allying herself with such an unhistorical people as the Hittites, as narrated in 2 Kings vii.6. But those utterances have vanished into thin air (1907, pp. 75-76).

In his classic text, *Lands of the Bible*, J.W. McGarvey remarked:

> A fictitious narrative, located in a country with which the writer is not personally familiar, must either avoid local allusions or be found frequently in conflict with the peculiarities of place and of manners and customs. By this conflict the fictitious character of the narrative is exposed (1881, p. 375).

McGarvey then documented numerous instances in which the facts of the Bible can be checked, and in which it always passes the test. Are compass references accurate? Is Antioch of Syria "down" from Jerusalem, even though it lies to the north of the holy city (Acts 15:1)? Is the way from Jerusalem to Gaza "south" of Samaria (Acts 8:26)? Is Egypt "down" from Canaan (Genesis 12:10)? McGarvey noted that "in not a single instance of this kind has any of the Bible writers been found at fault" (p. 378). Further, as Wayne Jackson has commented:

> In 1790, William Paley, the celebrated Anglican scholar, authored his famous volume, *Horae Paulinae* (*Hours with Paul*). In this remarkable book, Paley demonstrated an amazing array of "undesigned coincidences" between the book of Acts and the epistles of Paul, which argue for the credibility of the Christian revelation. "These coincidences," said Paley, "which are often incorporated or intertwined in references and allusions, in which no art can be discovered, and no contrivance traced, furnish numerous proofs of the truth

> of both these works, and consequently that of Christianity" (1839 edition, p. xvi). In 1847, J.J. Blunt of Cambridge University released a companion volume titled, *Undesigned Coincidences in the Writings of Both the Old Testament and New Testament*. Professor Blunt argued that both Testaments contain numerous examples of "consistency without contrivance" which support the Scriptures' claim of a unified origin from a supernatural source, namely God (1884, p. vii) [1991a, pp. 2-3].

A sampling of the information within Paley's and Blunt's books provides startling evidence of the fact that the writers simply could not have "contrived" their stories. Often the writers were separated from one another by centuries, yet their stories dovetail with astounding accuracy, and provide additional proof of the Bible's inspiration.

When Joseph was seventeen years old, he was sold into Egyptian slavery by his brothers. While serving in the house of an Egyptian named Potiphar, Joseph found himself the object of affection of Potiphar's wife, whose advances he rejected. Her anger aroused, she fabricated a story that resulted in Joseph's being thrown into prison where the king's captives were "bound" (Genesis 39:20). In the context of this passage, the word "bound" is of critical importance because hundreds of years after the fact the psalmist would state of Joseph: "His feet they hurt with fetters: He was laid in chains of iron" (Psalm 105:18). Contrivance—or consistency?

When Pharaoh stubbornly refused to release the Israelites from bondage, God rained down plagues on the Egyptian monarch and his people, including a plague of hail that destroyed the **flax** in the fields (Exodus 9:31). Eventually, the Israelites were released, traveled to the wilderness of Sinai, were found faithless in God's sight, and were forced to wander for four decades while everyone over the age of twenty perished (except for the houses of Joshua and Caleb—Numbers 14:29-30). Finally, however, the Hebrews were allowed to enter the promised land of Canaan. The arrival of the younger generation was exactly forty years after Moses had led them out of Egypt (Joshua 4:19), and thus shortly before the anniversary of that eighth plague which destroyed the flax. The book of Joshua mentions that their entrance into Canaan was near harvest time (3:15). Interestingly, when spies were sent to investigate the city of Jericho, the Bible notes that they were concealed by Rahab under drying stalks of **flax** upon the rooftop of her house (Joshua 2:6). Coincidence—or concordance?

In Exodus 1:11, the story is told of how the Israelites were forced to build the treasure cities of Pithom and Raamses for the Egyptian ruler. Exodus 5 records that, initially, the slaves made bricks containing straw, but later were forced to use stubble because Pharaoh ordered his taskmasters not to provide any more straw. Excavations at Pithom in 1883 by Naville, and in 1908 by Kyle, discovered that the lower layers of the structures were made of bricks filled with good, chopped straw. The middle layers had less straw with some stubble. The upper layers contained bricks that were made of pure clay, with no straw whatsoever (see Pfeiffer, 1966, p. 459). Contrivance—or correctness?

The Tell-el-Armarna tablets (c. 1450 B.C.) record the custom of bowing down seven times when meeting a superior. Thus the statement in Genesis 33:3—"And he [Jacob] himself passed over before them, and bowed himself to the ground **seven times**, until he came near to his brother [Esau]"—is confirmed as an act of respect. Coincidence—or consistency?

In at least two places, the Old Testament speaks of the Horites (Genesis 14:6; 36:21). Until approximately 1925, no one ever had heard of the Horites. Once again, however, archaeology revealed the factual accuracy of the Bible. Around 1925, archaeological discoveries helped explain the existence of this formerly unknown nation. Free and Vos have commented that "Horite" derives from the Egyptian *Hurru*, which is "...a general term the Egyptians applied to southern Transjordan...," and that "...the Hebrews adopted it from the Egyptians" (1992, p. 66). Thus, both Egyptian and Hebrew cultures were intertwined with the Horites. Contrivance—or concordance?

On one occasion during His earthly ministry, Jesus miraculously provided a meal for more than 5,000 people. Mark records that the Lord seated the people upon the "green grass" (6:39). Such a statement agrees completely with John's reference to the fact that this event occurred near the time of the Passover (6:44), which occurs in the spring—exactly the time in Palestine when the grass should be green. Coincidence—or correctness?

In Acts 28:20, Luke described Paul's Roman imprisonment, and quoted the apostle as proclaiming: "Because of the hope of Israel I am bound with this chain." During this incarceration, Paul penned four important letters (Ephesians, Philippians, Colossians, and Philemon). In his epistle to the Ephesians, Paul alluded to his "chain" (6:20). In Philippians he referred to his "bonds" (1:7,13-14,17). Similarly, see the references to his "bonds" in Colossians 4:3 and Philemon 1:13. Coincidence—or consistency?

In his second letter to Timothy, Paul admonished the young man by stating that "from a babe thou hast known the sacred writings which are able to make thee wise unto salvation through faith which is in Christ Jesus" (2 Timothy 3:15). The reference to the "sacred writings" is an allusion to the Old Testament. Since Timothy had known those writings from his earliest days, certainly it would be safe to suggest that his background was Jewish. As a matter of fact, the book of Acts states Timothy was "the son of a Jewess that believed, but his father was a Greek" (Acts 16:1). Of further interest is the fact that when Paul commended Timothy for his strong faith (2 Timothy 1:5), he alluded to the spirituality of both the young man's mother and grandmother, yet made no mention of Timothy's father. Coincidence—or concordance?

When Jesus died, His disciples desired to prepare His body for burial by embalming it. In his Gospel, John declared that the Jewish ruler, Nicodemus, brought a hundred pounds of spices (myrrh and aloes) for this purpose (19:39). It would be safe to conclude, therefore, that large quantities of these kinds of spices would be required for the embalming process. It is an undisputed fact of secular history that the Egyptians were experts in embalming. When Jacob died, the physicians of Egypt embalmed him (Genesis 50:2). Likewise, Joseph was embalmed upon his demise (50:26). The Egyptians required vast quantities of spices—like myrrh—for their embalming purposes. Not surprisingly, then, the Old Testament teaches that myrrh was imported by camel caravans into Egypt (Genesis 37: 24). Contrivance—or inspiration?

In their book, *A General Introduction to the Bible*, Geisler and Nix wrote: "Confirmation of the Bible's accuracy in factual matters lends credibility to its claims when speaking on other subjects" (1986, p. 195). Indeed it does! After previewing most of the above facts, and others of a similar nature, Wayne Jackson concluded:

> The Bible critic is likely to trivialize these examples as they are isolated from one another. When, however, literally hundreds and hundreds of these incidental details are observed to perfectly mesh, one begins to suspect that what have been called "undesigned coincidences" (from the human vantage point) become very obvious cases of divinely designed harmony—tiny footprints that lead only to the conclusion that God was the guiding Force behind the composition of the Sacred Scriptures (1991a, 11:3).

The Prophecy of the Bible

One of the most impressive internal proofs of the Bible's inspiration is its prophetic utterances. Rex A. Turner, Sr. has suggested:

> Predictive prophecy is the highest evidence of divine revelation. The one thing that mortal man cannot do is to know and report future events in the absence of a train of circumstances that naturally suggest certain possibilities...(1989, p. 12).

If the Bible is inspired of God, it should contain valid, predictive prophecy. In fact, the Bible's prophecy—completely foretold to the minutest detail, and painstakingly fulfilled with the greatest precision—has confounded its critics for generations. The Bible contains prophecies about individuals, lands, nations, and even the predicted Messiah.

Thomas H. Horne defined predictive prophecy as "a miracle of knowledge, a declaration or representation of something future, beyond the power of human sagacity to discern or to calculate" (1970, 1:272). The Bible confirms that definition:

> But the prophet, that shall speak a word presumptuously in my name, which I have not commanded him to speak, or that shall speak in the name of other gods, that same prophet shall die. And if thou say in thy heart, How shall we know the word which Jehovah hath not spoken? when a prophet speaketh in the name of Jehovah, if the thing follow not, nor come to pass, that is the thing which Jehovah hath not spoken: the prophet hath spoken it presumptuously, thou shalt not be afraid of him (Deuteronomy 18:20-22).

The prophet Isaiah based the credibility of his message on prophecy. To the promoters of idolatry in his day, he issued the following challenge: "Let them bring forth, and declare unto us what shall happen: declare ye the former things, what they are, that we may consider them, and know the latter end of them; or show us things to come" (Isaiah 41:22). His point was this: It is one thing to make the prediction; it is entirely another to see that prediction actually come true and be corroborated by subsequent history.

In order for a prophecy to be valid, it must meet certain criteria. First, it must be a specific, detailed declaration, as opposed to being nebulous, vague, or general in nature. Arthur Pierson wrote: "The particulars of the prophecy should be so many and minute that there shall be no possibility of accounting by shrewd guesswork for the accuracy of the fulfillment" (1913, pp. 75-76). Bernard Ramm has suggested: "The prophecy must be more than a good guess or a conjecture. It must possess sufficient precision as to be capable of verification by means of the fulfillment" (1971, p. 82).

Second, there must be a sufficient amount of time between the prophetic statement and its fulfillment. Suggestions as to what "might" happen in the future do not qualify as prophetic pronouncements. Rather, the prophecy must precede the fulfillment in a significant fashion, and there must be no chance whatsoever of the prophet having the ability to influence the outcome.

Third, the prophecy must be stated in clear, understandable terms. Roger Dickson has noted: "Prophecies must be sufficiently clear in order for the observer to be able to link pronouncement with fulfillment. If a prophecy is not understandable enough so as to allow the observer to depict its fulfillment, then what good would the prophecy be?" (1997, p. 346).

Fourth, the prophecy must not have historical overtones. In other words, true prophecy should not be based on past (or current) societal or economic conditions. Pierson amplified this point by stating: "There should have been nothing in previous history which makes it possible to forecast a like event in the future" (1913, p. 75). Fifth, a clear, understandable, exact prophecy must have a clear, understandable, exact fulfillment. It is not enough to suggest that a certain event came true with a "high degree of probability." The fulfillment must be unmistakable, and must match the prophecy in every detail.

Two questions, then, are in order: (1) does the Bible employ predictive prophecy; and (2) if it does, can the predictive prophecy be proven true? The answer to both questions is a resounding, "Yes!" Further, the Bible's prophecy fits the above standards perfectly—each and every time. Consider just a few brief examples.

Within the Sacred Volume, numerous prophecies are presented regarding the rise, decline, and eventual fall of kings, cities, and even nations. (1) The Bible foretells the destruction of the city of Tyre with miraculous precision. Ezekiel predicted that Nebuchadnezzar, king of Babylon, would destroy the city (Ezekiel 26:7-8). Many nations were to come up against Tyre (26:3). The city would be leveled and scraped clean like a bare rock (26:4). The city's stones, timbers, and soil would be cast into the sea (26:12). The surrounding area would become a place for the spreading of fishermen's nets (26:5). And, finally, the city never would be rebuilt to its former glory (26:14).

History records that each of these predictions came true. Tyre, a coastal city from ancient times, had a somewhat unusual arrangement. In addition to the inland city, there was an island about three-fourth's of a mile offshore. Nebuchadnezzar besieged the mainland city in 586 B.C., but when he finally was able to inhabit the city in about 573 B.C., his victory was hollow. Unbeknownst to him, the inhabitants had vacated the city and moved to the island—a situation that remained virtually unchanged for the next 241 years. Then, in 332 B.C., Alexander the Great conquered the city—but not with ease. To get to the island, he literally had his army "scrape clean" the inland city of its debris, and he then used those materials (stones, timbers, and soil) to build a causeway to the island. But even though Alexander inflicted severe damage on the city, it still remained intact. In fact, it waxed and waned for the next 1,600 years until finally, in A.D. 1291, the Muslims thoroughly crushed Tyre.

The city never regained its once-famous position of wealth and power. The prophet Ezekiel looked 1,900 years into the future and predicted that Tyre would be a bald rock where fishermen gathered to open their nets. And that is exactly what history records as having happened (see Bromling, 1994, p. 96; Major, 1996, pp. 93-95).

(2) During a time in the history of Israel in which God's people had delved deeply into idolatry, the prophet Isaiah foretold that God would raise up the Assyrians as His "rod of anger" in order to punish the disobedient Hebrews (Isaiah 10:5-6). But, Isaiah noted, after that had been accomplished, God would see to it that the Assyrians themselves were punished for their own wicked deeds (Isaiah 10:12,24-25).

Archaeology has revealed some impressive facts regarding this prophecy. Assyrian records discovered in recent years discuss the fact that in the reign of Hosea, king of Israel, Shalmanesar, ruler of Assyria, assaulted Samaria, the capital city of Israel. However, he died before completing the assault, which was taken up by his successor, Sargon, who captured the city (cf. 1 Kings 18:10). An Assyrian clay prism comments on the fact that 27,290 Israelite captives were taken in the conflict. Almost twenty-five years later, the Assyrian king Sennacherib once again invaded Palestine (2 Kings 18:13ff.). Archaeological records report that 46 Judean cities were seized and that 200,150 Israelites were captured. But Jerusalem was not conquered—a fact that is noteworthy since 2 Kings 19:32-34 predicted that Sennacherib would be unable to take the holy city.

The Taylor Cylinder, discovered at Nineveh in 1830, presents the history of the Assyrians' assault, and states that king Hezekiah of Judah was "shut up like a bird in a cage." But was Jerusalem itself spared? It was. And were the wicked Assyrians punished? They were. The account in 2 Kings 19:35 indicates that in one night God annihilated 185,000 Assyrian soldiers who had encircled Jerusalem. In addition, the prophecy stated that Sennacherib would return to his home and there fall by the sword (2 Kings 19:7). Some twenty years later, he was assassinated by his own sons, who smote him with the sword while he was worshiping pagan deities (Isaiah 37:37-38).

(3) King Josiah had his life's work foretold (his name even being provided within the prophetic utterance) **more than three hundred years before he was born** (1 Kings 13:2).

(4) But Josiah was not the only king who was called by name prior to birth. Cyrus, the future king of Persia, likewise was named more than a century-and-a-half prior to his birth (Isaiah 44:28; 45:1), and some of his activities as king were foretold. As always, the prophecies of the biblical record came true in exacting detail.

(5) The Old Testament contains more than three hundred messianic prophecies. As Hugo McCord has said, "Testimony about Jesus was the chief purpose of prophecy. To him all the prophets gave witness (Acts 10:43)" (1979, p. 332). The Prophesied One would be born of a woman (Genesis 3:15; Galatians 4:4), of the seed of Abraham (Genesis 22:18; Luke 3:34), of the tribe of Judah (Gen-

esis 49:10; Hebrews 7:14), of the royal lineage of David (2 Samuel 7:12; Luke 1:32), in Bethlehem (Micah 5:2; Matthew 2:1), to the virgin Mary (Isaiah 7:14; Matthew 1:22), in order to bruise the head of Satan (Genesis 3:15; Galatians 4:4; Hebrews 2:12-14).

His Galilean ministry was foretold (Isaiah 9:1-2), and it was prophesied that a forerunner would announce His arrival (Isaiah 40:3; Matthew 3:1-3). He would appear during the days of the Roman reign (Daniel 2:44; Luke 2:1), while Judah still possessed her own king (Genesis 49:10; Matthew 2:22). He would be killed some 490 years after the command to restore Jerusalem at the end of the Babylonian captivity (457 B.C.), i.e., A.D. 30 (Daniel 9:24ff.). He was to be both human and divine; though born, He was eternal (Micah 5:2; John 1:1,14); though a man, He was Jehovah's "fellow" (Zechariah 13:7; John 10:30; Philippians 2:6). He was to be gentle and compassionate in His dealings with mankind (Isaiah 42:1-4; Matthew 12:15-21). He would submit perfectly to His heavenly Father (Psalm 40:8; Isaiah 53:11; John 8:29; 2 Corinthians 5:21; 1 Peter 2:22).

The prophecy was that He would be rejected and know grief (Isaiah 53:3), and be betrayed by a friend (Psalm 41:9) for thirty pieces of silver (Zechariah 11:12). He was (John 13:18; Matthew 26:15). He would be spit upon and beaten (Isaiah 50:6; 53:5), and in death His hands and His feet were to be pierced (Psalm 22:16). This is exactly what happened (Matthew 27:30; Luke 24:39). The Scriptures foretold that He would be numbered among criminals (Isaiah 53:12), which He was (Matthew 27:38). He would be mocked, not only with scornful words (Psalm 22:7-8), but with bitter wine (Psalm 22:18). So He was (Matthew 27:39,48). Although He would die and be placed in a rich man's tomb (Isaiah 53:9; Matthew 27:57), His bones would not be broken (Psalm 34:20; John 19:33), and His flesh would not see corruption, because He would be raised from the dead (Psalm 16:10; Acts 2:22ff.), and eventually ascend into heaven (Psalm 110:1-3; 45:6; Acts 1:9-10).

Time and again biblical prophecies are presented, and fulfilled, with exacting detail. Jeremiah wrote: "When the word of the prophet shall come to pass, then shall the prophet be known, that Jehovah hath truly sent him" (28:9). Horne was correct when he said:

> The book which contains these predictions is stamped with the seal of heaven: a rich vein of evidence runs through the volume of the Old Testament; the Bible is true; infidelity is confounded forever; and we may address its patrons in the language of Saint Paul, "Behold, ye despisers, and wonder and perish!" (1970, 1:291).

The Scientific Foreknowledge of the Bible

Among the many intriguing proofs of the Bible's inspiration is its unique scientific foreknowledge. From anthropology to zoology, the Bible presents astonishingly accurate scientific information that the writers, on their own, simply could not have known. Henry Morris has suggested: "One of the most arresting evidences of the inspiration of the Bible is the great number of scientific truths that have lain hidden within its pages for thirty centuries or more, only to be discovered by man's enterprise within the last few centuries or even years" (1969, p. 5). In her book, *Science in the Bible*, Jean S. Morton commented:

> Many scientific facts, which prove the infallibility of Scripture, are tucked away in its pages. These proofs are given in nonscientific language; nevertheless, they substantiate the claims of authenticity of the Holy Scriptures.... In some cases, scientific concepts have been known through the ages, but these concepts are mentioned in a unique manner in Scripture. In other cases, scientific topics have been mentioned hundreds or even thousands of years before man discovered them (1978, p. 10).

Space limitations prohibit an in-depth examination of the Bible's scientific foreknowledge, but I would like to mention a few of the more prominent examples. For those who might desire additional information, I have dealt with this theme elsewhere in a more extensive fashion (Thompson, 1981, 1:33-36; Thompson and Jackson, 1992, pp. 125-137).

From the Field of Astronomy

1. Isaiah, in speaking of God, stated (40:22), "It is he who sitteth upon the circle of the earth." The Hebrew word Isaiah used for "circle" is the word *khug*, which means literally something with "roundness," a "sphere." But, of course, the people of Isaiah's day thought the Earth was flat. And that was the concept of the many generations of people who followed Isaiah. Later, it was discovered that the Earth was not flat; rather it was a *khug* (circle). Isaiah had been correct all along, even when the people of his day emphatically stated the opposite. How did Isaiah know the Earth to be a sphere? Just a lucky guess?

[NOTE: In recent years some have suggested that Isaiah's statement contains no foreknowledge since in chapter 40 he is dealing solely with the subject of God's sovereignty, and it therefore was not his intent to teach "scientific truths" (cf. England, 1983, pp. 135ff.). I repudiate such a claim. There can be no doubt that Isaiah's treatise is dealing with the sovereign nature of the Israelite God. Chapter 40 is, in fact, one of the most beautiful and stirring passages in the Bible dealing with that very subject. At the same time, however, Isaiah did set forth a "scientific truth" while acknowledging an important "spiritual truth." One does not preclude the other. Isaiah made two points: (1) God **is** sovereign and; (2) the Earth **is** a sphere (*khug*). How could Isaiah have known either, unless God had revealed them both?]

2. Psalm 19:5-6 contains several interesting scientific facts. In speaking of the Sun, the psalmist suggested that "his going forth is from the end of the heaven, and his circuit unto the ends of it; and there is nothing hid from the heat thereof." For years Bible critics scoffed at Bible believers, stating that this verse taught the false concept of geocentricity (i.e., the Sun revolves around the Earth). Then it was discovered that the Sun was the center of our solar system, not the Earth. People subsequently felt that the Sun was stationary, with the Earth revolving around it.

Only recently has it been discovered that rather than being fixed in space, the Sun actually is in an orbit of its own. In fact, it is estimated to be moving through space at the rate of 600,000 miles per hour, in a path that is so large it would take approximately 220,000,000 years to complete just one orbit. How did the psalmist portray such accurate statements—when people of this day, and for years afterward, taught that just the opposite was true? And by the way, there is another gem packed away in these two verses. The psalmist hinted at the fact that the Sun is the source of energy for the Earth ("and there is nothing hid from the heat thereof"). An amazing statement, is it not, considering when it was written and by whom?

3. Concerning light and darkness, the Lord asked Job: "Where is the way to the dwelling of the light? And as for darkness, where is the place thereof?" (38:19). Light is said to travel in a "way" (Hebrew, *derek*), which is literally a traveled path or road (cf. Genesis 16:7), whereas darkness is said to be a "place" (Hebrew, *maxim*) which means a place, a spot, as standing (cf. Genesis 1:9; 28:11). Until the seventeenth century, it was believed that light was transmitted instantaneously. Then Sir Isaac Newton suggested that light is composed of small particles that travel in a straight line. Christian Huygens proposed the wave theory of light and Olaus Roemer measured the velocity of light as evinced by its delay while traveling through space. Scientists now know that light is a form of energy called radiant energy, and that it travels in electromagnetic waves in a straight line at the speed of over 186,000 miles per second (660 million miles per hour). For example, it takes about eight minutes for light to travel its "path" from the Sun to the Earth.

Scientists use the speed of light to measure distances in our vast Universe. Our solar system is said to be about 26,000 light years (the distance light would travel in 26,000 years at the rate of 186,000+ miles per second) from the edge of our galaxy. Some evolutionists, who deny the chronological data found in the Bible, have suggested that light, which spans the distances from stars to us, proves the Universe is billions of years old. They overlook, of course, the fact that God created the heavenly lights already in place (Genesis 1:14-16) to serve as a "witness" of His infinite power and for man's benefit (Psalm 19:1). God, in making His perfect, mature Universe, formed the stars so that their light could be seen on Earth.

Jehovah also inquired of Job? "By what way is light parted?" (38:24). The word "parted" is from the Hebrew *halaq*, meaning to divide, allot, apportion (cf. Numbers 26:53). Though the Lord simply may have been asking the patriarch if he knew how light is distributed on Earth, nonetheless it is an amazing scientific fact that light literally can be parted. When a narrow beam of sunlight passes at a slant into a triangular, transparent prism, the sunlight is broken into a band of seven colored lights called a spectrum. Sir Isaac Newton eventually discovered this, yet the writer of the book of Job knew it first.

From the Field of Oceanography

1. Long ago, Solomon wrote, "All the rivers run into the sea, yet the sea is not full; unto the place whither the rivers go, thither they go again" (Ecclesiastes 1:7). This statement, considered by itself, may not seem profound at first glance. But when considered with additional evidence and other biblical passages, it becomes all the more remarkable. For example, the Mississippi River, when moving at normal speed, dumps approximately **6,052,500 gallons** of water **per second** into the Gulf of Mexico. And that is just one river! Where, pray tell, does all that water go? The answer, of course, lies in the hydrologic cycle so well illustrated in the Bible. Ecclesiastes 11:3a states that "if the clouds be full of rain, they empty themselves upon the earth." Amos 9:6b tells us that "He...calleth for the waters of the sea, and poureth them out upon the face of the earth; the Lord is His name." The idea of a complete water cycle was not fully understood or accepted until the sixteenth and seventeenth centuries. The first substantial evidence came from ex-

periments of Pierre Perrault and Edme Mariotte. These scientists demonstrated that the flow of the Seine River could be accounted for by precipitation. Astronomer Edmund Halley also contributed valuable data to the concept of a complete water cycle. More that 2,000 years prior to their work, however, the Scriptures had indicated a water cycle. How?

2. Job was asked by God (38:16), "Hast thou entered into the springs of the sea? Or hast thou walked in the recesses of the deep?" The Hebrew word for "recesses" (or "trenches") refers to that which is "hidden, and known only by investigation." What were these "recesses of the deep" (the Hebrew word for "deep" is the word for seas or oceans)? Man, in previous centuries, considered the seashore as nothing but a shallow, sandy extension from one continent to another. Then, in 1873 a team of British scientists working in the Pacific Ocean found a "recess" 5½ miles deep. Later, another team of researchers discovered another trench 35,800 feet deep (over 6 miles down). Trenches now are known to be found in all three major oceans, but the Pacific Ocean is unique in that it has a semicontinuous peripheral belt of trenches and deep sea troughs. Extensive studies have now been conducted on the Marianas Trench off the coast of Guam. The bathyscaph *Trieste* has traveled down almost seven miles into that trench. The best known trench is perhaps the one off the coast of Puerto Rico, with its deepest point known as the Milwaukee Depth. How did Job know about these "recesses in the deep," when we didn't discover them for centuries? A lucky guess?

3. God told Noah (Genesis 6:15) to build an ark that measured 300 cubits in length, 50 cubits in width, and 30 cubits in height. This is a ratio of 30 to 5 to 3, length to breadth to height. Until approximately 1858, the ark was the largest seagoing vessel of which we have any written record. Using the most conservative estimate available for a cubit (17½ to 18 inches), the ark would have been roughly 450 feet long (a football-field-and-a-half) and would have contained approximately 1.5 million cubic feet of space. In 1844,

when Isambard K. Brunnel built his giant ship, the *Great Britain*, he constructed it to almost the exact dimensions of the ark—30:5:3. As it turns out, these dimensions are the perfect ratio for a huge boat build for seaworthiness and not for speed. Obviously the ark was not built for speed; it had nowhere to go! In fact, shipbuilders during World War II used that 30:5:3 ratio to build the boat that eventually was nicknamed "the ugly duckling"—a barge-like boat built to carry tremendous amounts of cargo. It had the same ratio as the ark. How did Noah know the perfect seagoing ratio to use in building the ark? Upon whose knowledge did he draw? Brunnel and others like him had many generations of shipbuilding knowledge upon which to draw, but Noah's literally was the first of its kind.

From the Field of Physics

1. Moses (Genesis 2:1) stated, "And the heavens and the earth were finished, and all the host of them." This is an extremely interesting assessment of the situation, because Moses chose the Hebrew past definite tense for the verb "finished," indicating an action completed in the past, never to occur again. Moses stated that the creation was "finished"—once and for all. That is exactly what the First Law of Thermodynamics states. This law (often referred to as the Law of Conservation of Energy/Matter) states that neither matter nor energy can be created or destroyed. It was because of this law that Sir Fred Hoyle's "Steady State" (or "Continuous Creation") Theory was discarded several years ago. Hoyle stated that at points in the Universe called "irtrons" matter was being created constantly. But the First Law states just the opposite. The Bible says that God "ended His work which He had made" (Genesis 2:2). As Henry M. Morris has suggested: "This is the most universal and certain of all scientific principles and it states conclusively that, so far as empirical observation has shown, there is **nothing** now being created anywhere in the known universe" (1974a, p. 235, emp. in orig.).

It is because God has finished His creation that nothing new is being created. But, as a corollary to that, why is it that nothing is being destroyed? This is the second half of the statement of the law. Matter/energy may change form, but the total amount in the Universe remains the same. Nothing is being destroyed, even though its form may change. Once again, the answer can be found in the science of the Bible. Nehemiah provided a portion of the answer when he stated: "Thou hast made heaven, the heaven of heavens, with all their host, the earth, and all things that are therein, the seas, and all that is therein, and thou preservest them all" (9:6). Hebrews 1:3 points out that God "upholds all things by the word of His power." If God is upholding it, then man will not destroy it. Other verses make that clear in this regard (cf. Isaiah 40:26, Ecclesiastes 3:14, and 2 Peter 3:7). Thus, we see that the biblical writers penned accurate scientific statements long before such statements were known to be scientific. How? Just a lucky guess?

2. In three places in the Bible (Hebrews 1:11; Isaiah 51:6; Psalm 102:26) the indication is given that the Earth, like a garment, is wearing out. This, of course, is exactly what the Second Law of Thermodynamics states. This law, also known as the Law of Increasing Entropy, governs all processes; there is not a single known exception. The law states that as time progresses, entropy increases. Entropy is the scientific word which simply means that things become more disorderly, more random, more unstructured. In other words, a flower blooms, fades, and dies. A child grows into adolescence, adulthood, senility, and dies. The house we build today, in 250 years will be a heap of junk. The car we buy today, given 30 or 40 years, will rust and fall apart. Everything is running down. Everything is wearing out. Energy is becoming less available for work. Eventually then (theoretically speaking) the Universe, left to itself, will experience a "heat death" when no more energy is available for use. We did not discover these things until fairly recently, yet the Bible writers portrayed them accurately thousands of years ago. What was the source of their knowledge?

From the Field of Medicine

1. Moses told the Israelites (Leviticus 17:11-14) that "the life of the flesh is in the blood." He was correct. Because the red blood cells can carry oxygen (due to hemoglobin in the cells), life is possible. In fact, human red blood cells carry, for example, approximately 270,000,000 molecules of hemoglobin per cell (see Perutz, 1964, pp. 64-65).

If there were any less, there would not be enough residual oxygen to sustain life after, say, a hard sneeze or a hefty pat on the back. We know today that the "life of the flesh is in the blood." But we didn't know that in George Washington's day. How did the "father of our country" die? We bled him to death (see Havron, 1981, p. 62). People felt that the blood was where evil "vapors" were found, and that getting rid of the blood would make a person well again. Today, of course, we know that is not true. Think of how often blood transfusions have made life possible for those who otherwise would have died. Today we know the truth of the matter. How did the biblical writer know it?

2. Genesis 3:15 teaches plainly that both the male and the female possess the "seed of life." This was not the commonly held position in Moses' day, however. Nor was it the commonly held position just a few centuries ago. Several writers of days gone by, including some of Moses' day, felt that only the male possessed the seed of life and that the woman actually was little more than a "glorified incubator." One writer even suggested that the male seed could be deposited in warm mud, and the end result would be the same as placing it in the woman's womb. But Moses spewed forth no such nonsense. Rather, he stated the truth of the matter. But how did he know? Upon whose knowledge of such facts did he draw?

3. Leviticus 17:15 teaches that an animal that has died **naturally** is not to be eaten. Moses obviously was highly trained in public health procedures, for he certainly knew that of which he spoke. Today it is against local, state, and federal public health laws to

take an animal that has died naturally to a slaughterhouse in order to be prepared for human consumption. What if the animal had died of rabies, anthrax, brucellosis, or a similar disease? Obviously, it would not be suitable for human consumption because if the animal died, something was wrong. Even today this practice is one of our basic public health standards. But how did Moses possess such knowledge?

4. While the Old Testament placed no restrictions on the eating of fruits and vegetables, severe limitations were given for the eating of certain meats. Among land animals, only those that had a split hoof and chewed the cud were approved as edible (Leviticus 11:3). Of the water-living animals, only those with fins and scales were acceptable (Leviticus 11:9; of interest is the fact that poisonous fish have no scales). Birds of prey were prohibited, as were almost all insects. But perhaps the best known among these biblical injunctions was eating the meat of a pig. To the Jew, pork was considered unclean, and thus was inedible.

Today, we know there is good scientific reasoning behind such a prohibition. The pig is a scavenger and therefore will eat almost anything. In so doing, on occasion it ingests the parasite, *Trichinella spiralis*, which is the cause of trichinosis in humans. Left untreated, this disease can be debilitating or even deadly. Pigs also are known carriers (as intermediate hosts) of the tapeworm *Taenia solium*, and of the parasite *Echinococcus granulosis*, which causes tumors in the liver, lungs, and other parts of the body. Raw or undercooked pork can be quite dangerous when consumed by humans. Pigs can provide safe meat if they are fed properly and if the muscle tissue is cooked correctly. But such conditions often did not prevail in ancient times.

Were the Israelites "ahead of their times" in regard to their extensive public health and personal hygiene laws? Archaeologists admit that they have yet to find civilizations as ancient as the Israelites with rules and regulations that could rival those of the Jewish people in regard to complexity and scientific accuracy. The Egyptians, for example, were quite brilliant in many respects when it came to their medical technology. Yet the Jews had access to this kind of information (and much more) that not even the Egyptians possessed. Interestingly, even today in some countries (like Germany) raw pork is considered a delicacy—in spite of the knowledge we possess about the potential dangers of eating it.

5. In Deuteronomy 23:12-14, Moses instructed the Israelites always to bury human waste products. Today, of course, with centuries of experience behind us, we know that this is an excellent sanitary hygienic practice. But the common course of action in Moses' day, and for centuries to follow, was to dump waste products in any convenient place. History has recorded the folly of this kind of action. In Europe, during the Middle Ages, "Black Plague" swept over the continent on two different occasions, slaughtering more than 13 million people in the process. Why did this happen—not once, but twice? Europeans routinely dumped waste products of all kinds out their windows and into the public streets—where decomposition took place, allowing a variety of microorganisms to flourish.

One of those microorganisms—the one we know today as *Yersinia pestis*—grew in the waste products and contaminated the fleas associated with those waste products. The fleas, using rats as their hosts, subsequently traveled into the people's houses. Once inside a dwelling, the fleas then jumped from the rats onto the humans, biting them and infecting them with the plague organism. As this cycle was repeated over and over, millions perished. Yet if the people simply had obeyed God's injunction, as given by Moses to the Israelites, all of the death and horror of two separate epidemics could have been avoided. How did Moses know to instruct the Israelites regarding such public health hygiene laws, when none of the nations surrounding God's people enlisted such practices—and would not for centuries?

6. In Genesis 17:12, God commanded Abraham to circumcise newborn males on the **eighth** day. But why day eight? In humans, blood clotting is dependent upon three factors: (a) platelets; (b) vitamin K; and (c) prothrombin. In 1935, professor H. Dam proposed the name "vitamin K" for the factor that helped prevent hemorrhaging in chicks. We now realize that vitamin K is responsible for the production (by the liver) of prothrombin. If the quantity of vitamin K is deficient, there will be a prothrombin deficiency and hemorrhaging may occur.

Interestingly, it is only on the fifth to seventh days of a newborn's life that vitamin K (produced by the action of bacteria in the intestinal tract) is present in adequate quantities. Vitamin K—coupled with prothrombin—causes blood coagulation, which is important in any surgical procedure. A classic medical text, *Holt Pediatrics*, corroborates the fact that a newborn infant has

> ...peculiar susceptibility to bleeding between the second and fifth days of life.... Hemorrhages at this time, though often inconsequential, are sometimes extensive; they may produce serious damage to internal organs, especially to the brain, and cause death from shock and exsanguination (1953, pp. 125-126).

Obviously, then, if vitamin K is not produced in sufficient quantities until days five through seven, it would be wise to postpone any surgery until sometime after that. But why did God specify day **eight**?

On the eighth day, the amount of prothrombin present actually is **elevated above 100 percent of normal**. In fact, day eight is the only day in the male's life in which this will be the case under normal conditions. If surgery is to be performed, day eight is the perfect day to do it.

S.I. McMillen, the renowned medical doctor who authored *None of These Diseases*, wrote concerning this information:

> ...as we congratulate medical science for this recent finding, we can almost hear the leaves of the Bible rustling. They would like to remind us that four thousand years ago, when God

> **initiated** circumcision with Abraham, He said "And he that is eight days old shall be circumcised...." Abraham did not pick the eighth day after many centuries of trial-and-error experiments. Neither he nor any of his company from the ancient city of Ur in the Chaldees had ever been circumcised. It was a day picked by the Creator of vitamin K (1963, p. 21, emp. in orig.).

The medical information employed by Abraham, and confirmed by Moses, was accurate scientifically then, and still remains so to this very day. No culture around the Israelites possessed such scientific acumen, which, by the way, was light-years ahead of its time. How, then, did Abraham and Moses come to know the best time for circumcision, unless, of course, this particular fact was revealed to them by God, and recorded in His Word through inspiration?

From the Field of Biology

1. Moses stated (Genesis 1:11,12,21,24) that things reproduce "after their kind." This, of course, is no surprise to us today because we understand genetics and the laws of heredity which ensure that things do indeed reproduce "after their kind." If a farmer plants corn seed, he knows full well that he will not be harvesting wheat. If he breeds a bull to a heifer, he knows that the end result will not be a baby colt. Corn produces corn; cows produce cows. Why? Because all living things reproduce "after their kind" Even today, in nature these things hold true. But how did Moses know that—many years before the science of genetics (which came into existence only around 1900) was discovered?

2. Paul stated that it is God who giveth all life (Acts 17:25). For centuries men have been trying to "create life" through processes of spontaneous generation. Even though men like Spallanzani, Redi, Pasteur and hundreds of others have proven time and again that spontaneous generation is impossible, evolutionists still keep on trying. But, to date, no one ever has "created" life. They do well, in fact, even to get one of the simplest "building blocks"—amino acids. Paul knew long ago that it was God who gives life. Just a lucky guess?

3. Paul also stated that there are **four** fleshes—those of men, beasts, birds and fishes (1 Corinthians 15:39). Today even evolutionists accept this fact of science. These fleshes are indeed different in their biochemical make-up. But how did Paul, an itinerant preacher of the first century A.D., know this?

From the Field of Archaeology

1. The Moabite Stone, found in 1868 by a German missionary, was cut in 850 B.C., in the reign of Mosha, king of Moab. It tells of his being subjected to the Israelites. It also mentions that Omri, the captain of the Israelite host, was made king in that day. The Scriptures speak of that very event in 1 Kings 16:16. With every scoop of dirt that the spade overturns, archaeology proves biblical statements to be factual.

2. The Bible plainly speaks of a king by the name of Belshazzar (Daniel 5:22; 7:1; 8:1). It was common practice for Bible critics to ridicule the Bible regarding its references concerning Belshazzar, because secular records never had been found that substantiated what the Bible said. Then, in 1876 Sir Henry Rawlinson discovered more than 2,000 tablets concerning Babylon. They disclosed records of a man named Belshazzar who, in the absence of his father Nabonidus, became king. The Bible had been right all along.

The incredible accuracy of the Bible's science is yet another example of God's superintending guidance, and one that provides an impressive proof of its inspiration.

Conclusion

Those who have set their face against God have railed against the Bible for generations. King Jehoiakim took his penknife, slashed the Old Testament Scriptures to pieces, and tossed them into a fire (Jeremiah 36:22-23). During the Middle Ages, attempts were made to keep the Bible from the man on the street. In fact, those people caught translating or distributing the Scriptures often were subjected to imprisonment, torture, and even death. Centuries later, the French skeptic Voltaire boasted that "within fifty years, the Bible no longer will be discussed among educated people." His braggadocio notwithstanding, the Bible still is being discussed among educated people, while the name of Voltaire languishes in relative obscurity.

In the early 1900s, American infidel Robert Ingersoll claimed regarding the Bible: "In fifteen years, I will have this book in the morgue." But, as history records, Ingersoll ended up in the morgue, while the Bible lives on. Like the blacksmith's anvil—which wears out many hammers but itself remains unaffected—the Bible wears out the skeptics' innocuous charges, all the while remaining unscathed. An unknown poet once wrote:

Last eve I passed beside a blacksmith's door,
And heard the anvil ring the vesper chime;
Then looking, I saw upon the floor,
Old hammers, worn with beating years of time.
"How many anvils have you had," said I,
"To wear and batter all these hammers so?"
"Just one," said he, and then with twinkling eye;
"The anvil wears the hammers out, ye know."
And so, thought I, the anvil of God's Word,
For ages skeptic blows have beat upon;
Yet though the noise of falling blows was heard
The anvil is unharmed...the hammers gone.

Governments come and go. Nations rise and fall. People live and die. Jesus warned that "heaven and earth shall pass away" (Matthew 24:35), but went on to note that "my words shall not pass away." Isaiah wrote: "The grass withereth, the flower fadeth; but the word of our God shall stand forever" (40:8). I believe it is fitting that we close this portion of our study with these words from Kenny Barfield's book, *Why the Bible is Number 1*:

We have seen how the biblical materials are unique. They are no run-of-the-mill religious writings, but—quite the contrary—reveal a remarkable understanding of the universe. ...How did the biblical writers manage to avoid the erroneous world views of their contemporaries? What made these men capable of producing painstakingly accurate scientific statements far in advance of their actual discovery? We want answers to those important questions....

One answer has been suggested by the biblical writers themselves. If their materials are so radically different from other sources, surely we must listen to their explanation. Rather than finding confusion or uncertainty in their ranks, we find calm unanimity.

They refused to be called geniuses and scorned personal glory. Even more significant, they denied having figured it out for themselves. In fact, there is reason to believe that they never really understood the far-reaching implications of the words they wrote.

Humbly, without a dissenting voice, these writers gave credit to a superior being. One of their favorite phrases was: "This is the Word of God." They sensed a far-greater intelligence behind this universe than that of any mortal. They stood in awe before that wisdom and power. They even wrote words on their papyri and scrolls that made little earthly sense. "All Scripture is given by inspiration of God." It was the only answer they ever gave.

It is the thesis of this study that one must simply look at the trademark, the signature of authorship.... Unless we can devise a more suitable explanation, it seems reasonable to believe that the seemingly incongruous wisdom was placed in the Bible by an intelligence far greater than that of man. That intelligence is God's alone (1988, pp. 182,184-185).

CHAPTER 10

JESUS CHRIST—LORD AND SAVIOR

On Tuesday, prior to the Christ's crucifixion the following Friday, Jesus engaged in a discussion with the Pharisees, who made no secret of their hatred for Him. When Matthew recorded the scene in his Gospel, he first commented on an earlier skirmish the Lord had with the Sadducees: "But the Pharisees, when they heard that he had put the Sadducees to silence, gathered themselves together" (22:34).

Jesus—with penetrating logic and an incomparable knowledge of the Old Testament Scriptures—had routed the Sadducees completely. No doubt the Pharisees thought they could do better. Yet they were about to endure the same embarrassing treatment.

In the midst of His discussion with the Pharisees, Jesus asked: "What think ye of the Christ? Whose son is he?" (Matthew 22:42). They were unable to answer the questions satisfactorily because their hypocrisy prevented them from comprehending both Jesus' nature and His mission. The questions the Lord asked on that day, however, are ones that every rational, sane person must answer eventually.

The two questions were intended to raise the matter of Christ's deity. The answers—had the Pharisees' spiritual myopia not prevented them from responding correctly—were intended to confirm it. Today, these questions still raise the spectre of Christ's identity. Who is Jesus? Is He, as He claimed to be, the Son of God? Was He, as many around Him claimed, God incarnate? Is He, as the word "deity" implies, of divine nature and rank?

Christ as a Historical Figure

The series of events that eventually would lead to Jesus' becoming the world's best-known historical figure began in first-century Palestine. There are four primary indicators of this fact. First, when Daniel was asked by king Nebuchadnezzar to interpret his wildly imaginative dream, the prophet revealed that God would establish the Messianic kingdom during the time of the Roman Empire (viz., the fourth kingdom represented in the king's dream; see Daniel 2: 24-45). Roman domination of Palestine began in 63 B.C. and continued until A.D. 476.

Second, the Christ was promised to come before "the scepter" departed from Judah (Genesis 49:10). Bible students recognize that this prophecy has reference to the Messiah ("Shiloh") arriving before the Jews lost their national sovereignty and judicial power (the "scepter" of Genesis 49). Thus, Christ had to have come prior to the Jews' losing their power to execute capital punishment (John 18:31). When Rome deposed Archelaus in A.D. 6, Coponius was installed as Judea's first procurator. Interestingly, "the...procurator held the power of jurisdiction with regard to capital punishment" (Solomon, 1972, 13:117). Therefore, Christ was predicted to come sometime prior to A.D. 6 (see also McDowell, 1972, pp. 176-178).

Third, Daniel predicted that the Messiah would bring an end to "sacrifice and offering" before the destruction of Jerusalem (cf. Daniel 9:24-27 and Matthew 24:15; see also Jackson, 1997a). History records that the Temple was obliterated by the Romans in A.D. 70.

Fourth, the Messiah was to be born in Bethlehem of Judea (Micah 5:2). It also is a matter of record that Jesus was born in Beth lehem while Palestine was under Roman rule, before Judah lost her judicial power, and before the destruction of Jerusalem (see also Matthew 2:3-6; Luke 2:2-6).

In an excellent, thought-provoking article titled "The Historical Christ—Fact or Fiction?," Kyle Butt examined the hostile testimony from both Romans and Jews that inadvertently (yet powerfully!) documented Christ's historicity. In commenting on the records available to us from secular sources, he remarked:

> Interestingly, the first type of records comes from what are known commonly as "hostile" sources—writers who mentioned Jesus in a negative light or derogatory fashion. Such penmen certainly were not predisposed to further the cause of Christ or otherwise to add credence to His existence. In fact, quite the opposite is true. They rejected His teachings and often reviled Him as well. Thus, once can appear to them without the charge of built-in bias.... Even a casual reader who glances over the testimony of the hostile Roman witnesses who bore testimony to the historicity of Christ will be struck by the fact that these ancient men depicted Christ as neither the Son of God nor the Savior of the world. They verbally stripped him of His Sonship, denied His glory, and belittled His magnificence. They described Him to their contemporaries, and for posterity, as a mere man. Yet even though they were wide of the mark in regard to the truth of **Who** He was, through their caustic diatribes they nevertheless documented **that** He was. And for that we are indebted to them.... Faced with such overwhelming evidence, it is unwise to reject the position that Jesus Christ actually walked the streets of Jerusalem in the first century (2000, 20:1,3,6, emp. in orig).

Christ in the Old Testament

The Old and New Testaments portray a portrait of Christ that presents valuable evidence for the person desiring to answer the questions, "What think ye of the Christ?," and "Whose son is he?" In Isaiah 7:14, for example, the prophet declared that a virgin would conceive, bear a son, and name him "Immanuel," which means "God with us" (a prophecy that was fulfilled in the birth of Christ; Matthew 1:22-23). Later, Isaiah referred to this son as "Mighty God" (9:6). In fact, in the year that king Uzziah died, Isaiah said he saw "the Lord" sitting upon a throne (see Isaiah 6:1ff.). Overpowered by the scene, God's servant exclaimed: "Woe is me,...for mine eyes have seen the King, Jehovah of hosts" (6:5). In the New Testament, John wrote: "These things said Isaiah, because he saw His [Christ's —BT] glory; and he spake of him" (John 12:41).

Isaiah urged God's people to sanctify "Jehovah of hosts" (8:12-14), a command applied to Jesus by Peter (1 Peter 3:14-15). Furthermore, Isaiah's "Jehovah" was to become a stone of stumbling and a rock of offense (8:14), a description that New Testament writers applied to Christ (cf. Romans 9:33, 1 Peter 2:8). Isaiah foretold that John the Baptizer would prepare the way for the coming of **Jehovah** (40:3). It is well known that John was the forerunner of **Christ** (cf. Matthew 3:3, John 1:23).

Isaiah pictured Christ not only as a silent "lamb" (53:7), but as a man Who "a bruised reed will he not break, and a dimly burning wick will he not quench" (42:3; cf. Matthew 12:20). J.W. McGarvey explained the imagery in these verses as follows:

> A bruised reed, barely strong enough to stand erect...a smoking flax (a lamp wick), its flame extinguished and its fire almost gone, fitly represent the sick, and lame, and blind who were brought to Jesus to be healed. ...he would heal their bruises and fan their dying energies into a flame (1875, p. 106).

Other Old Testament writers illuminated Christ in their writings as well. The psalmist suggested He would be known as zealous for righteousness (Psalm 69:9), that He would be hated without cause (Psalm 22), and that He would triumph over death (Psalm 16:8-11). Daniel referred to His coming kingdom as one that would "stand forever" (12:44). The prophets' portrait of Christ was intended not only to foreshadow His coming, but to make Him all the more visible to the people in New Testament times as well (see Bromling, 1991b).

Christ in the New Testament

The New Testament is equally explicit in its commentary regarding the Christ, and offers extensive corroboration of the Old Testament declarations concerning Him. The prophets had portrayed the Messiah's demise as unjust, painful, and vicarious (Isaiah 53: 4-6; Psalm 22). In the New Testament, Paul reiterated that fact (Romans 5:6-8). The prophets predicted that He would be betrayed by a friend (Psalm 41:9) for a mere thirty pieces of silver (Zechariah 11:12), and He was (Luke 22:47-48; Matthew 26:15). They said that He would be mocked (Psalm 22:7-8), spat upon (Isaiah 50:6), numbered among common criminals (Isaiah 53:12), pierced through (Zechariah 12:10), and forsaken by God (cf. Psalm 22:1), and He was (Luke 23:35; Matthew 26:67; Matthew 27:46; Mark 15:27-28; John 19:37; John 20:25; Mark 15:34). Without any explanation, an inspired prophet predicted that the suffering servant's hands and feet would be pierced (Psalm 22:16). Later revelation reveals the reason for such a statement: He was nailed to a cross (Luke 23:33).

The prophets had said that He would be raised from the dead so that He could sit upon the throne of David (Isaiah 9:7). This occurred, as Peter attested in his sermon on Pentecost following the resurrection (Acts 2:30). He would rule, not Judah, but the most powerful kingdom ever known. As King, Christ was to rule (from heaven) the kingdom that "shall never be destroyed" and that "shall break in pieces and consume all these [earthly] kingdoms, and... shall stand forever" (Daniel 2:44). The New Testament establishes the legitimacy of His kingdom (Colossians 1:13; 1 Corinthians 15:24-25). The subjects of this royal realm were to be from every nation on Earth (Isaiah 2:2), and were prophesied to enjoy a life of peace and harmony that ignores any and all human distinctions, prejudices, or biases (cf. Isaiah 2:4 and Galatians 3:28). This King would be arrayed, not in the regal purple of a carnal king, but in the humble garments of a holy priest (Psalm 110:4; Hebrews 5:6). Like

Melchizedek, the Messiah was to be both Priest and King (Genesis 14:18), guaranteeing that His subjects could approach God without the interference of a clergy class. Instead, as the New Testament affirms, Christians offer their petitions directly to God through their King—Who mediates on their behalf (cf. Matthew 6:9; John 14:13-14; 1 Timothy 2:5; Hebrews 10:12,19-22). It would have been utterly impossible for the New Testament writers to provide any clearer answers than they did to the questions that Christ asked the Pharisees.

Christ as a Man

The Scriptures teach that Jesus possessed two natures—divine and human. As an eternal Being (Isaiah 9:6; Micah 5:2; John 1:1ff.), He was God; yet, He became man (1 Timothy 2:5), made in the likeness of sinful flesh (Romans 8:3), though without sin (Hebrews 4:15). Isaiah observed that Christ would be "a **man** of sorrows, and acquainted with grief" Who would **grow up** "as a tender plant, and as a root out of dry ground" (Isaiah 53:2-3).

As a human, the prophets had said, Christ was to be the seed of woman (Genesis 3:15), and a descendant of Abraham, Isaac, Jacob, and David (Genesis 22:18; 26:4; 28:14; 2 Samuel 7:12-13). The New Testament confirms that indeed, He was born of a woman (Galatians 4:4) who was a virgin (Matthew 1:23), and that He was the descendant of Abraham, Isaac, Jacob, and David (Matthew 1:1ff.). The apostle John stated that He had become flesh and had dwelt among men (John 1:14). Paul wrote that Christ was recognized "in fashion as a man" (Philippians 2:7-8). From his position as a physician, Luke wrote that Christ "advanced in wisdom and stature, and in favor with God and men" (Luke 2:52). He was able to learn (Hebrews 5:8). He experienced hunger (Matthew 4:2), thirst (John 19:28), weariness (John 4:6), anger (Mark 3:5), frustration (Mark 9:19), joy (John 15:11), sadness (John 11:35), and grief (Luke 19:41; Hebrews 5:7). He was "in all points tempted as we are, yet without sin" (Hebrews 4:15). But most significantly, He was able to die (Mark 15:44). In every respect, He was as human as you and I, which is why He could, and did, refer to Himself as the "Son of Man" (see Matthew 1:20; 9:6; et al.).

But the impact He had on the world was not due to His physical appearance. In fact, Isaiah foretold that He would have "no form nor comeliness; and when we see Him, there is no beauty that we should desire Him" (Isaiah 53:2). Rather, it was His nature and His character that made Him so intriguing, so commanding a figure, and so worthy of honor, respect, and worship. Here we see a man—but no mere man, for He is the only man ever to be born of a virgin (Isaiah 7:14; Matthew 1:18), and to whom the inspired prophets dared to apply the revered name of "Jehovah" (Isaiah 40:3).

Why do the Scriptures place importance upon the **human** nature of Christ? Wayne Jackson has suggested:

> If Christ had not become a man, He could not have died. Deity, as pure Spirit-essence, possesses **immortality** (1 Tim. 6:16—the Greek word denotes deathlessness). The writer of Hebrews makes it wonderfully plain that Christ partook of "flesh and blood" that "through death he might bring to nought him that had the power of death, that is, the devil" (Heb. 2:14). If Christ had not died, there would have been no atonement, no forgiveness of sins—the human family would have been hopelessly lost forever! Thank God for Christ's humanity (1979, p. 66, emp. in orig.).

Christ as God

The Scriptures do not speak of Christ as **just** a man, however. They also acknowledge His divine nature. In most of its occurrences, the name "Jehovah" is applied to the first person of the Godhead (i.e., the Father—Matthew 28:19). For example: "Jehovah said unto my Lord, Sit thou at my right hand, until I make thine enemies thy footstool" (Psalm 110:1). Jesus later explained that this verse pictures the Father addressing the Christ (Luke 20:42).

Yet the name "Jehovah" also is used on occasion to refer to Christ. For example, Isaiah prophesied concerning the mission of John the Baptizer: "The voice of one that crieth, Prepare ye in the wilderness the way of Jehovah; make level in the desert a highway for our God" (Isaiah 40:3; cf. Matthew 3:3, Mark 1:3, Luke 3:4). John was sent to prepare the way for Jesus Christ (John 1:29-34). But Isaiah said that John would prepare the way of **Jehovah**. Clearly, Jesus and Jehovah are the same.

The writer of Hebrews quoted the Father as addressing His Son in this way: "Thou, Lord [Jehovah—Psalm 102:25], in the beginning did lay the foundation of the earth, and the heavens are the works of thy hands" (Hebrews 1:10). This verse not only applies the word "Jehovah" to Jesus, **but actually attributes the quotation to the mouth of God**. Again, Jesus and Jehovah are used synonymously (see Bromling, 1991a).

Furthermore, Jesus spoke and acted like God. He affirmed that He was "one" with the Father (John 10:30). He forgave sins—a prerogative of God alone (Mark 2:5,7). He accepted the worship of men (John 9:38) which is due only to God (Matthew 4:10), and which good angels (Revelation 22:8-9) and good men (Matthew 4:10) refuse.

In addition, Jesus plainly is called "God" a number of times within the New Testament. In John 1:1, regarding Him "Who became flesh and dwelt among men" (1:14), the Bible says that "the Word was God." And in John 20:28, one of the disciples, Thomas, upon being confronted with empirical evidence for the Lord's resurrection, proclaimed: "My Lord and my God!" Significantly (and appropriately), Christ accepted the designation. Additional passages that reveal Christ as God include Philippians 2:5ff., 2 Corinthians 4:4, Colossians 1:15, and many others.

Choices Regarding Christ's Deity

When Jesus was put on trial before the Sanhedrin, the Jewish high priest asked: "Are you the Christ, the Son of the Blessed?" To that question Christ replied simply, "I am" (Mark 14:62). In view of the exalted nature of such a claim, and its ultimate end results, there are but three possible views one may entertain in reference to Christ's claim of being deity: (1) He was a liar and con-artist; (2) He was a madman; or (3) He was exactly Who He said He was.

In his book, *Evidence that Demands a Verdict*, Josh McDowell titled one chapter: "The Trilemma—Lord, Liar, or Lunatic?" His purpose was to point out that, considering the grandiose nature of Christ's claims, He was either a liar, a lunatic, or the Lord. McDowell introduced his chapter on Christ's deity with a quotation from the famous British apologist of Cambridge University, C.S. Lewis, who wrote:

> I am trying here to prevent anyone saying the really foolish thing that people often say about Him: "I'm ready to accept Jesus as a great moral teacher, but I don't accept His claim to be God." That is the one thing we must not say. A man who was merely a man and said the sort of things Jesus said would not be a great moral teacher. He would either be a lunatic—on a level with the man who says he is a poached egg —or else he would be the Devil of Hell. You must make your choice. Either this man was, and is, the Son of God: or else a madman or something worse. You can shut Him up for a fool, you can spit at Him and kill Him as a demon; or you can fall at His feet and call Him Lord and God. But let us not come up with any patronising nonsense about His being a great human teacher. He has not left that open to us. He did not intend to (1952, pp. 40-41).

Was Christ a Liar?

Was Christ a liar? A charlatan? A "messianic manipulator"? In his book, *The Passover Plot*, Hugh J. Schonfield claimed that He was all three. Schonfield suggested that Jesus manipulated His life in such a way as to counterfeit the events described in the Old Testament prophecies about the Messiah. At times, this required "contriving those events when necessary, contending with friends and foes to ensure that the predictions would be fulfilled" (1965, p. 7). Schonfield charged that Jesus "plotted and schemed with the utmost skill and resourcefulness, sometimes making secret arrangements, taking advantage of every circumstance conducive to the attainment of his objectives" (p. 155). He further asserted that Jesus even planned to fake His own death on the cross. Unfortunately, however, Jesus had not counted on having a Roman soldier pierce His side with a spear. Thus, instead of recovering from His stupor, Jesus died unexpectedly. On Saturday night, His body was moved to a secret place so that His tomb would be empty on the next day, thus leaving the impression of His resurrection and, simultaneously, His deity (pp. 161,165). One writer has asked, however:

> But does this reconstruction of the life of Christ ring true? Even if a charlatan **could** beguile a few followers into believing that he had fulfilled a few of the prophecies (either by coincidence, or by contrivance), how could he possibly fulfill those which were beyond his control? How could an impostor have planned his betrayal price? How could he have known the money would be used to buy the potter's field (cf. Zechariah 11:13, Matthew 27:7)? How could he have known that men would gamble for his clothing (cf. Psalm 22:17-18, Matthew 27:35-36)? Yet, these are just a few of the prophecies over which he would have no control. Jesus fulfilled every single one of them (Bromling, 1991b, 11:47, emp. in orig.).

In considering the possibility that Christ was little more than an accomplished liar, renowned biblical historian Philip Schaff wrote:

> How in the name of logic, common sense, and experience, could an impostor—that is a deceitful, selfish, depraved man—have invented, and consistently maintained from the beginning to end, the purest and noblest character known in history with the most perfect air of truth and reality? How could he have conceived and successfully carried out a plan of unparalleled beneficence, moral magnitude, and sublimity, and sacrificed his own life for it, in the face of the strongest prejudices of his people and ages? (1913, pp. 94-95).

Further, the question must be asked: What sane man would be willing to **die** for what he **knows** is a lie? As McDowell summarized the matter: "Someone who lived as Jesus lived, taught as Jesus taught, and died as Jesus died could not have been a liar" (1972, p. 106).

Was Christ a Lunatic?

Was Jesus merely a psychotic lunatic Who sincerely (albeit mistakenly) viewed Himself as God incarnate? Such a view rarely has been entertained by anyone cognizant of Christ's life and teachings. Schaff inquired:

> Is such an intellect—clear as the sky, bracing as the mountain air, sharp and penetrating as a sword, thoroughly healthy and vigorous, always ready and always self-possessed—liable to a radical and most serious delusion concerning His own character and mission? Preposterous imagination! (1913, pp. 97-98).

Would a raving lunatic teach that we should do unto others as we would have them do unto us? Would a lunatic teach that we should pray for our enemies? Would a lunatic teach that we should "turn the other cheek," and then set an example of exactly how to do that—even unto death? Would a lunatic present an ethical/moral code like the one found within the text of the Sermon on the Mount? Hardly! Lunacy of the sort ascribed to Christ by His detractors does not produce such genius. Schaff wrote:

> Self-deception in a matter so momentous, and with an intellect in all respects so clear and so sound, is equally out of the question. How could He be an enthusiast or a madman who never lost the even balance of His mind, who sailed serenely over all the troubles and persecutions, as the sun above the clouds, who always returned the wisest answer to tempting questions, who calmly and deliberately predicted His death on the cross, His resurrection on the third day, the outpouring of the Holy Spirit, the founding of His Church, the destruction of Jerusalem—predictions which have been literally fulfilled? A character so original, so completely, so uniformly consistent, so perfect, so human and yet so high above all human greatness, can be neither a fraud nor a fiction. The poet, as has been well said, would be in this case greater than the hero. It would take more than a Jesus to invent a Jesus (1910, p. 109).

Was Christ Deity?

If Jesus was not a liar or a lunatic, then the questions that Jesus asked the Pharisees still remain: "What think ye of the Christ? Whose son is He?" Was Jesus, in fact, exactly Who He claimed to be? Was He God incarnate? The evidence suggests that, indeed, He was.

Evidence for the Deity of Christ

In Mark 10, an account is recorded concerning a rich young ruler who, in speaking to Christ, addressed Him as "Good Teacher." Upon hearing this reference, Jesus asked the man: "Why callest thou me good? None is good, save one, even God" (Mark 10:17).

Was Christ suggesting that His countryman's loyalty was misplaced, and that He was unworthy of being called "good" (in the sense that ultimately only God merits such a designation)? No. In fact, Christ was suggesting that He **was worthy** of the appellation. He wanted the ruler to understand the significance of the title he had used. R.C. Foster paraphrased Jesus' response as follows: "Do you know the meaning of this word you apply to me and which you use so freely? There is none good save God; if you apply that term to me, and you understand what you mean, you affirm that I am God" (1971, p. 1022).

What evidence establishes Christ's deity? Among other things, it includes Christ's fulfillment of Old Testament prophecies, His confirmation of His Sonship via the miracles He performed, His crucifixion and subsequent resurrection, and His post-resurrection appearances.

Fulfillment of Old Testament Prophecies

Scholars have documented over 300 messianic prophecies in the Old Testament (Lockyer, 1973, p. 21). From Genesis through Malachi, the history of Jesus is foretold in minute detail. Bible critics who wish to disprove Christ's deity, must refute fulfilled prophecy. To accomplish this, one would have to contend that Jesus did not fulfill the prophecies **genuinely**; rather, He only **appeared** to fulfill them. Yet with over 300 prophecies relating to Christ—none of which can be dismissed flippantly—this is an impossible task (see Bromling, 1989).

Could Christ have fulfilled 300+ prophetic utterances **by chance**? P.W. Stoner and R.C. Newman selected eight specific prophecies and then calculated the probability of one man fulfilling only those eight. Their conclusion was that 1 man in 10^{17} could do it (1971, p. 106). The probability that a single man could fulfill—by chance—**all** of the prophecies relating to Christ and His ministry would be practically incalculable, and the idea that a single man did so would be utterly absurd.

Performance of Genuine Miracles

Christ also backed up His claims by working miracles. Throughout history, God had empowered other people to perform miracles. But while their miracles confirmed they were **servants** of God, Jesus' miracles were intended to prove that He **is** God (John 10:37-38; cf. John 20:30-31).

While in prison, John the Baptizer sent his followers to ask Jesus: "Art thou he that cometh, or look we for another?" (Matthew 11:3). Jesus' response was: "Go and tell John...the blind receive their sight and the lame walk, the lepers are cleansed, the deaf hear, and the dead are raised up, and the poor have good tidings preached to them" (Matthew 11:4-5). "Over seven hundred years earlier, the prophet Isaiah predicted that those very things would be done by the Messiah (Isaiah 35:5-6; 61:1). Jesus wasn't merely saying, 'Look at all the good things I am doing.' He was saying: 'I am doing **exactly what the Coming One is supposed to do**!'" (Bromling, 1995, 15:19, emp. added).

When Peter addressed the very people who had put Jesus to death, he reminded them that Christ's unique identity had been proved "by mighty works and wonders and signs which God did by him in the midst of you, even as ye yourselves know" (Acts 2: 22). The key phrase here is "even as ye yourselves know." The Jews had witnessed Christ's miracles occurring among them on practically a daily basis. And, unlike the pseudo-miracles allegedly performed by today's "spiritualists," Jesus' miracles were feats that truly defied naturalistic explanation. In the presence of many witnesses, the Nazarene not only gave sight to the blind, healed lepers, fed thousands from a handful of food, and made the lame to walk, but also calmed turbulent seas and raised the dead! Although not overly eager to admit it, Jesus' critics often were brought face-to-face with the truth that no one could do what Jesus did unless God was with Him (John 3:2; see also John 9).

The Resurrection, and Post-Resurrection Appearances

Likely, however, the most impressive miracle involving Jesus was His resurrection. In agreement with Old Testament prophecy, and just as He had promised, Christ came forth from the tomb three days after His brutal crucifixion (Matthew 16:21; 27:63; 28:1-8). His resurrection was witnessed by the soldiers who had been appointed to guard His tomb. In the end, those soldiers had to be bribed to change their story so that the Jewish leaders would not lose credibility, and in order to prevent the Jewish people from recognizing their true Messiah (Matthew 28:11-15). It is a matter of history that Christ's tomb was empty on that Sunday morning almost 2,000 years ago. If Jesus were not raised from the dead, how came His guarded and sealed tomb to be empty?

That Christ had been raised from the dead was witnessed by many different types of people: the soldiers who guarded His tomb; the women who came early in the morning to anoint Him with spices; eleven apostles; and more than 500 other witnesses (1 Corinthians 15:4-8). When they saw the living, breathing Jesus—days after His death—they had concrete proof that He was Who He claimed to be all along! Even his detractors could not deny successfully the fact, and significance, of the empty tomb.

Thousands of people go annually to the graves of the founders of the Buddhist and Muslim religions to pay homage. Yet Christians do not pay homage at the grave of Christ—for the simple fact that **the tomb is empty**. A dead Savior is no good! For those who accept, and act upon, the evidence for Christ's deity provided by the resurrection, life is meaningful, rich, and full (see Paul's discussion in 1 Corinthians 15). For those who reject the resurrection, the vacant tomb will stand forever as eternity's greatest mystery, and one day will serve as their silent judge.

Conclusion

Who is Jesus of Nazareth? He had no formal rabbinical training (John 7:15). He possessed no material wealth (Luke 9:58; 2 Corinthians 8:9). Yet, through His teachings, He turned the world upside down (Acts 17:6). Clearly, as the evidence documents, He was, and is, both the Son of Man and the Son of God. He lived, and died, to redeem fallen mankind. He gave Himself a ransom (Matthew 20:28). He is God, Who predates, and will outlast, time itself (Philippians 2:5-11).

CHAPTER 11

GOD'S PLAN FOR MAN'S SALVATION

> "And Jehovah God formed man of the dust of the ground, and breathed into his nostrils the breath of life; and man became a living soul" (Genesis 2:7).

Of all the living beings that dwell on planet Earth, one solitary creature was made "in the image of God." On day six of His creative activity, God said: "Let us make man in our image, after our likeness. And God created man in his own image, in the image of God created he him; male and female created he them" (Genesis 1:26-27).

Mankind was not created in the physical image of God, of course, because God, as a Spirit Being, has no physical image (John 4:24; Luke 24:39; Matthew 16:17). Rather, mankind was fashioned in the spiritual, rational, emotional, and volitional image of God (Ephesians 4:24; John 5:39-40; 7:17; Joshua 24:15; Isaiah 7:15). Humans are superior to all other creatures. No other living being was given the faculties, the capacities, the capabilities, the potential, or the dignity that God instilled in each man and woman. Indeed, humankind is the peak, the apex, the pinnacle of God's creation.

In its lofty position as the zenith of God's creative genius, mankind was endowed with certain responsibilities. Men and women were to be the stewards of the entire Earth (Genesis 1:28). They were to glorify God in their daily existence (Isaiah 43:7). And, they were to consider it their "whole duty" to serve the Creator faithfully throughout their brief sojourn on the Earth (Ecclesiastes 12:13).

Man's Predicament: Disobedience and Death

Unfortunately, the first man and woman used their volitional powers—and the free moral agency based on those powers—to rebel against their Maker. Finite man made some horribly evil choices, and so entered the spiritual state biblically designated as "sin." The Old Testament not only presents in vivid fashion the entrance of sin into the world through Adam and Eve (Genesis 3), but also alludes to the ubiquity of sin within the human race when it says: "There is no man that sinneth not" (1 Kings 8:46). Throughout its thirty-nine books, the Old Covenant discusses time and again both sin's presence amidst humanity and its destructive consequences. The great prophet Isaiah reminded God's people: "Behold, Jehovah's hand is not shortened that it cannot save; neither his ear heavy that it cannot hear: but your iniquities have separated between you and your God, and your sins have hid his face from you, so that he will not hear" (59:1-2).

The New Testament is no less clear in its assessment. The apostle John wrote: "Every one that doeth sin doeth also lawlessness; and sin is lawlessness" (1 John 3:4). Thus, sin is defined as the act of transgressing God's law. In fact, Paul observed that "where there is no law, neither is there transgression" (Romans 4:15). Had there been no law, there would have been no sin. But God **had** instituted divine law. And mankind freely chose to transgress that law. Paul reaffirmed the Old Testament concept of the universality of sin (1 Kings 8:46) when he stated that "all have sinned, and fall short of the glory of God" (Romans 3:23).

As a result, mankind's predicament became serious indeed. Ezekiel lamented: "The soul that sinneth, it shall die" (18:20a). Once again, the New Testament writers reaffirmed such a concept. Paul wrote: "Therefore, as through one man sin entered into the world, and death through sin; and so death passed unto all men, for that all sinned" (Romans 5:12). He then added that "the wages of sin is death" (Romans 6:23). Years later, James would write: "But each man is tempted, when he is drawn away by his own lust, and enticed. Then the lust, when it hath conceived, beareth sin: and the sin, when it is full-grown, bringeth forth death" (1:15-16).

As a result of mankind's sin, God placed the curse of death on the human race. While all men and women must die physically as a result of Adam and Eve's sin, each person dies spiritually for his or her own sins. Each person is responsible for himself, spiritually speaking. The theological position which states that we inherit the guilt of Adam's sin is false. We do not inherit the **guilt**; we inherit the **consequences**. And there is a great difference between the two.

Consider, as an illustration of this point, the family in which a drunken father arrives home late one evening, and in an alcoholic stupor severely beats his wife and children. His spouse and offspring suffer the consequences of his drunkenness, to be sure. But it would be absurd to suggest that they are guilty of it! The same concept applies in the spiritual realm. People die **physically** because of Adam's sin, but they die **spiritually** because of their own personal transgression of God's law. In Ezekiel 18:20, quoted earlier, the prophet went on to say: "The son shall not bear the iniquity of the father, neither shall the father bear the iniquity of the son: the righteousness of the righteous shall be upon him, and the wickedness of the wicked shall be upon him."

The Reality of Sin

The reality of sin is all around us, is it not? Consider the ways in which mankind has been affected by sin.

Physically—Disease and death were introduced into this world as a direct consequence of man's sin (Genesis 2:17; Romans 5:12).

Geophysically—Many features of the Earth's surface that allow for such tragedies as earthquakes, tornadoes, hurricanes, violent thunderstorms, etc. can be traced directly to the Great Flood of Noah's day (which came as the result of man's sin, Genesis 6:5ff.).

Culturally—The numerous communication problems that man experiences, due to the multiplicity of human languages, are traceable to ambitious rebellion on the part of our ancestors (Genesis 11: 1-9).

Psychologically—Man generally is without the peace of mind for which his heart longs (look at the number of psychiatrists in the Yellow Pages of any telephone book!). Isaiah opined: "They have made them crooked paths; whosoever goeth therein doth not know peace" (59:8; cf. 57:21).

Spiritually—By sinning, man created a chasm between himself and God (Isaiah 59:2). Unless remedied, this condition will result in man's being unable to escape the "judgment of hell" (Matthew 23:33), and in his being separated from God throughout all eternity (Revelation 21:8; 22:18-19).

The key phrase in the discussion above is that man's sin will result in an eternal separation from God **unless remedied**. The question then becomes: Has God provided such a remedy? Thankfully, the answer is: Yes, He has.

God's Remedy for Sin

Regardless of how desperate, or how pitiful, man's condition has become, one thing is certain: God had no **obligation** to provide a means of salvation for the ungrateful creature who so haughtily turned away from Him, His law, and His beneficence. The Scriptures make this apparent when they discuss the fact that angels sinned (2 Peter 2:4; Jude 6), and yet "not to angels doth he give help, but he giveth help to the seed of Abraham" (Hebrews 2:16).

The rebellious creatures that once inhabited the heavenly portals were not provided a redemptive plan. But man was! Little wonder the psalmist inquired: "What is **man**, that thou art mindful of **him**?" (8:4, emp. added).

Why would God go to such great lengths for mankind, when His mercy was not even extended to the angels that once surrounded His throne? Whatever answers may be proffered, there can be little doubt that the Creator's efforts on behalf of sinful man are the direct result of pure love. As a loving God (1 John 4:8), He acted out of a genuine concern, not for His own desires, but rather for those of His creation. And let us be forthright in acknowledging that Jehovah's love for mankind was completely **undeserved**. The Scriptures make it clear that God decided to offer salvation—our "way home"—even though we were ungodly, sinners, and enemies (note the specific use of those terms in Romans 5:6-10). The apostle John rejoiced in the fact that: "Herein is love, not that we loved God, but that He loved us" (1 John 4:10).

God's love is universal, and thus not discriminatory in any fashion (John 3:16). He would have **all men** to be saved (1 Timothy 2:4)—**if they would be** (John 5:40)—for He is not willing that **any** should perish (2 Peter 3:9). And, Deity's love is unquenchable. Read Romans 8:35-39 and be thrilled! Only man's wanton rejection of God's love can put him beyond the practical appropriation of heaven's offer of mercy and grace.

God's Plan In Preparation

Did God understand that man would rebel, and stand in eventual need of salvation from the perilous state of his own sinful condition? The Scriptures make it clear that He did. Inspiration speaks of a divine plan set in place even "before the foundation of the world" (Ephesians 1:4; 1 Peter 1:20). After the initial fall of man, humankind dredged itself deeper and deeper into wickedness. When approximately a century of preaching by the righteous Noah failed to bring mankind back into a right relationship with God, Jehovah sent a worldwide flood to purge the Earth (Genesis 6-8). From the faithful Noah, several generations later, the renowned Abraham was descended, and, through him, eventually the Hebrew nation would be established. From that nation, the Messiah—God incarnate—would come.

Some four centuries following Abraham, the Lord, through His servant Moses, gave to the Hebrews the written revelation that came to be known as the Law of Moses. Basically, this law-system had three distinct purposes. First, its intent was to define sin and sharpen Israel's awareness of it. To use Paul's expression in the New Testament, the law made "sin exceeding sinful" (Romans 7:7,13). Second, the law was designed to show man that he could not, by his own merit or efforts, save himself. For example, the law demanded perfect obedience, and since no mere man could keep it perfectly, all stood condemned (Galatians 3:10-11). Thus, the law underscored the need for a **Savior**—Someone Who could do for us what we were unable to do for ourselves. Third, in harmony with that need, the Old Testament pointed the way toward the coming of the Messiah. He was to be Immanuel—"God with us" (Matthew 1:23).

Mankind was prepared for the coming of the Messiah in several ways. **Theophanies** were temporary appearances of God in various forms (see Genesis 16:7ff.; 18:1ff.; 22:11ff., et al.). A careful examination of the facts leads to the conclusion that many of these manifestations were of the preincarnate Christ. In addition, the Old Testament contains **types** (pictorial previews) of the coming Messiah. For example, every bloody sacrifice was a symbol of the "Lamb of God that taketh away the sin of the world" (John 1: 29). Finally, there are more than 300 **prophecies** containing countless minute details that speak of the coming Prince of Peace. These prophecies name the city in which He was to be born, the purpose of His earthly sojourn, and even the exact manner of His death.

The simple fact is, Jehovah left no stone unturned in preparing the world for the coming of the One Who would save mankind. Through a variety of avenues, He alerted Earth's inhabitants to the importance of Him Who was yet to come, and to the urgency of complete belief in Him.

God's Plan In Action

One of God's attributes, as expressed within Scripture, is that He is an absolutely **holy** Being (see Revelation 4:8; Isaiah 6:3). As such, He cannot, and will not, ignore the fact of sin. The prophet Habakkuk wrote: "Thou that art of purer eyes than to behold evil, and thou canst not look on perverseness" (1:13). Yet another of God's attributes is that He is absolutely **just**. Righteousness and justice are the very foundation of His throne (Psalm 89:14). The irresistible truth arising from the fact that God is both holy and just is that **sin must be punished!**

If God were a cold, vengeful Creator (as some infidels wrongly assert), He simply could have banished mankind from His divine presence forever and that would have been the end of the matter. But the truth is, He is not that kind of God! Our Creator is loving (1 John 4:8) and "rich in mercy" (Ephesians 2:4). Thus, the problem became: How could a loving, merciful God pardon rebellious humanity?

Paul addressed this very matter in Romans 3. How could God be just, and yet a justifier of sinful man? The answer: He would find someone to stand in for us—someone to receive His retribution, and to bear our punishment. That "someone" would be Jesus Christ, the Son of God. He would become a substitutionary sacrifice, and personally would pay the price for human salvation. In one of the most moving tributes ever written to the Son of God, Isaiah summarized the situation like this:

> But he was wounded for our transgressions, he was bruised for our iniquities; the chastisement of our peace was upon

> him; and with his stripes we are healed. All we like sheep have gone astray; we have turned every one to his own way; and Jehovah hath laid on Him the iniquity of us all (53:5-6).

Jehovah's intent was to extend His grace and mercy freely—through the redemptive life and death of His Son (Romans 3:24ff.). As a member of the Godhead, Christ took upon Himself the form of a man. He came to Earth as a human being (John 1:1-4,14; Philippians 2:5-11; 1 Timothy 3:16), and thus shared our full nature and life-experiences. He even was tempted in all points, just we are, yet He never yielded to that temptation (Hebrews 4:15).

But what has this to do with us? Since Christ was tried (Isaiah 28:16), and yet found perfect (2 Corinthians 5:21; 1 Peter 2:22), He alone could satisfy heaven's requirement for justice. He alone could serve as the "propitiation" (atoning sacrifice) for our sins. Just as the lamb without blemish that was used in Old Testament sacrifices could be the (temporary) propitiation for the Israelites' sins, so the "Lamb of God" (John 1:29) could be the (permanent) propitiation for mankind's sins.

In the gift of Christ, Heaven's mercy was extended; in the death of the Lamb of God, divine justice was satisfied; and, in the resurrection of Christ, God's plan was documented and sealed historically forever!

Mankind's Appropriation of God's Gift of Salvation

As wonderful as God's gift of salvation is, there is one thing it is not. It is not **unconditional**. Mankind has a part to play in this process. While the gift of salvation itself is free (in the sense that the price levied already has been paid by Christ), God will not **force** salvation on anyone. Rather, man must—by the exercise of his personal volition and free moral agency—do something to accept the pardon that heaven offers. What is that "something"?

In His manifold dealings with mankind, Jehovah has stressed repeatedly the principle that man, if he would be justified, must live "by faith" (see Habakkuk 2:4; Romans 1:17; Galatians 3:11; Hebrews 10:38). Salvation has been available across the centuries, conditioned upon God's foreknowledge of the atoning death of Christ upon the Cross at Calvary (see Galatians 4:4-5; Hebrews 9:15-17; 10:1ff.). Yet "living by faith" never denoted a mere "mental ascent" of certain facts. Instead, "living by faith" denoted **active obedience**.

Faith consists of three elements: (1) an acknowledgment of historical facts; (2) a willingness to trust the Lord; and (3) a wholehearted submission (obedience) to the divine will. Furthermore, we should remember that faith has not always—for all men, in all circumstances—required the same things. It always has required obedience, but obedience itself has not always demanded the same response.

For example, in God's earliest dealings with men, obedient faith required that those men offer animal sacrifices at the family altar (Genesis 4:4). Later, God dealt with the nation of Israel, giving them the law at Mount Sinai (Exodus 20). Under that law, animal sacrifices continued, along with the observance of certain feast days and festivals. Acceptable faith, under whatever law that was then in force, demanded obedience to the will of God.

The Scriptures are clear that "obedience of faith" (Romans 1:5; 16:26) is based on the Word of God (Romans 10:13), and that both the faith and the obedience are demonstrated by **action**. Hebrews 11, in fact, devotes itself to an examination of that very concept. "By faith" Abel **offered**. "By faith" Noah **prepared**. "By faith" Abraham **obeyed**. "By faith," Moses **refused**. And so on. Even the casual reader cannot help but be impressed with the heroes of faith listed in Hebrews 11:32-40, and the **action** they took **because of their faith**. Writing by inspiration, James observed that faith, divorced from obedience, is dead (James 2:26). What, then, is involved in this "obedience of faith" in regard to salvation? What must a person **do** to be saved?

Several critically important questions need to be asked here. First, where is salvation found? Paul told Timothy: "Therefore I endure all things for the elect's sake, that they also may obtain **the salvation which is in Christ Jesus** with eternal glory" (2 Timothy 2:10, emp. added).

Second, where are all spiritual blessings found? They are found only "in Christ." Paul wrote in Ephesians 1:3: "Blessed be the God and Father of our Lord Jesus Christ, who hath blessed us with every spiritual blessing in the heavenly places **in Christ**" (emp. added).

Third, and most importantly, how, then, does one get "into Christ"? In other words, how does the alien sinner rid himself of his soul-damning sin? What "obedience of faith" is required to appropriate the free gift of salvation that places him "in Christ"?

The Road Home: Salvation Through "Obedience of Faith"

The only way to find the "road home" to heaven is to follow God's directions **exactly**. There are numerous things God has commanded that a person **must do** in order to enjoin the "obedience of faith" and thereby receive the free gift of salvation. According to God's Word, in order to be saved a person must do the following.

First, the sinner must **hear** God's Word (Romans 10:17). Obviously, one cannot follow God's commands if he has not heard them, so God commanded that people hear what He has said regarding salvation.

Second, one who is lost cannot be saved if he does not **believe** what he hears. So, God commanded that belief ensue (John 3:16; Acts 16:31).

Third, one who is lost cannot obtain salvation if he is unwilling to **repent** of his sins and seek forgiveness (Luke 13:3). Without repentance he will continue in sin; thus, God commanded repentance.

Fourth, since Christ is the basis of our salvation, God commanded the penitent sinner to **confess** before men a belief in Him as the Son of God (Romans 10:9-10).

However, this is not all that God commanded. Hearing, believing, repentance, and confession—as important and as essential as they are—will not rid a person of sin. The overriding question is: **How does one get rid of sin**? Numerous times within the pages of the New Testament, that question is asked and answered. The Jews who had murdered Christ, and to whom Peter spoke on the Day of Pentecost when he ushered in the Christian age, asked that question. Peter's sermon had convicted them. They were convinced that they were sinners and, as such, desperately in need of salvation at the hand of an almighty God. Their question then became: "Brethren, what shall we do?" (Acts 2:37). Peter's response could not have been any clearer than it was. He told them: "Repent ye, and **be baptized** every one of you in the name of Jesus Christ **unto the remission of your sins**" (Acts 2:38, emp. added). Saul, who later would become Paul, the famous apostle to the Gentiles, needed an answer to that same question. While on a trip to Damascus for the explicit purpose of persecuting Christians, Saul was blinded (see Acts 22). Realizing his plight, he asked: "What shall I do, Lord?" (Acts 22:10). When God's servant, Ananias, appeared to Saul in the city, he answered Saul's question by commanding: "And now why tarriest thou? Arise, and **be baptized, and wash away thy sins**" (Acts 22:16, emp. added).

What, then, is the correct, biblical answer regarding how one rids himself of soul-damning sin? The biblical solution is that the person who has heard the gospel, who has believed its message, who has repented of past sins, and who has confessed Christ as Lord must then—in order to receive remission (forgiveness) of sins—be baptized. [The English word "baptize" is a transliteration of the Greek word *baptizo,* meaning to immerse, dip, plunge beneath, or submerge (Thayer, 1958, p. 94).]

Further, it is baptism that puts a person "in Christ." Paul told the first-century Christians in Rome:

> Or are ye ignorant that all we who were baptized into Christ Jesus were baptized into his death? We were buried therefore with him through baptism into death: that like as Christ was raised from the dead through the glory of the Father, so we also might walk in newness of life (Romans 6:3-4).

Paul told the Galatians: "For as many of you as were **baptized into Christ** did put on Christ" (3:37, emp. added). Little wonder, then, that Peter spoke of baptism as that which saves (1 Peter 3:21).

Numerous New Testament writers made the point that it is only when we come into contact with Christ's blood that our sins can be washed away (Ephesians 1:7-8; Revelation 5:9; Romans 5:8-9; Hebrews 9:12-14). The question arises: **When** did Jesus shed His blood? The answer, of course, is that He shed His blood on the Cross at His death (John 19:31-34). Where, and how, does one come into contact with Christ's blood to obtain the forgiveness of sin that such contact ensures? Paul answered that question when he wrote to the Christians in Rome. It is only in baptism that contact with the blood, and the death, of Christ is made (Romans 6:3-11). Further, the ultimate hope of our resurrection (to live with Him in heaven) is linked to baptism. Paul wrote of "having been buried with him in baptism, wherein ye were raised with him through faith in the working of God, who raised him from the dead" (Colossians 2:12). If we are not baptized, we remain in sin. If we are not baptized, we have no hope of the resurrection that leads to heaven.

Baptism, of course, is no less, or more, important than any other of God's commands regarding what to do to be saved (see Jackson, 1997c). But it is **essential**, and one cannot be saved without it. Is baptism a command of God? Yes (Acts 10:48). Is baptism where the remission of sins occurs? Yes (Acts 2:38; Acts 22:16; 1 Peter 3:21).

Some, who no doubt mean well, teach that a person is saved by "faith only." That is, people are taught simply to "pray and ask Jesus to come into their hearts" so that they might be saved from their sins. This teaching, though widespread, is completely at odds with the Bible's specific instructions regarding what one must do to be saved.

First, the Scriptures teach quite clearly that God does not hear (i.e., hear to respond with forgiveness) the prayer of an alien sinner (Psalm 34:15-16; Proverbs 15:29; Proverbs 28:9). Thus, the sinner can pray as long and as hard as he wants, but God has stated plainly exactly how a person is to be saved. This makes perfect sense, since in John 14:6 Christ taught: "I am the way, and the truth, and the life; no one cometh to the Father but by me." The alien sinner cannot approach God on his own, and, as an alien sinner, has no advocate to do so on his behalf. That is one of the spiritual blessings reserved for Christians (Ephesians 1:3). Thus, it is fruitless for an alien sinner to pray to God to "send Jesus into his heart." God does not hear (i.e., hear to respond to) such a request.

Second, the Scriptures plainly teach that man **cannot be saved by faith alone**. James, in his epistle, remarked that indeed, a man may be justified (i.e., saved), but "not only by faith" (James 2:24). This, too, makes perfectly good sense. As James had observed only a few verses earlier: "Thou believest that God is one; thou doest well; the demons also believe, and shudder" (James 2:19). It is not enough merely to believe. Even the demons who inhabit the eternal regions of hell believe. But they hardly are saved (see 2 Peter 2:4). It is obvious, therefore, that mere faith **alone** is insufficient to save mankind.

Also, where, exactly, in the Scriptures does it teach that, in order to be saved, one should to "pray to ask Jesus to come into his heart"? Through the years, I have asked many within various religious groups this important question. But I have yet to find anyone who could provide a single biblical reference to substantiate such a claim.

Salvation is not conditioned on prayer; it is conditioned on the "obedience of faith." The case of Saul provides a good example. As Christ's enemy-turned-penitent, he prayed earnestly while living in his blind state in the city of Damascus. Yet the fact remains that his sins were removed ("washed away") only when he obeyed God's command (as verbalized by Ananias) to be baptized. Prayer could not wash away Saul's sins. But the Lord's blood could—at the point of baptism (Hebrews 9:22; Ephesians 5:26).

Objections to God's Plan of Salvation

Whenever the topic of salvation is discussed, it is not unusual to hear certain objections to God's designated plan. At times, such objections result from a misunderstanding of the steps involved in the salvation process (or the reasons for those steps). On occasion, however, the objections result from a stubborn refusal to acquiesce to God's commands regarding what constitutes salvation. I would like to consider three such objections here.

Is Salvation the Result of "Baptismal Regeneration"?

Is the forgiveness of sins that results from being baptized due to some special power within the water? No. "Baptismal regeneration" is the idea that there is a miraculous power in the water that produces salvation (i.e., regeneration). As Wayne Jackson has noted: "...the notion that baptism is a 'sacrament' which has a sort of mysterious, innate power to remove the contamination of sin—independent of personal faith and a volitional submission to God's plan of redemption"—is plainly at odds with biblical teaching (1997b, 32:45). An examination of the Old Testament (which serves as our "tutor" [Galatians 3:24] and contains things "for our learning" [Romans 15:4]) provides important instruction regarding this principle. When Naaman the leper was told by Elijah to dip seven times in the Jordan River, at first he refused, but eventually obeyed—and was healed. However, there was no meritorious power in the muddy waters of the Jordan. Naaman was healed because He did exactly what God commanded him to do, in exactly the way God commanded him to do it.

This was true of the Israelites' salvation as well. On one occasion when they sinned, and God began to slay them for their unrighteousness, those who wished to repent and be spared were commanded to look upon a brass serpent on a pole in the midst of the camp (Numbers 21:1-9). There was no meritorious power in the serpent. Rather, the Israelites were saved from destruction because they did exactly what God commanded them to do, in exactly the way God commanded them to do it.

The New Testament presents the same principle. Jesus once encountered a man born blind (John 9). Then Lord spat on the ground, made a spittle/clay potion, and placed it over the man's eyes. He then instructed the man to "go, wash in the pool of Siloam" (John 9:7). Was there medicinal power in Siloam's waters? No. It was the man's obedient faith that produced the end-result, not some miraculous power in the water.

What would have happened if the man had refused to obey Christ, or had altered the Lord's command? Suppose the man had reasoned: "If I wash in Siloam, some may think I am trusting in the **water** to be healed. Others may think that I am attempting to perform some kind of 'work' to 'merit' regaining my sight. Therefore I simply will 'have faith in' Christ, but I will **not** dip in the pool of Siloam." Would the man have been healed? Most certainly not!

What if Noah, during the construction of the ark, had followed God's instructions to the letter, except for the fact that he decided to build the ark out of a material other than the gopher wood that God had commanded? Would Noah and his family have been saved? Most certainly not! Noah would have been guilty of violating God's commandments, since he had not done **exactly** as God commanded him. Did not Jesus Himself say: "If ye love me, ye will **keep My commandments**" (John 14:15, emp. added)?

Peter used the case of Noah to discuss the relationship of baptism to salvation. He stated unequivocally that baptism is involved in salvation when he noted that, just as Noah and his family were transported from a polluted environment of corruption into a realm of deliverance, so in baptism we are moved from the polluted environment of defilement into a realm of redemption. It is by baptism that one enters "into Christ" (Romans 6:4; Galatians 3:27), wherein salvation is found (2 Timothy 2:10). In Ephesians 5:26 and Titus 3:35, Paul described baptism as a "washing of water" or a "washing of regeneration" wherein the sinner is "cleansed" or "saved." [Baptist theologian A.T. Robertson admitted that both of these passages refer specifically to water baptism (1931, 4:607).] The power of baptism to remove sin lies not in the water, but in the God Who commanded the sinner to be baptized in the first place.

Is Baptism a Human Work?

Is baptism a meritorious human work? No. But is it required for a person to be saved? Yes. How is this possible? The Bible clearly teaches that we are **not** saved by works (Titus 3:4-7; Ephesians 2: 9). Yet the Bible clearly teaches we **are** saved by works (James 2: 14-24). Since inspiration guarantees that the Scriptures never will contradict themselves, it is obvious that **two different kinds of works** are under consideration in these passages.

The New Testament mentions at least four kinds of works: (1) works of the Law of Moses (Galatians 2:16; Romans 3:20); (2) works of the flesh (Galatians 5:19-21); (3) works of merit (Titus 3:4-7); and (4) works resulting from obedience of faith (James 2:14-24). This last category often is referred to as "works of God." This phrase does not mean works **performed by** God; rather, the intent is "works **required and approved by** God" (Thayer, 1958, p. 248; cf. Jackson, 1997c, 32:47). Consider the following example from Jesus' statements in John 6:27-29:

> Work not for the food which perisheth, but for the food which abideth unto eternal life.... They said therefore unto him, What must we do, that we may work the **works of God**? Jesus answered and said unto them, This is the **work of God**, that ye believe on him whom he hath sent.

Within this context, Christ made it clear that there are certain works that humans must perform in order to receive eternal life. Moreover, the passage affirms that believing itself is a work ("This is the **work** of God, that ye **believe** on him whom he hath sent"). It therefore follows that if one is saved **without any type of works**, then he is saved **without faith**, because **faith is a work**. Such a conclusion would throw the Bible into hopeless confusion!

In addition, it should be noted that repentance from sin is a divinely appointed work for man to perform prior to his reception of salvation. The people of ancient Nineveh "repented" at Jonah's preaching (Matthew 12:41), yet the Old Testament record relates that "God saw their **works**, that they turned from their evil way" (Jonah 3:10). Thus, if one can be saved without **any kind** of works, he can be saved **without repentance**. Yet Jesus Himself declared that without repentance, one will surely perish (Luke 13:3,5).

But what about baptism? The New Testament **specifically excludes** baptism from the class of human meritorious works unrelated to redemption. The context of Titus 3:4-7 reveals the following information. (1) We **are not saved** by works of righteousness that we do by ourselves (i.e., according to any plan or course of action that we devised—see Thayer, p. 526). (2) We **are saved** by the "washing of regeneration" (i.e., baptism), exactly as 1 Peter 3:21 states. (3) Thus, baptism is excluded from all works of human righteousness that men contrive, but is itself a "work of God" (i.e., required and approved by God) necessary for salvation. When one is raised from the watery grave of baptism, it is according to the "working of God" (Colossians 2:12), and not any man-made plan. No one can suggest (justifiably) that baptism is a meritorious work of human design. When we are baptized, we are completely passive, and thus hardly can have performed any kind of "work." Instead, we have obeyed God through saving faith. Our "works of God" were belief, repentance, confession, and baptism—all commanded by the Scriptures of one who would receive salvation as the free gift of God (Romans 6:23).

Is the Baptism Associated with Salvation Holy Spirit Baptism?

To circumvent the connection between water baptism and salvation, some have suggested that the baptism discussed in passages such as Acts 2:38, Acts 22:16, and 1 Peter 3:21 is Holy Spirit baptism. But such a position cannot be correct. Christ commanded His followers—after His death and ascension—to go into all the world and "make disciples of all the nations, baptizing them into the name of the Father and of the Son and of the Holy Spirit" (Matthew 28:18-20). That same command applies no less to Christians today.

During the early parts of the first century, we know there was more than one baptism in existence (e.g., John's baptism, Holy Spirit baptism, Christ's baptism, etc.). But by the time Paul wrote his epistle to the Christians who lived in Ephesus, **only one** of those baptisms remained. He stated specifically in Ephesians 4:4-5: "There is one body, and one Spirit, even as also ye were called in one hope of your calling; one Lord, one faith, **one baptism**." Which **one** baptism remained? One thing we know for certain: Christ never would give His disciples a command that they could not carry out.

The Scriptures, however, teach that Jesus administers baptism of the Holy Spirit (Matthew 3:11; Luke 3:15-17). Yet Christians were commanded to baptize those whom they taught, and who believed (John 3:16), repented of their sins (Luke 13:3), and confessed Christ as the Son of God (Matthew 10:32). It is clear, then, that the baptism commanded by Christ was not Holy Spirit baptism. If it were, Christ would be put in the untenable position of having commanded His disciples to do something they could not do—baptize in the Holy Spirit. However, they **could** baptize in **water**, which is exactly what they did. And that is exactly what we still are doing today. Baptism in the Holy Spirit no longer is available; only water baptism remains, and is the one true baptism commanded by Christ for salvation (Ephesians 4:4-5; Mark 16:16; Acts 2:38).

When a person does precisely what the Lord has commanded, he has not "merited" or "earned" salvation. Rather, his obedience is evidence of his faith (James 2:18). Are we saved by God's grace? Indeed we are (Ephesians 2:8-9). But the fact that we are saved by grace does not negate human responsibility in obeying God's commands. Every person who wishes to be saved must exhibit the "obedience of faith" commanded within God's Word (Romans 1:5; 16:26). A part of that obedience is adhering to God's command to be baptized.

Conclusion

The biblical message—from Genesis 1 to Revelation 22—is that mankind is in a woefully sinful condition and desperately in need of help in order to find his way "back home." A corollary to that message is that God takes no pleasure in the death of the wicked (Ezekiel 18:23; 33:11) and genuinely desires that all should be saved (John 3:16). But in order to be saved, one must do **exactly** what God commanded, in **exactly** the way God commanded it. When a person hears, believes, repents, confesses, and is baptized for the forgiveness of his sins, that person becomes a Christian—nothing more, and nothing less. God Himself then adds that new Christian to His Son's one true body—the church. The child of God who remains faithful even unto death (Revelation 2:10) is promised a crown of life and eternity in heaven as a result of his faith, his obedience, God's mercy, and God's grace (John 14:15; Ephesians 2:8-9; Romans 1:5). What a joyous thought—to experience the "abundant life" (John 10:10b) with a "peace that passeth understanding" (Philippians 4:7) here and now, and then to be rewarded with a home in heaven in the hereafter (John 14:2-3). What a joyous thought indeed!

CHAPTER 12

THE ESSENTIALITY AND SINGULARITY OF CHRIST'S CHURCH

But when the fulness of the time came," the apostle Paul wrote, "God sent forth his Son, born of a woman, born under the law, that he might redeem them that were under the law, that we might receive the adoption of sons" (Galatians 4:4-5). God incarnate had come to Earth, bringing the "good news" about the last and final covenant that Heaven would make with man. The series of events that began with the birth of Christ in Bethlehem, and culminated in His death, burial, and resurrection outside Jerusalem approximately thirty-three years later, stirred a whirlwind of controversy in the first century. Nineteen centuries later, it still does.

To the Christian, there is little of more importance than the proclamation and defense of the Old Jerusalem Gospel that is able to save men's souls. Christianity did not come into the world with a whimper, but a bang. It was not in the first century, neither is it intended to be in the twentieth, something "done in a corner." Instead, it arrived like a trumpet's clarion call.

Christ spent three-and-a-half years teaching in order to make disciples. When finally He was ready to call them to action, it was not for a quiet retreat into the peaceful, nearby hills. He never intended that they be "holy men" who set themselves apart to spend each hour of every day in serene meditation. Rather, they were to be soldiers—fit for a spiritual battle against the forces of evil (Ephesians 6: 10-17). Jesus called for action, self-denial, uncompromising love for truth, and zeal coupled with knowledge. His words to those who would follow Him were: "If any man would come after me, let him deny himself, and take up his cross, and follow me" (Mark 8:34). And many did.

The teaching did not stop when Christ left to return to His home in heaven. He had trained others—apostles and disciples—to continue the task He had begun. They were sent to the uttermost parts of the Earth with the mandate to proclaim the gospel boldly via preaching and teaching (Matthew 28:18-20). This they did daily (Acts 5:42). The result was additional, new disciples. They too, then, were instructed and grounded in the fundamentals of God's Word (Acts 2:42) and sent on their way to teach still others.

The results were extraordinary indeed. In a single day, in a single city, over 3,000 constituted the original church as a result of the teaching they had heard from Christ's apostles (see Acts 2:41). In fact, so effective was this kind of instruction that the enemies of Christianity attempted to prohibit any further public teaching (Acts 4:18; 5:28), yet to no avail. Nineteen centuries later, the theme of the Cross still is alive, vibrant, and forceful. Christianity's central message, the manner in which that message was taught, and the dedication of those into whose hands it had been placed, were too powerful for even its bitterest foes to abate or defeat. That Christianity continues to be taught, and continues to thrive, is evidence aplenty of this fact.

While it may be true to say that some religions flourish best in secrecy, such is not the case with Christianity. It is intended both to be presented, and to be defended, in the marketplace of ideas. In addition, while some religions eschew open investigation and critical evaluation, Christianity welcomes both. Of all the major religions based upon an individual rather than a mere ideology, it is the only one that claims, and can document, an empty tomb for its Founder.

Furthermore, Christians, unlike adherents to some other religions, do not have an option regarding the distribution and/or dissemination of their faith. The efficacy of God's saving grace—as made possible through His Son, Jesus Christ—is a message that all accountable people need to hear, and one that Christians are commanded to proclaim (John 3:16; Matthew 28:18-20; cf. Ezekiel 33:7-9).

Christ's Church—His Singular, Unique Body of Saved Believers

At Caesarea Philippi, situated at the base of Mount Hermon that rises several thousand feet above it, Jesus asked His disciples how the public viewed Him. "Who do men say that the Son of man is?," He inquired (Matthew 16:13). The reply of the disciples was: "Some say, John the Baptist; some, Elijah; and others, Jeremiah, or one of the prophets" (16:14). But Jesus delved deeper when He asked the disciples: "But who say ye that I am?" (16:15). Ever the impulsive one, Simon Peter quickly answered: "Thou art the Christ, the Son of the living God" (16:16). Jesus' response to Peter was this:

> Blessed art thou, Simon Bar-Jonah: for flesh and blood hath not revealed it unto thee, but my Father who is in heaven. And I also say unto thee, that thou art Peter, and upon this rock I will build my church; and the gates of Hades shall not prevail against it (16:17-18).

Jesus had come—"in the fulness of time"—to bring the one thing that all the Earth's inhabitants needed. From Cain, the first murderer, to the lawless men who eventually would put Him to death on the cross, mankind desperately needed the salvation that the heavenly plan would provide. In writing to the young evangelist Timothy, Paul observed that it had been God's plan to save men through Christ even before the foundation of the world. He wrote of God, "who saved us, and called us with a holy calling, not according to our works, but according to his own purpose and grace, which was given us in Christ Jesus before times eternal" (2 Timothy 1: 9). Through His foreknowledge, God knew that man one day would need redemption from sin. In fact, throughout the history of Israel, God made both promises and prophecies concerning a coming kingdom and its King. The promise was that from David's seed, God would build a "house" and "kingdom" (2 Samuel 7:11-17—a promise, incidentally, that was reaffirmed in Psalm 132:11 and preached as reality by Peter in Acts 2:29-34 when the church began). Seven hundred years before Christ's arrival, the prophet Isaiah foretold:

> For unto us a child is born, unto us a son is given; and the government shall be upon his shoulder: and his name shall be called Wonderful, Counsellor, Mighty God, Everlasting Father, Prince of Peace. Of the increase of his government and of peace there shall be no end, upon the throne of David, and upon his kingdom, to establish it, and to uphold it with justice and with righteousness from henceforth even for ever. The zeal of Jehovah of hosts will perform this (Isaiah 9:6-7).

Thus, Christ's exclamation to Peter that the building of His church would be upon a "rock" was nothing more than what the Old Testament prophets had foretold hundreds of years before. Isaiah prophesied: "Therefore, thus saith the Lord Jehovah, Behold, I lay in Zion for a foundation a stone, a tried stone, a precious corner-stone of sure foundation: he that believeth shall not be in haste" (Isaiah 28: 16). Later, Peter himself—through inspiration, and no doubt with the events of Caesarea Philippi still fresh on his mind—would make reference to this very rock foundation when he wrote about the "living stone, rejected indeed of men.... The stone which the builders rejected, the same was made the head of the corner" (1 Peter 2:4,7). In fact, even Jesus Himself mentioned the "rejected stone" of Old Testament allusion. In Matthew 21:42, Mark 12:10, and Luke 20:17, He made reference to the psalmist's statement about "the stone which the builders rejected is become the head of the corner" (Psalm 118:22), and applied the rejection of the stone by the builders to the Sanhedrin's rejection and repudiation of Him.

Sadly, some today erroneously teach that Christ's church was established out of desperation as an "emergency measure" set in motion when the Jews rejected Him as Savior. The basis for such a view is the idea that Jesus presented Himself to the Jewish nation as its Messiah but was rebuffed—a rejection that came as an unexpected surprise to Him and His Father. Christ's failure to convince the Jews of His rightful place as their King forced Him to have to re-evaluate, and eventually delay, His plans—His intention being to re-establish His kingdom at some distant point in the future. In the meantime, the story goes, He established the church in order to allay temporarily the complete failure of His mission.

However, such a view ignores the inspired writers' observations that "before times eternal" God had set in motion His plan for man's salvation as His Son's church. [The Greek word *ekklesia*, translated "church" in the English, denotes God's "called out."] It ignores the Old Testament prophecies that specifically predicted Christ's rejection by the Jews. And, it ignores Christ's own allusions to those prophecies during His earthly ministry. But worst of all, it impeaches the omniscience of both God and His Son by suggesting that they were "caught off guard" by the Jews' rejection of Christ as the Messiah, thus causing Heaven's emissary to have to rethink His plans. What an offensive and unscriptural view this is!

Jesus was a man with a mission—and He completed successfully what He had come to accomplish. Deity had come to Earth, taking the form of a servant (Philippians 2:7) to communicate the truth (John 8:32) about the lost state in which man now found himself (Romans 3:23; 6:23), and to pay the ransom for man (Matthew 20:28), thereby extricating him from a situation from which he could not extricate himself (Jeremiah 10:23).

When Christ died upon the cross, it was not for any sin that He personally had committed. Though He was tempted in all points like as we are, He did not sin (Hebrews 4:15). When Peter wrote that Jesus "did not sin," he employed a verbal tense which suggests that the Lord never sinned—not even once (1 Peter 2:22). Isaiah repeatedly emphasized the substitutionary nature of the Lord's death when he wrote: "But he was wounded for our transgressions, he was bruised for our iniquities; the chastisement of our peace was upon him; and with his stripes we are healed.... Jehovah hath laid on him the iniquity of us all" (Isaiah 53:5-6). When the prophet declared that our "iniquity" was laid upon the Son of God, he employed a figure of speech known as metonymy (wherein one thing is used to designate another). In this case, the cause is being used for the effect. In other words, God did not actually put our **sins** upon Christ; He put the **penalty** of our wrongs upon His Son at Calvary. Yet, in spite of the fact that all sinners deserve to be lost, God provided a way to "escape the judgment of hell" (Matthew 23:33).

Jesus made it clear that He would provide this way of escape through a plan that would result in the establishment of His church —i.e., His body of "the called out." The first messianic prophecy was to be fulfilled: Satan would bruise the Lord's heel, but the Lord would triumph and bruise Satan's head (Genesis 3:15). Against the building of Christ's church, not even the Gates of Hades could prevail (Matthew 16:18).

Further, there would be one and only one church. Paul wrote that Christ "is the head of **the body, the church**" (Colossians 1: 18). In Ephesians 1:22, he stated concerning Christ that God "gave him to be head over all things to the church, **which is his body**." Thus, Paul clearly identified the body as the church. Three chapters later, however, in Ephesians 4:4, Paul stated: "There is **one body**." Expressed logically, one might reason as follows:

> There is one body (Ephesians 4:4).
>
> But Christ is the Savior of the body (Ephesians 5:22).
>
> Thus, Christ is the Savior of **one body.**

And,

Christ is the Savior of one body.

But the body is the church (Eph. 1:22-23; Col.1:18,24).

Thus, Christ is the Savior of **one** church.

The body, Christ's church, would be known as "the church of the Lord" (Acts 20:28), "the church of God" (1 Corinthians 1:2; Galatians 1:13), "the house of God" (1 Timothy 3:15), "the household of faith" (Galatians 6:10), and "the kingdom of God" (Acts 28:23, 31). The Lord's people were to bear Christ's name (Acts 11:26; 26:28; 1 Peter 4:16). The church would be His bride (Revelation 21:2), His wife (Revelation 19:7-8), and His kingdom (Revelation 1:9). Those in it would be victorious over Satan and death forever (1 Corinthians 15:26,54-56; 2 Timothy 1:9-10).

Unfortunately, men sought to alter the divine plan and to infuse it with their own personal belief systems. Thus, the concept of denominationalism was born. Denominationalism, however, is unknown to, and unauthorized by, the Word of God. A denomination is defined as "a class or kind having a specific name or value." We speak of various monetary denominations—a five-dollar bill, a ten-dollar bill, etc. They all are different. The same is true of religious denominations. They all are different.

Denominationalism ignores the singularity and uniqueness of the true church, and instead establishes various groups teaching conflicting doctrines that are antagonistic both to the Bible and to each other. It also ignores the church's relationship to Christ, which is described so beautifully in Ephesians 5 where Paul reminded first-century Christians that "the husband is the head of the wife, as Christ also is the head of the church" (5:23). The apostle's point is well taken. In a physical context, the wife is the bride and the husband is the bridegroom; in a spiritual context, the church is the bride and Christ is the bridegroom (the same point reiterated by John in Revelation 21:9). In Acts, Peter discussed Christ's relationship to His church when he observed that "neither is there any other name under heaven, that is given among men, wherein we must be saved" (4:12).

Denominations are man-made institutions that neither are recognized in, nor sanctioned by, the Word of God. The simple truth of the matter is that John the Baptist—while a marvelous harbinger of the Messiah—did not die to establish the church. Why, then, be a member of a denomination bearing his name? As great a reformer as Martin Luther was, the fact remains that he did not die to establish the church. Why, then, be a member of a denomination bearing his name? The early church's presbyters (i.e., elders, bishops, overseers) did not give their lives on a cross to establish the church. Why, then, be a member of a denomination named after such men? The Bible—although it accurately prophesies the coming of the church and historically documents its arrival—did not make possible the church. Why, then, be a member of a "Bible church"? Instead, should not Christians seek to be simply a member of the singular church that honors Christ's authority, and that He purchased with His blood? It is His bride; He is its bridegroom. His congregations are called the "churches of Christ" (Romans 16:16).

Those who are true New Testament Christians are those who have done exactly what God has commanded them to do to be saved, in exactly the way God has commanded that it be done. In so doing, they have not "joined" some man-made religious denomination that, like a five-dollar bill is one denomination among many others, is simply one religious group among many others. If the church is the body, and there is only one body, then there is only one church. Further, one does not "join" the church. The Scriptures teach that as a person is saved, God Himself "adds" that person to the one true church (Acts 2:41) that bears His Son's name.

Christ's Church—His Divinely Designed, Blood-Bought, Spirit-Filled Kingdom

During His earthly ministry, Jesus taught: "All authority hath been given unto me in heaven and on earth" (Matthew 28:18). Having such authority from His Father, He alone possessed the right to be Head of the church, His singular body of believers (Ephesians 1:22-23; Colossians 1:18). Recognizing Christ's position as authoritative Head of the church, Paul was constrained to remind Christians: "And whatsoever ye do, in word or in deed, do all in the name of [by the authority of—BT] the Lord Jesus" (Colossians 3:17).

Christ announced while on Earth that He would build His church (Matthew 16:18). It would be divinely designed (John 10:25; Acts 2:23), blood bought (Acts 20:28), and Spirit filled (1 Corinthians 6:19-20; Romans 8:9-10). On Pentecost following the Lord's death, burial, and resurrection, Peter rebuked the Jews for their duplicity in killing God's Son, and convicted them of their sin of murder (Acts 2:22-23). Luke recorded that they were "pricked in their heart" and sought to make restitution and be forgiven (Acts 2:27). On that fateful day, at least 3,000 people were added together by God to constitute Christ's church (Acts 2:41). Later, Luke noted that great fear fell upon the **whole church** as a result of God's having disciplined sinners within it (Acts 5:11). There is no doubt that the church was established in Christ's generation.

The Bible speaks of the church as Christ's kingdom. Jesus said the time for its coming had been "fulfilled" (Mark 1:15) and that the kingdom was as near as the very generation of people to whom He spoke, since some of them would not taste of death before they saw the kingdom of heaven come (Mark 9:1). Paul taught that the church is constituted of saints (1 Corinthians 1:1-2). But when he wrote his epistle to the Colossians (c. A.D. 62), he specifically stated that by that time the saints in the church at Colossae were subjects in "the kingdom of the Son of his love" (Colossians 1:13).

If the kingdom had not been established, then Paul erred in saying that the Colossians already were in it. [Those who teach that the church and the kingdom are separate, and that the kingdom has yet to arrive, must contend that there are living on the Earth today some of the very people to whom Jesus spoke nearly 2,000 years ago—since He stated that some who heard Him **would not die until the kingdom had come** (Mark 9:1).]

The New Testament teaches that the **church** is composed of individuals purchased with the blood of Christ (Acts 20:28), and that those so purchased were made to be a **kingdom** (Revelation 1:5-6; 5:9-10). Since the church and the kingdom both are composed of blood-purchased individuals, the church and the kingdom must be the same. And since the Christians that constitute the church were themselves translated into the kingdom, it is conclusive that the church and the kingdom **are the same**. The establishment of the kingdom coincided with the establishment of the church. Not only did the Lord foretell both the establishment of the kingdom and the church in His generation, but the New Testament writers spoke of both the church and the kingdom as being in existence during the very generation of His arrival (i.e., the first century).

Christ's Triumphant Church

From the first to the last of His earthly ministry, Jesus admonished those who would be His disciples that they would be both controversial and persecuted. He warned them:

> Think not that I came to send peace on the earth: I came not to send peace, but a sword. For I came to set a man at variance against his father and the daughter against her mother, and the daughter in law against her mother in law: and a man's foes shall be they of his own household (Matthew 10: 34-36).

Jesus wanted no misunderstanding about the trials and tribulations His followers would endure. He constantly reminded them of such (Matthew 10:16,39; 16:24; 24:9; John 15:2,18,20; 16:1-2; 21:18-19). While He desired that men be at peace with men, His primary goal was to bring men to a peaceful, covenant relationship with God. In addressing the Christians at Rome, Paul wrote:

> Who shall separate us from the love of Christ? shall tribulation, or anguish, or persecution, or famine, or nakedness, or peril, or sword?... Nay, in all these things we are more than conquerors through him that loved us. For I am persuaded that neither death, nor life, nor angels, nor principali-

> ties, nor things present, nor things to come, nor powers, nor height, nor depth, nor any other creature, shall be able to separate us from the love of God, which is in Christ Jesus our Lord (Romans 8:35,37-39).

Christ alerted His followers to the pressure yet to be brought upon them by other religions (Matthew 10:17), by civil governments (Matthew 10:18), and even by some of their own (2 Thessalonians 4:1ff.). He said: "And ye shall be hated of all men for my name's sake" (Matthew 10:22). History records that Christ's words accurately depicted what was to befall those early saints. As James O. Baird has noted: "In actuality, Christianity was opposed more vigorously than any other religion in the long history of Rome" (1978, p. 29).

Persecution against the church was, and is, rooted in the nature and work of Christ: "But me it hateth, because I testify of it, that its works are evil" (John 7:7). The world hated Christ because of the judgment He brought against what the world is, does, and loves. It will hate those in the church who remind it—by word and by deed —of this judgment. Jesus lamented: "If the world hateth you, ye know that it hath hated me before it hated you" (John 15:18). Hatred often results in persecution. The church, if true to its mission, will be opposed. But Jesus also said:

> Blessed are ye when men shall reproach you, and persecute you, and say all manner of evil against you falsely, for my sake. Rejoice, and be exceeding glad: for great is your reward in heaven: for so persecuted they the prophets that were before you (Matthew 5:11-12).

One thing, however, was beyond doubt. Those saints who remained faithful—even unto death if necessary—would be triumphant (Revelation 2:10). As the great Restorationist, F.G. Allen, so beautifully wrote:

> One by one will we lay our armor down at the feet of the Captain of our salvation. One by one will we be laid away by tender hands and aching hearts to rest on the bosom of Jesus. One by one will our ranks be thus thinned, till erelong we shall all pass over to the other side. But our cause will live.

> Eternal truth shall never perish. God will look down from His habitation on high, watch over it in His providence, and encircle it in the arms of His love. God will raise up others to take our places; and may we transmit the cause to them in its purity! Though dead, we shall thus speak for generations yet to come, and God grant that we shall give no uncertain sound! Then may we from our blissful home on high, watch the growth of the cause we love, till it shall cover the whole earth as the waters cover the face of the great deep (1949, pp. 176-177).

Conclusion: How Humanity Should Serve God

In His manifold dealings with mankind, God consistently has reiterated the fact that, as Sovereign of the Universe, He alone is worthy to be worshipped. When He provided the Israelites with their cherished ten commandments, for example, He reminded them in no uncertain terms:

> I am Jehovah thy God, who brought thee out of the land of Egypt, out of the house of bondage. Thou shalt have no other gods before me. Thou shalt not make unto thee a graven image, nor any likeness of anything that is in heaven above, or that is in the earth beneath, or that is in the water under the earth; thou shalt not bow down thyself unto them; for I Jehovah thy God am a jealous God (Exodus 20:2-5).

It was not enough, however, for man merely to worship God. Through the millennia, God provided specific instructions concerning not only the fact that He was to be worshipped, but the **manner** in which He was to be worshipped. A straightforward reading of the Scriptures reveals that apparently these instructions were set forth very early in human history. The author of the book of Hebrews substantiated this when he commented on events that transpired shortly after Adam and Eve's expulsion from the Garden of Eden, and the subsequent birth of two of their children, Cain and Abel. The inspired writer observed that "by faith Abel offered unto God a more excellent sacrifice than Cain, through which he had witness borne to him that he was righteous, God bearing witness in respect of his gifts" (Hebrews 11:4).

Whatever else might be gleaned from the Bible's statements about these two brothers, one thing is certain: Abel's worship to God was acceptable; Cain's was not. The conclusion, therefore, is inescapable: Abel had obeyed whatever instructions God had given the first family regarding their worship of Him, while Cain had ignored those same instructions.

These two brothers are not the only siblings from whom such a lesson can be drawn. In the Old Testament Book of Leviticus, the story is told of two of Aaron's sons, Nadab, his firstborn, and Abihu. Leviticus 10 presents a chilling commentary on the two boys' ill-fated attempt to worship God according to their own desires, rather than as God had commanded.

> And Nadab and Abihu, the sons of Aaron, took each of them his censer, and put fire therein, and laid incense thereon, and offered strange fire before Jehovah, which he had not commanded them. And there came forth fire from before Jehovah, and devoured them and they died before Jehovah (Leviticus 10:1-2).

The key to understanding the account, of course, is in the fact that they offered "strange fire" that God "had not commanded." Aaron's two sons suffered a horrible death because they ignored Jehovah's specific commands relating to **how** He was to be worshipped.

In referring to the Old Testament, the apostle Paul commented: "For whatsoever things were written aforetime were written for our learning, that through patience and through comfort of the scriptures we might have hope" (Romans 15:4). From the accounts of Cain and Abel, and Nadab and Abihu, we can learn a critically important lesson regarding how God views man's worship of Him. That lesson is this: **God places a premium on foundational knowledge, proper understanding, correct mental attitude, contrite spirit, and reverent obedience** in matters relating to worship offered to Him!

A New Testament example not only bears this out, but brings the matter more clearly into focus. In Matthew 6:1ff., Jesus condemned the Pharisees for their public display of ritualistic religion when He said:

> Take heed that ye do not your righteousness before men, to be seen of them: else ye have no reward with your Father who is in heaven. When therefore thou doest alms, sound not a trumpet before thee, as the hypocrites do in the synagogues and in the streets, that they may have glory of men. Verily I say unto you, They have received their reward.... And when ye pray, ye shall not be as the hypocrites: for they love to stand and pray in the synagogues and in the corners of the streets, that they may be seen of men. Verily I say unto you, They have received their reward.... Moreover, when ye fast, be not, as the hypocrites, of a sad countenance: for they disfigure their faces, that they may be seen of men. Verily I say unto you, They have received their reward (Matthew 6: 1-2,5,16).

Consider the Pharisees that Christ used as an example of how **not** to worship God. They gave alms; they prayed; they fasted. Under normal circumstances, would each of these acts be acceptable to God? Yes. But the Pharisees performed them for the wrong reason—"to be seen of men." In other words, although the act itself was correct, the **purpose** for which they did it, and the **attitude** with which they did it, were wrong. Hence, **God would not accept their worship!**

Consider also additional New Testament passages that come to bear on this issue. In 2 Corinthians 9:7, Paul discussed a person's giving of his financial means to the Lord, and stated that "each man" was to "do according as he hath purposed in his heart; not grudgingly, or of necessity: for God loveth a cheerful giver." Both the purpose of the act, as well as the understanding and attitude of the worshiper, were critical. Further, in Luke 22:19, in speaking of the memorial supper that He was instituting, Christ commanded: "This do in remembrance of me." The Scriptures make it clear, however, that it is possible to partake of the Lord's supper in an incorrect way (see 1 Corinthians 11:27-29), thus making it null and void in its effects. In other words, foundational knowledge, proper understanding, correct mental attitude, contrite spirit, and reverent obedience are all vitally important. And when they are missing, the act of worship is vain.

An additional point needs to be examined as well. Sincerity alone is not enough to make an act pleasing and acceptable to God. In 2 Samuel 6, the story is told of a man by the name of Uzzah who was accompanying the Ark of the Covenant of God as it was being moved from one location to another at the command of King David. The Ark had been placed on an ox cart, and the text says simply that "the oxen stumbled" (2 Samuel 6:6). Uzzah—no doubt believing that the precious cargo was about to be tumble from its perch on the cart and be damaged or destroyed—reached up to steady the Ark (2 Samuel 6:6). But Jehovah had commanded that no man, under any circumstances, was to touch the holy things of God (Numbers 4:15). And so, the moment Uzzah touched the Ark, God struck him dead (2 Samuel 6:7).

Was Uzzah sincere in what he did? Undoubtedly. But his sin cerity counted for nothing because he disobeyed. Note specifically the Bible's statement that "God smote him there for his **error**" (2 Samuel 6:7b). God does not want just sincerity; He wants obedience. Jesus Himself said: "If ye love me, ye will keep my commandments" (John 14:15). Furthermore, the way of the Lord is both restrictive and narrow, as Jesus made clear in His beautiful Sermon on the Mount (read specifically Matthew 7:13-14). In fact, Christ observed: "Not everyone that saith unto me, Lord, Lord, shall enter into the kingdom of heaven; but he that doeth the will of my Father who is in heaven" (Matthew 7:21). Jesus later commented on the attitude of the people of His day when He said: "This people honoreth me with their lips, but their heart is far from me. But in vain do they worship me, teaching as their doctrines the precepts of men" (Matthew 15:8-9).

These people of whom Jesus spoke did not have the foundational knowledge, proper understanding, correct mental attitude, contrite spirit, or reverent obedience God demands of those who would worship and serve Him as He has commanded. There is a valuable lesson in each of these accounts for those of us today who seek to worship and serve God. That lesson is this: we must do **exactly** what God has commanded, in **exactly** the way He has commanded that we do it. Nothing can take the place of simple obedience to the law of God. Neither sincerity nor good intentions will suffice. Only the person who reverently obeys because of adequate foundational knowledge, a proper understanding, a correct mental attitude, and a contrite spirit will be acceptable to God. That being the case, let us all strive not only to worship and serve God, but to worship and serve Him in a scriptural fashion.

CHAPTER 13

THE MERCY AND GRACE OF GOD

The mercy and grace of God are at the core of one of the most beautiful, yet one of the most heart-rending, accounts in all the Bible—the story of Peter's denial of His Lord, and Jesus' reaction to that denial. Christ had predicted that before His crucifixion Peter would deny Him three times (John 13:36-38). Peter did just that (John 18:25-27). First, he was asked by a maid who controlled the door to the court of the high priest if he was a disciple of Jesus. Peter denied that he was. Second, he was asked by servants of the high priest if he was indeed the Lord's disciple. Again, he denied knowing Jesus. Third, he was asked if he was with the Lord when they arrested Him in the Garden of Gethsemane. One last time, Peter vehemently denied the Lord. The cock crowed, and the Lord looked across the courtyard. As their eyes met, the text says simply that Peter "went out and wept bitterly" (Luke 22:61-62).

When next we see Peter, he has given up. In fact, he said "I go a fishing" (John 21:3). Peter's life as a follower of Christ was finished, so far as he was concerned. He had decided to go back to his former vocation. No doubt Peter felt that his sin against the Lord was so grievous that even though he now believed the Lord to be risen, there could be no further use for him in the kingdom. It was, then, to fishing that he would return.

It is a compliment to Peter's innate leadership ability that the other disciples followed him even on this sad occasion. As Peter and his friends fished one morning, the Lord appeared on the shore and called to them. When they brought the boat near, they saw that Christ had prepared a meal of fish and bread over an open fire. They sat, ate, and talked. As they did, the Lord asked Peter, "Simon, lovest thou me more than these?" (John 21:15). Peter assured Jesus that he did. But Christ appeared unsatisfied with Peter's response. He inquired a second time, and a third. After the last query, the text in dicates that Peter was "grieved because Christ said unto him a third time, 'lovest thou me?' " (John 21:17).

Peter's uneasiness was saying, in essence, "What are you trying to do to me, Lord?" Jesus was asking: "Peter, can you comprehend—in spite of your denying heart—that I have forgiven you? Do you understand that the mercy and grace of God have been extended to you? There is still work for you to do. Go, use your immense talents in the advancement of the kingdom." Jesus loved Peter. And He wanted him back. Jesus simply was putting into action that which He had taught personally. Forgive, yes, even "70 times 7."

Perhaps during these events one of Christ's parables came to Peter's mind. He no doubt was familiar with the teaching of the Lord in Luke 7:36-50 (see the similar account found in Matthew 18:23-35). Jesus was eating with Simon, a Pharisee. Simon saw a worldly woman come into the Lord's presence, and thought: "This man, if he were a prophet, would have perceived who and what manner of woman this is that toucheth him, that she is a sinner" (Luke 7:39). Simon's point, of course, was that Christ should have driven away the sinful woman. But Jesus, knowing Simon's thoughts, presented a parable for his consideration.

Two servants owed their lord; one owed an enormous debt, and the other only a small amount. Yet the master forgave both of the debts. Jesus asked Simon: "Which of them therefore will love him the most?" (Luke 7:42). Simon correctly answered: "He, I suppose, to whom he forgave the most" (Luke 7:43). Jesus, through this parable, was saying to Simon: "I came here today and you would not even extend to me the common courtesy of washing my feet. This woman entered, cried, washed my feet with her tears, and dried them with her hair. I have forgiven her. She, therefore, should love me the most."

This woman had been a recipient of God's mercy and grace. She gratefully expressed devotion for the forgiveness offered by the Son of God. Simon, on the other hand, was too religious to beg, and too proud to accept it if offered. It is a sad-but-true fact that man will treat forgiveness lightly so long as he treats sin lightly. The worldly, fallen woman desperately desired the saving mercy and grace of God—and accepted it when it was extended. Christ's point to Simon was that man can appreciate **to what** he has been elevated (God's saving grace) only when he recognizes **from what** he has been saved (his own sinful state).

In this context, Christ's point to Peter becomes clear. "Peter, you denied me, not just once, but three times. Have I forgiven you? Yes, I have." Peter, too, had been the recipient of God's mercy and grace. He had much of which to be forgiven. Yet, **he had been forgiven**! The problem that relates to mercy and grace is not to be found in heaven; rather, it is to be found here on the Earth. Man often finds it difficult to accept God's mercy and grace. And often he finds it just as difficult to forgive himself. We do not stand in need of an accuser; God's law does that admirably, as the seventh chapter of Romans demonstrates. What we need is an Advocate (1 John 2:1-2)—someone to stand in our place, and to plead our case. We—laden with our burden of sin—have no right to stand before the majestic throne of God, even with the intent to beg for mercy.

But Jesus the Righteous has that right. He made it clear to His disciples, and likewise has made it clear to us, that He is willing to be just such an Advocate on our behalf. The author of the book of Hebrews wrote:

> Having then a great high priest, who hath passed through the heavens, Jesus the Son of God, let us hold fast our confession. For we have not a high priest that cannot be touched with the feeling of our infirmities; but one that hath been in all points tempted as we are, yet without sin (4: 14-15).

The entire story of the Bible centers on man's need for mercy and grace. That story began in Genesis 3, and has been unfolding ever since. Fortunately, "the Lord is full of pity, and merciful" (James 5:11). Even when Cain—a man who had murdered his own brother—begged for mercy, God heard his plea and placed a mark on him for his protection. God never has wanted to punish anyone. His words to that effect were recorded by Ezekiel: "Have I any pleasure in the death of the wicked? saith the Lord Jehovah; and not rather that he should return from his way, and live?... I have no pleasure in the death of him that dieth, saith the Lord Jehovah" (18:23,32). Similarly, in the times of Hosea sin was rampant. Life was barren. Worship to God had been polluted. The effects of Satan's rule were felt everywhere on the Earth. The Lord, suggested Hosea, "hath a controversy with the inhabitants of the land, because there is no truth, nor goodness, nor knowledge of God in the land" (4:1). Evidence of God's mercy and grace is seen, however, in the words spoken by Hosea on God's behalf:

> How shall I give thee up, O Ephraim! How shall I cast thee off, Israel! ...my heart is turned within me, my compassions are kindled together. I will not execute the fierceness of mine anger, I will not return to destroy Ephraim; for I am God and not man; the Holy One in the midst of thee; and I will not come in wrath (11:8-9).

Solomon said that those who practice mercy and truth will find "favor and good understanding in the sight of God and man" (Proverbs 3:4). Many are those in the Bible who desperately sought the mercy and grace of God. Cain needed mercy and grace. Israel needed mercy and grace. Peter needed mercy and grace. And to all it was given, as God deemed appropriate. We must understand, however, several important facts about God's mercy and grace.

God is Sovereign in Delegating His Mercy and Grace

First, we must realize that God is sovereign in granting both His mercy and His grace. When we speak of God's sovereign nature, it is a recognition on our part that whatever He wills is right. He alone determines the appropriate course of action; He acts and speaks at the whim of no outside force, including mankind.

When humans become the recipients of heaven's grace, the unfathomable has happened. The apostle Paul wrote: "For all have sinned, and fall short of the glory of God.... For the wages of sin is death; but the free gift of God is eternal life in Christ Jesus our Lord" (Romans 3:23; 6:23). God—our Justifiable Accuser—has become our Vindicator. He has extended to us His wonderful love, as expressed by His mercy and His grace.

Mercy has been defined as feeling "sympathy with the misery of another, and especially sympathy manifested in act" (Vine, 1940, 3:61). Mercy is more than just sympathetic feelings. It is sympathy in concert with action. Grace often has been defined as the "unmerited favor of God." If grace is unmerited, then none can claim it as an unalienable right. If grace is undeserved, then none is entitled to it. If grace is a gift, then none can demand it. Grace is the antithesis of justice. After God's grace has been meted out, there remains only divine justice. Because salvation is through grace (Ephesians 2:8-9), the very chief of sinners is not beyond the reach of divine grace. Because salvation is by grace, boasting is excluded and God receives the glory.

When justice is meted out, we **receive what we deserve**. When mercy is extended, we **do not receive what we deserve**. When grace is bestowed, we **receive what we do not deserve**. Perhaps no one could appreciate this better than Peter. It was he who said: "And if the righteous is scarcely saved, where shall the ungodly and sinner appear?" (1 Peter 4:18). Paul reminded the first-century Christians in Rome that "scarcely for a righteous man will one die: for peradventure for the good man some one would even dare to die. But God commendeth his own love toward us, in that, while we were yet sinners, Christ died for us" (Romans 5:7-8).

Yet because mercy is a free gift, and thus unearned, it remains within God's sovereign right to bestow it as He sees fit. A beautiful expression of this fact can be seen in the prayers of two men who found themselves in similar circumstances—in that both were under the sentence of death. In Numbers 20, the story is told of God's commanding Moses to speak to the rock in the wilderness, so that it would yield water for the Israelites. Rather than obey the command of God to speak to the rock, however, Moses struck it instead. The Lord said to him: "Because ye believed not in me, to sanctify me in the eyes of the children of Israel, therefore ye shall not bring this assembly into the land which I have given them" (Numbers 20:12). Years later, God called Moses to the top of Mount Nebo and allowed him to look across into the promised land, but He vowed that Moses would not enter into Canaan with the Israelites. Moses begged God to permit him to go (Deuteronomy 3:26), but his plea was denied.

Yet king Hezekiah, likewise under a sentence of death, petitioned God to let him live—and God added 15 years to his life. Moses wrote: "The Lord would not hear me," and died. But to Hezekiah it was said: "I have heard thy prayer" (2 Kings 20:1-6), and his life was spared. What a beautiful illustration and amplification of Romans 9:15: "For he saith unto Moses, I will have mercy on whom I have mercy, and I will have compassion on whom I have compassion." God is sovereign in His mercy and His grace.

God's Grace Does Not Mean a Lack of Consequences to Sin

Second, we must recognize that God's granting mercy and grace does not somehow negate the consequences of sin here and now. While mercy may ensue, so may sin's consequences. Perhaps the most touching story in the Bible illustrating this eternal truth is the account of King David. How could a man of David's faith and righteousness commit the terrible sins attributed to him? David was about 50 years old at the time. Fame and fortune were his as Israel's popular, beloved king. He had taken his vows before God (see Psalm 101). He had insisted on righteousness in his nation. The people had been taught to love, respect, and honor the God of heaven. David, their king, also was their example. He was a man after God's own heart (1 Samuel 13:14).

But he committed the sin of adultery with Bathsheba (2 Samuel 11-12), and then had her husband, Uriah, murdered. One cannot help but be reminded of the sin of Achan (Joshua 7) when he took booty from a war and hid it under the floor of his tent after the Israelites were commanded specifically not to take any such items. Achan said, "I saw..., I coveted..., I took..., I hid..." (Joshua 7:21). Is that not what King David did? But Achan and David also could state, "I paid." Achan paid with his life; David paid with twenty years of heartbreak, strife, and the loss of a child that meant everything to him.

The prophet Nathan was sent by God to the great king. He told David the story of a rich man who had many sheep in his flock, and of a poor man who had but one small ewe that practically was part of the family. When a visitor appeared at the rich man's door, the rich man took the single ewe owned by the poor man and slaughtered it for the visitor's meal. Upon hearing what had happened, David was overwhelmed with anger and vowed, "As Jehovah liveth, the man that hath done this is worthy to die" (2 Samuel 12:5).

Nathan looked the powerful king in the eye and said, "Thou art the man" (2 Samuel 12:7). The enormity of David's sin swept over him and he said, "I have sinned" (2 Samuel 12:13). David, even through his sin, was a man who loved righteousness. Now that Nathan had shown him his sin, he felt a repulsion which demanded a cleansing that could come only from God. His description of the consequences of sin on the human heart is one of the most vivid in all of Scripture, and should move each of us deeply. His agonizing prayer is recorded in Psalm 51. David cried out: "Have mercy upon me, O God, according to thy lovingkindness."

David needed a new heart; sin had defiled his old one. He likewise realized that he needed to undergo an inner renewal; pride and lust had destroyed his spirit. So, David prayed for a proper spirit. He could do nothing but cast himself on the mercy and grace of God. David laid on the altar his own sinful heart and begged God to cleanse, recreate, and restore his life. God did forgive. He did cleanse. He did recreate. He did restore.

But the consequences of David's sin remained. The child growing in Bathsheba's womb died after birth. In addition, the prophet Nathan made it clear to David that "the sword shall never depart from thy house," and that God would "raise up evil against thee out of thine own house" (2 Samuel 12:10-11). David's life never again would be the same. His child was dead, his reputation was damaged, his influence was all but destroyed.

David learned that the penalty for personal sin often is felt in the lives of others as well. He prayed that those who loved and served the Lord would not have to bear his shame, but such was not to be. The shame of the one is the shame of the many; as God's people, we are bound together. More often than not, what affects one of us affects all of us.

It is to David's credit that once his sin was uncovered, he did not try to deny it. Solomon, his son, later would write: "He that covereth his transgressions shall not prosper; but whoso confesseth and forsaketh them shall obtain mercy" (Proverbs 28:13).

Mercy and Grace Are Expensive

Third, we should realize that the mercy and grace God uses to cover mankind's sins are not cheap. They cost heaven its finest jewel —the Son of God. The popular, old song says it well:

I owed a debt I could not pay
He paid a debt He did not owe
I needed someone to wash my sins away.
So now I sing a brand new song—amazing grace
Christ paid the debt I could never pay.

Jesus' death represented His total commitment to us. Isaiah prophesied:

> Surely he hath borne our griefs, and carried our sorrows; yet we did esteem him stricken, smitten of God, and afflicted. But he was wounded for our transgressions, he was bruised for our iniquities; the chastisement of our peace was upon him; and with his stripes we are healed. All we like sheep have gone astray; we have turned everyone to his own way; and Jehovah hath laid on him the iniquity of us all.... He bare the sin of many, and made intercession for the transgressors (53: 4-6,12).

Paul wrote: "Him who knew no sin he made to be sin on our behalf that we might become the righteousness of God in him" (2 Corinthians 5:21).

Grace does not **eliminate** human responsibility; rather, grace **emphasizes** human responsibility. Grace, because it cost God so much, delivers agonizing duties and obligations. It is seemingly a great paradox that Christianity is free, yet at the same time is so very costly. Jesus warned: "If any man will come after me, let him deny himself, and take up his cross, and follow me" (Matthew 16:24). Paul summarized it like this: "I have been crucified with Christ; and it is no longer I that live, but Christ liveth in me: and that life which I now live in the flesh I live in faith, the faith which is in the Son of God, who loved me, and gave himself up for me. I do not make void the grace of God" (Galatians 2:20-21).

Grace does not make one **irresponsible**; rather, it makes one **more responsible**! Paul asked: "What shall we say then? Shall we continue in sin, that grace may abound? God forbid" (Romans 6: 1-2). God's grace is accessed through willful obedience to the "perfect law of liberty" (James 1:25). It is God's law that informs us of the availability of grace, of the manner in which we appropriate it, and of the blessings that stem from living within it.

The testimony of Scripture is abundantly clear when it speaks of the importance of the "obedience of faith" (Romans 1:5). We are to be obedient to God by returning to Him from an alien, sinful state, and, once redeemed, through our continued faithfulness as evinced by our works. Grace and works of obedience are not mutually exclusive.

Neither are grace and law mutually exclusive, as some have suggested. One who is "in Christ" does not live under the dominion of sin, since Christianity is a system of grace. The apostle to the Gentiles stated: "Ye are not under the law, but under grace" (Romans 6:14). He cannot mean that we are under no law at all, because in the following verses he spoke of early Christians being "obedient from the heart to that form of teaching" delivered to them (6:17). These Christians had obeyed God's law, and were living faithfully under that law. They understood that "faith worketh by love" (Galatians 5:6). The terms "law," "works," and "grace" are not at odds, but like all things within God's plan, exist in perfect harmony.

We Are Saved Through Grace

Fourth, let us remember that our salvation is by **atonement**, not **attainment**. Because salvation is a free gift (Romans 6:23), man never can earn it. Unmerited favor cannot be merited! God did for us what we, on our own, could not do. Jesus paid the price we could not pay. From beginning to end, the scheme of redemption—including all that God has done, is doing, and will do—is one continuous act of grace. The Scriptures speak of God "reconciling the world unto himself, not reckoning unto them their trespasses, and having committed unto us the word of reconciliation" (2 Corinthians 5:19). Peter stated:

> Knowing that ye were redeemed, not with corruptible things, with silver or gold, from your vain manner of life handed down from your fathers; but with precious blood, as of a lamb without blemish and without spot, even the blood of Christ (1 Peter 1:18-19).

God has promised mercy and grace to those who believe on His Son (John 3:16), repent of their sins (Luke 13:3), and have those sins remitted through baptism (Acts 2:38; 22:16). Subsequent to the Day of Pentecost, Peter called upon his audiences to: "Repent ye therefore, and turn again, that your sins may be blotted out" (Acts 3: 19). The word for "blotted out" derives from the Greek word meaning to "wipe out, erase, or obliterate." The New Testament uses the word to refer to "blotting out" the old law (Colossians 2:14) and to "blotting out" a person's name from the Book of Life (Revelation 3: 5). One of the great prophetical utterances of the Old Testament was that "their sin will I remember no more" (Jeremiah 31:34).

Our sins were borne by Jesus on the cross. He paid our debt so that we, like undeserving Barabbas, might be set free. In this way, God could be just, and at the same time Justifier of those who believe in and obey His Son. By refusing to extend mercy to Jesus on the cross, God was able to extend mercy to me—**if** I submit in obedience to His commands.

There was no happy solution to the justice/mercy dilemma. There was no way that God could remain just (since justice demands that the wages of sin be paid) and yet save His Son from death. Christ was abandoned to the cross so that mercy could be extended to sinners who stood condemned (Galatians 3:10). God could not save sinners by fiat—upon the ground of mere authority alone—without violating His own attribute of divine justice. Paul discussed God's response to this problem in Romans 3:24-26:

> Being justified freely by his grace through the redemption that is in Christ Jesus; whom God set forth to be a propitiation, through faith, in his blood...for the showing of his righteousness...that he might himself be just and the justifier of him that hath faith in Jesus.

Man's salvation was no arbitrary arrangement. God did not decide merely to consider man a sinner, and then determine to save him upon a principle of mercy. Sin placed man in a state of antagonism toward God. Sinners are condemned because they have violated God's law, and because God's justice cannot permit Him to ignore sin. Sin could be forgiven only as a result of the vicarious death of God's Son. Because sinners are redeemed by the sacrifice of Christ, and not their own righteousness, they are sanctified by the mercy and grace of God.

Our Response to God's Mercy and Grace

What, then, should be our response to mercy and grace? (1) Let us remember that "blessed are the merciful, for they shall obtain mercy" (Matthew 5:7). It is a biblical principle that unless we extend mercy, we cannot obtain mercy. Jesus taught: "For if ye forgive men their trespasses, your heavenly Father will also forgive you; but if ye forgive not men their trespasses, neither will your Father forgive your trespasses" (Matthew 6:14-15). We would do well to recall the adage that "he who cannot forgive destroys the bridge over which he, too, one day must pass." If we expect to be forgiven, then let us be prepared to forgive.

(2) Let us remember that mercy and grace demand action on our part. Mercy is to feel "sympathy with the misery of another, and especially sympathy manifested in act." Luke recorded an example of Christ's mercy in healing ten lepers who "lifted up their voices saying, 'Jesus, Master, have mercy on us' " (Luke 17:13). Did these diseased and dying men want merely a few kind words uttered in their direction? Hardly. They wanted to be healed! When the publican prayed so penitently, "God, be thou merciful to me a sinner" (Luke

18:13), he was asking for more than tender feelings of compassion. He wanted something done about his pitiful condition. Mercy and grace are compassion in action.

(3) Let us remember that nothing must take precedence over our Savior. If we must choose between Christ and a friend, spouse, or child, Christ comes first. He demands no less (Luke 4:25-35)—but His demands are consistent with His sufferings on our behalf. He insists that we take up our cross: He took up His. He insists that we lose our life to find it: He lost His. He insists that we give up our families for His sake: He gave up His for ours. He demands that we give up everything for Him: He had nowhere to lay His head, and His only possession—the robe on His back—was taken from Him. Yes, the costs sometimes are high; but the blessings that we receive in return are priceless. He dispenses mercy and grace, and offers eternal salvation to all those who will believe in and obey Him.

Conclusion

In Luke 15, Jesus spoke of a wayward son who had sinned against his father and squandered his precious inheritance. Upon returning home, he decided to say to his father: "Make me as one of thy hired servants" (15:19). He was prepared for the worst.

But he received the best. His father, "while he was yet afar off, ...was moved with compassion, and ran, and fell on his neck, and kissed him" (Luke 15:20). The son did not receive what he **deserved**; he received **what he did not deserve**. He received mercy and grace. His father wanted him back!

Does our heavenly Father want us back? Oh, yes! Paul wrote: "For ye were bought with a price" (1 Corinthians 6:20). Let us yearn for the day when we can stand before His throne and thank Him for granting us mercy and grace—and for paying the debt we could not pay, and the debt He did not owe.

REFERENCES

Abelson, Phillip (1964), "Bigotry in Science," *Science*, April 24.

Albright, William F. (1953), *Archaeology and the Religion of Israel* (Baltimore, MD: Johns Hopkins University Press).

Allen, F.G. (1949), "The Principles and Objects of the Current Reformation," *Foundation Facts and Primary Principles*, ed. G.C. Brewer (Kansas City, MO: Old Paths Book Club).

Altizer, Thomas J.J. (1961), *Oriental Mysticism and Biblical Eschatology* (Philadelphia, PA: Westminster).

Altizer, Thomas J.J. (1966), *The Gospel of Christian Atheism* (Philadelphia, PA: Westminster).

Andrews, E.H. (1978), *From Nothing to Nature* (Welwyn, Hertfordshire, England: Evangelical Press).

Arndt, William (1955), *Does the Bible Contradict Itself?* (St. Louis, MO: Concordia).

Asimov, Isaac (1975), *Guide to Science* (London: Pelican Books).

Asimov, Isaac (1982), "Interview with Isaac Asimov on Science and the Bible," Paul Kurtz, interviewer, *Free Inquiry*, Spring, pp. 6-10. [See also: Hallman, Steve (1991), "Christianity and Humanism: A Study in Contrasts," *AFA Journal*, March, p. 11.]

Ayer, A.J. (1966), "What I Believe," ed. George Unwin, *What I Believe* (London: Allen and Unwin).

Baird, James O. (1978), "The Trials and Tribulations of the Church from the Beginning," *The Future of the Church*, ed. William Woodson (Henderson, TN: Freed-Hardeman College).

Bales, James D. (1967), *The God-Killer?* (Tulsa, OK: Christian Crusade).

Bales, James D. (1976), *How Can Ye Believe?* (Shreveport, LA: Lambert).

Bales, James D. and Robert T. Clark (1966), *Why Scientists Accept Evolution* (Grand Rapids, MI: Baker).

Barfield, Kenny (1988), *Why the Bible is Number 1* (Grand Rapids, MI: Baker).

Barnett, Lincoln (1959), *The Universe and Dr. Einstein* (New York: Mentor).

Bass, Thomas (1990), "Interview with Richard Dawkins," *Omni*, 12[4]: 57-60,84-89, January.

Baxter, Batsell Barrett (19710, *I Believe Because* (Grand Rapids, MI: Baker).

Beck, William (1971), *Human Design* (New York: Harcourt, Brace, Jovanovich).

Bertram, George (1971), "*moros*," *Theological Dictionary of the New Testament*, ed. Gerhard Kittel and Gerhard Friedrich (Grand Rapids, MI: Eerdmans).

Blinderman, Charles S. (1957), "Thomas Henry Huxley," *Scientific Monthly*, April.

Block, Irvin (1980), "The Worlds Within You," *Science Digest* special edition, pp. 49-53,118, September/October.

Blumenfeld, Samuel L. (1984), *NEA: Trojan Horse in American Education* (Boise, ID: Paradigm).

Blunt, J.J. (1884), *Undesigned Coincidences in the Writings of the Old and New Testaments* (London: John Murray).

Borek, Ernest (1973), *The Sculpture of Life* (New York: Columbia University Press).

Bromling, Brad T. (1989), "Jesus—My Lord and My God," *Reasoning from Revelation*, 1[9]:1-2, September.

Bromling, Brad T. (1991a), "Jesus and Jehovah—An Undeniable Link," *Reasoning from Revelation*, 3[2]:3, February.

Bromling, Brad T. (1991b), "The Prophets' Portrait of Christ," *Reason & Revelation*, 11:45-47, December.

Bromling, Brad T. (1994), "Prophetic Precision," *Reason & Revelation*, 14:96, December.

Bromling, Brad T. (1995), "Jesus: Truly God and Truly Human," *Reason & Revelation*, 15:17-20, March.

Brown, Colin (1984), *Miracles and the Critical Mind* (Grand Rapids, MI: Eerdmans).

Butt, Kyle (2000), "The Historical Christ—Fact or Fiction,?" *Reason & Revelation*, 20:1-6, January.

Carnell, Edward John (1948), *An Introduction to Christian Apologetics* (Grand Rapids, MI: Eerdmans).

Chafer, L.S. (1926), *Major Bible Themes* (Grand Rapids, MI: Zondervan).

Cheyne, T.K., ed. (1899), *Encyclopedia Biblica* (London: A&C Black).

Christlieb, Theodore (1878), *Modern Doubt and Christian Belief* (New York: Scribner's).

Clark, David K. and Norman L. Geisler (1990), *Apologetics in the New Age: A Critique of Pantheism* (Grand Rapids, MI: Baker).

Clark, Gordon H. (1957), *Thales to Dewey—A History of Philosophy* (Grand Rapids, MI: Baker, 1980 reprint).

Clark, Robert E.D. (1945), *Scientific Rationalism and Christian Faith* (London: Inter-Varsity Fellowship).

Clark, Robert E.D. (1948), *Darwin: Before and After* (London: Paternoster Press).

Clarke, William N. (1912), *An Outline of Christian Theology* (New York: Charles Scribner's Sons).

Coats, Wayne (1989), *The Providence of God*, ed. Thomas B. Warren and Garland Elkins (Southaven, MS: Southaven Church of Christ).

Corduan, Winfried (1993), *Reasonable Faith* (Nashville, TN: Broadman and Holman).

Darrow, Clarence (1988 reprint), "An Address Delivered to the Prisoners in the Chicago County Jail," *Philosophy and Contemporary Issues*, ed. John R. Burr and Milton Goldinger (New York: Macmillan), pp. 58-66.

Darwin, Charles (1870), *The Descent of Man* (New York: Modern Library). This is a two-volume edition in a single binding that also includes *The Origin of Species*.

Darwin, Francis (1898), *Life and Letters of Charles Darwin* (London: Appleton)

Davis, George (1958), "Scientific Revelations Point to a God," *The Evidence of God in an Expanding Universe*, ed. John C. Monsma (New York: G.P. Putnam's Sons).

Davis, Robert Gorham (1992), "Letter to the Editor," *New York Times*, July 5.

Dawkins, Richard (1982), "The Necessity of Darwinism," *New Scientist*, 94:130-132, April 15.

Dawkins, Richard (1986), *The Blind Watchmaker* (New York: W.W. Norton).

Dawkins, Richard (1989a), "Book Review" (of Donald Johanson and Maitland Edey's *Blueprint*), *The New York Times*, section 7, p. 34, April 9.

Dawkins, Richard (1989b), *The Selfish Gene* (Oxford: Oxford University Press).

Desmond, Adrian (1997), *Huxley* (Reading, MA: Addison-Wesley).

Desmond, Adrian and James Moore (1991), *Darwin* (New York: Warner).

Dickson, Roger (1979), "The Hermit-God Theology," *Gospel Advocate*, 121[8]:118-119, February 22.

Dickson, Roger E. (1997), *The Dawn of Belief* (Winona, MS: Choate).

Durant, Will (1961), *The Story of Philosophy* (New York: Simon & Schuster).

Durant, Will (1980), "We Are in the Last Stage of a Pagan Period," *Chicago Tribute Syndicate*, April.

Eaves, Thomas F. (1980), "The Inspired Word," *Great Doctrines of the Bible*, ed. M.H. Tucker (Knoxville, TN: East Tennessee School of Preaching).

Eccles, John (1984), "Modern Biology and the Turn to Belief in God," *The Intellectuals Speak Out About God*, ed. R.A. Varghese (Chicago, IL: Regnery Gateway).

Edwards, Jonathan (1879), *The Works of President Edwards* (New York: Robert Carter and Brothers).

Encyclopaedia Britannica (1997a), s.v. "Agnosticism," (London: Encyclopaedia Britannica, Inc.), 1:151.

Encyclopaedia Britannica (1997b), s.v. "Religious and Spiritual Belief, Systems of," (London: Encyclopaedia Britannica, Inc.), 26:530-577.

England, Donald (1983), *A Scientist Examines Faith and Evidence*, (Delight, AR: Gospel Light).

Erickson, Millard J. (1992), *Does It Matter What I Believe?* (Grand Rapids, MI: Baker).

Estling, Ralph (1994), "The Scalp-Tinglin', Mind-Blowin', Eye-Poppin', Heart-Wrenchin', Stomach-Churnin', Foot-Stumpin', Great Big Doodley Science Show!!!," *Skeptical Inquirer*, 18[4]:428-430, Summer.

Estling, Ralph (1995), "Letter to the Editor," *Skeptical Inquirer*, 19[1]: 69-70, January/February.

Farmer, Herbert H. (1942), *Towards Belief in God* (London: Student Christian Movement Press).

Ferguson, Wallace K. and Geoffrey Bruun (1937), *A Survey of European Civilization: 1500-Present* (Boston, MA: Houghton Mifflin).

Fletcher, Joseph (1966), *Situation Ethics: The New Morality*, (Philadelphia, PA: Westminster Press).

Foster, R.C. (1971), *Studies in the Life of Christ* (Grand Rapids, MI: Baker).

Free, Joseph P. and Howard F. Vos (1992), *Archaeology and Bible History* (Grand Rapids, MI: Zondervan).

Gardner, Martin (1988), *The New Age: Notes of a Fringe Watcher* (Buffalo, NY: Prometheus).

Geisler, Norman L. (1976), *Christian Apologetics* (Grand Rapids, MI: Baker).

Geisler, Norman L. (1981), *Options in Contemporary Christian Ethics* (Grand Rapids, MI: Baker).

Geisler, Norman L. (1997), *Creating God in the Image of Man* (Wheaton, IL: Bethany House).

Geisler, Norman L. and Ronald M. Brooks (1990), *When Skeptics Ask* (Wheaton, IL: Victor Books).

Geisler, Norman L. and William E. Nix (1986), *A General Introduction to the Bible* (Chicago, IL: Moody).

Geisler, Norman L. and Winfried Corduan (1988), *Philosophy of Religion* (Grand Rapids, MI: Baker).

Gliedman, John (1982), "Scientists in Search of the Soul," *Science Digest*, 90[7]:77-79,105, July.

Glueck, Nelson (1959), *Rivers in the Desert: A History of the Negev* (New York: Farrar, Strauss, and Cudahy).

Goodpasture, B.C. (1970), "Inspiration of the Bible," *The Church Faces Liberalism*, ed. T.B. Warren (Henderson, TN: Freed-Hardeman College).

Gore, Rick (1976), *National Geographic*, September.

Gould, Stephen Jay (1987), "Darwinism Defined: The Difference Between Fact and Theory," *Discover*, 8[1]:64-65,68-70, January.

Gould, Stephen Jay (1999a), *Rocks of Ages: Science and Religion in the Fullness of Life* (New York: Random House).

Gould, Stephen Jay (1999b), "Dorothy, It's Really Oz," *Time*, 154[8]: 59, August 23.

Gould, Stephen Jay and Niles Eldredge (1977), "Punctuated Equilibria: The Tempo and Mode of Evolution Reconsidered," *Paleobiology*, Spring.

Graber, Glenn C. (1972), *The Relationship of Morality and Religion: Language, Logic, and Apologetics* (Ann Arbor, MI: University of Michigan), doctoral dissertation.

Greene, John C. (1963), *Darwin and the Modern World View* (New York: New American Library).

Gribbin, John (1983), "Earth's Lucky Break," *Science Digest*, 91[5]:36-37,40,102, May.

Gruenler, Royce G. (1983), *The Inexhaustible God* (Grand Rapids, MI: Baker).

Guinness, Alma E., ed. (1987), *ABC's of the Human Body* (Pleasantville, NY: Reader's Digest).

Guth, Alan (1988), Interview in *Omni*, 11[2]:75-76,78-79,94,96-99, November.

Guth, Alan and Paul Steinhardt (1984), "The Inflationary Universe," *Scientific American*, 250:116-128, May.

Hall, Marshall and Sandra Hall (1974), *The Truth: God or Evolution?* (Grand Rapids, MI: Baker).

Halley, H.H. *Halley's Bible Handbook* (Grand Rapids, MI: Zondervan).

Harrison, Everett F. (1966), *Baker's Dictionary of Theology* (Grand Rapids, MI: Baker).

Havron, Dean (1981), "Curious Cure-Alls" *Science Digest*, 89[8]:62, September.

Hawking, Stephen W. (1988), *A Brief History of Time* (New York: Bantam).

Hayes, Judith (1996), *In God We Trust: But Which One?* (Madison, WI: Freedom From Religion Foundation).

Heeren, Fred (1995), *Show Me God* (Wheeling, IL: Searchlight Publications).

Holt, L.E. and R. McIntosh (1953), *Holt Pediatrics* (New York: Appleton-Century-Crofts), twelfth edition.

Hoover, Arlie J. (1976), *Ideas and Their Consequences* (Abilene, TX: Biblical Research Press).

Hoover, Arlie J. (1981), "Starving the Spirit," *Firm Foundation*, 98[4]: 6, January.

Horne, Thomas H. (1970 reprint), *An Introduction to the Critical Study and Knowledge of the Holy Scriptures* (Grand Rapids, MI: Baker).

Hoyle, Fred (1981a), "The Big Bang in Astronomy," *New Scientist*, November 19.

Hoyle, Fred (1981b), "Hoyle on Evolution," *Nature*, November 12.

Hoyle, Fred and Chandra Wickramasinghe (1981), *Evolution from Space* (London: J.M. Dent & Sons).

Huff, Darrell (1959), *How to Take a Chance* (New York: W.W. Norton).

Hull, David (1974), *Philosophy of Biological Science* (Englewood Cliffs, NJ: Prentice-Hall)

Humanist Manifestos I & II (1973), (Buffalo, NY: Prometheus).

Hurst, Jr., William R. (1971), "Editor's Report," *The [Los Angeles] Herald-Examiner*, section A, p. 4, November 14.

Huxley, Aldous (1966), "Confessions of a Professed Atheist," *Report: Perspective on the News*, 3:19, June.

Huxley, Julian (1960), "At Random: A Television Interview," *Issues in Evolution* (Volume 3 of *Evolution After Darwin*), ed. Sol Tax (Chicago, IL: University of Chicago), pp. 41-65.

Huxley, Julian (1964), *Essays of a Humanist* (New York: Harper & Row).

Huxley, Leonard (1900), *Life and Letters of Thomas Huxley* (New York: Appleton).

Huxley, Leonard (1903), *Life and Letters of Thomas Huxley* (New York: Macmillan).

Huxley, Thomas Henry (1894), *Collected Essays* (New York: Greenwood Press, 1968 reprint). [Quotation is from volume five of a nine-volume set published 1894-1908.]

Huxley, Thomas Henry (1896), *Darwiniana* (New York: Appleton).

Jackson, Wayne (1974), *Fortify Your Faith* (Stockton, CA: Courier Publications).

Jackson, Wayne (1979), "Isaiah 53: The Messiah," *Great Chapters of the Bible*, ed. Thomas F. Eaves (Knoxville, TN: East Tennessee School of Preaching and Missions).

Jackson, Wayne (1981), "'And He Could Do There No Mighty Work,'" *Reason and Revelation*, 1:13, April.

Jackson, Wayne (1982), *Biblical Studies in the Light of Archaeology* (Montgomery, AL: Apologetics Press).

Jackson, Wayne (1984), "Rules by Which Men Live," *Reason and Revelation*, 4:21-24), May.

Jackson, Wayne (1988), "The Earth: A Planet Plagued with Evil," *Reason and Revelation*, 8:49-52, December.

Jackson, Wayne (1991a), "Bible Unity—An Argument for Inspiration," *Reason & Revelation*, 11:1, January.

Jackson, Wayne (1991b), "The Holy Bible—Inspired of God," *Christian Courier*, 27[1]:1-3, May.

Jackson, Wayne (1993), *The Human Body: Accident or Design?* (Stockton, CA: Courier Publications).

Jackson, Wayne (1995), "The Case for the Existence of God—Part III," *Reason and Revelation*, 15:49-55), July.

Jackson, Wayne (1997a), "Daniel's Prophecy of the 'Seventy Weeks,'" *Reason & Revelation*, 17:49-53, July.

Jackson, Wayne (1997b), "The Matter of 'Baptismal Regeneration,'" *Christian Courier*, 32:45-46, April.

Jackson, Wayne (1997c), "The Role of 'Works' in the Plan of Salvation," *Christian Courier*, 32:47, April.

Jackson, Wayne and Tom Carroll (no date), "The Jackson-Carroll Debate on Atheism and Ethics," *Thrust*, ed. Jerry Moffitt, 2:98-154.

Jastrow, Robert (1977), *Until the Sun Dies* (New York: W.W. Norton).

Jastrow, Robert (1978), *God and the Astronomers* (New York: W.W. Norton).

Jastrow, Robert (1982), "A Scientist Caught Between Two Faiths," Interview with Bill Durbin, *Christianity Today*, August 6.

Jevons, W. Stanley (1928), *Elementary Lessons in Logic* (London: Macmillan).

Johnson, B.C. (1983), *The Atheist Debater's Handbook* (Buffalo, NY: Prometheus).

Kautz, Darrel (1988), *The Origin of Living Things* (Milwaukee, WI: Privately published by the author).

Keil, C.F. and F. Delitzsch (1981 reprint), *Commentary on the Old Testament* (Grand Rapids, MI: Eerdmans).

Kelcy, Raymond C. (1968), *The Living Word Commentary: The Letters of Paul to the Thessalonians* (Austin, TX: Sweet).

Kennedy, D. James (1997), *Skeptics Answered* (Sisters, OR: Multnomah).

Key, Bobby (1982), "Sin Is a Reproach to Any People," *Four State Gospel News*, 21[12]:2, December.

Koster, John (1989), *The Atheist Syndrome* (Brentwood, TN: Wolgemuth & Hyatt).

Kreeft, Peter and Ronald K. Tacelli (1994), *Handbook of Christian Apologetics* (Downers Grove, IL: InterVarsity Press).

Kung, Hans (1980), *Does God Exist?* (New York: Doubleday).

Kurtz, Paul (1973), "Scientific Humanism," *The Humanist Alternative*, ed. Paul Kurtz, (Buffalo, NY: Prometheus).

Lamont, Corliss (1949), *Humanism as a Philosophy* (New York: Philosophical Library).

Lawton, April (1981), "From Here to Infinity," *Science Digest*, 89[1]: 98-105, January/February.

Leakey, Richard and Roger Lewin (1977), *Origins*, New York: E.P. Dutton).

Lewis, C.S. (1952), *Mere Christianity* (New York: MacMillan).

Lewontin, Richard (1978), "Adaptation," *Scientific American*, 239[3]: 212-218,220,222,228,230, September.

Lewontin, Richard (1997), "Billions and Billions of Demons," *The New York Review*, January 9.

Liebman, Joshua (1946), *Peace of Mind* (New York: Simon & Schuster).

Lindsell, Harold (1976), *The Battle for the Bible* (Grand Rapids, MI: Zondervan).

Lipe, David (1987a), "The Foundations of Morality," *Reason and Revelation*, 7:25-27, July.

Lipe, David (1987b), "Religious Ethics and Moral Obligation," *Reason and Revelation*, 7:37-40, October.

Lippmann, Walter (1929), *A Preface to Morals* (New York: Macmillan).

Lockerbie, D. Bruce (1998), *Dismissing God* (Grand Rapids, MI: Baker).

Lockyer, Herbert (1964), *All the Doctrines of the Bible* (Grand Rapids, MI: Zondervan).

Lockyer, Herbert (1973), *All the Messianic Prophecies of the Bible* (Grand Rapids, MI: Zondervan).

MacLaine, Shirley (1983), *Out on a Limb* (New York: Bantam).

MacLaine, Shirley (1989), *Going Within* (New York: Bantam).

MacLaine, Shirley (1991), *Dancing in the Light* (New York: Bantam).

Major, Trevor J. (1996), "The Fall of Tyre," *Reason & Revelation*, 16: 93-95, December.

Major, Trevor J. (1998), "The Problem of Suffering," *Reason and Revelation*, 18:49-55, July.

Mathews, J.M. (1857), *The Bible and Men of Learning* (New York: Daniel Fanshaw).

Mayberry, Thomas C. (1970), "God and Moral Authority," *The Monist*, January.

McClintock, John and James Strong (1879), *Cyclopedia of Biblical, Theological, and Ecclesiastical Literature* (Grand Rapids, MI: Baker, 1970 reprint).

McCord, Hugo (1979), "Internal Evidences of the Bible's Inspiration," *The Holy Scriptures*, ed. Wendell Winkler (Fort Worth, TX: Winkler Publications).

McDowell, Josh (1972), *Evidence that Demands a Verdict* (San Bernardino, CA: Campus Crusade for Christ).

McGarvey, J.W. (1875), *The New Testament Commentary: Matthew and Mark* (Delight, AR: Gospel Light).

McGarvey, J.W. (1881), *Lands of the Bible* (Philadelphia, PA: Lippincott).

McGrath, Alister E. (1993), *Intellectuals Don't Need God* (Grand Rapids, MI: Zondervan).

McMillen, S.I. (1963), *None of These Diseases* (Old Tappan, NJ: Revell).

Medawar, Peter (1969), "On 'The Effecting of All Things Possible,'" *The Listener*, October 2.

Merideth, Noel (1972), "The Bible and Theories of Inspiration," *The Bible Versus Liberalism* (Henderson, TN: Freed-Hardeman College).

Miethe, Terry L. and Gary R. Habermas (1993), *Why Believe? God Exists!* (Joplin, MO: College Press).

Montgomery Advertiser (1999), "Atheists Move Headquarters," Section D, p. 3, April 3.

Moffitt, Jerry (1993), "Arguments Used to Establish an Inerrant, Infallible Bible," *Biblical Inerrancy*, ed. Jerry Moffitt (Portland, TX: Portland Church of Christ).

Morris, Henry M. (1963), *Twilight of Evolution* (Grand Rapids, MI: Baker).

Morris, Henry M. (1969), *The Bible and Modern Science* (Chicago, IL: Moody).

Morris, Henry M. (1971), *The Bible Has the Answer* (Nutley, NJ: Craig Press).

Morris, Henry M. (1974a), *Many Infallible Proofs* (San Diego, CA: Creation-Life Publishers).

Morris, Henry M. (1974b), *Scientific Creationism* (San Diego, CA: Creation-Life Publishers).

Morris, Henry M. (1989), *The Long War Against God* (Grand Rapids, MI: Baker).

Morton, Jean S. (1978), *Science in the Bible* (Chicago, IL: Moody).

Motulsky, Arno S. (1974), "Brave New World?," *Science*, 185:654.

Newman, John Henry (1887), *An Essay in Aid of a Grammar of Assent* (London: Longmans, Green and Co.).

Nielsen, Kai (1973), *Ethics Without God* (London: Pemberton).

O'Hair, Madalyn Murray (1983), "Introduction," *Sixty-five Press Interviews with Robert G. Ingersoll* (Austin, TX: American Atheist Press).

Orr, James (1969), *Revelation and Inspiration* (Chicago, IL: Moody).

Paley, William (1839), *The Works of William Paley* (Edinburgh: Thomas Nelson).

Perutz, H.F. (1964), *Scientific American*, pp. 64-65, November.

Pfeiffer, Charles F. (1966), *The Biblical World* (Grand Rapids, MI: Baker).

Pfeiffer, John (1964), *The Cell* (New York: Time).

Pierson, Arthur T. (1913), *The Scriptures: God's Living Oracles* (London: Revell).

Pink, Arthur (1976 reprint), *The Divine Inspiration of the Bible* (Grand Rapids, MI: Baker).

Pinnock, Clark (1972), *A Defense of Biblical Infallibility* (Grand Rapids, MI: Baker).

Popper, Karl R. and John C. Eccles (1977), *The Self and Its Brain* (New York: Springer International).

Porter, Walter L. (1974), "Why Do the Innocent Suffer?," *Firm Foundation*, 91[30]:467,475, July 23.

Prabhavananda, Swami and Christopher Isherwood (1972), "Appendix II: The Gita War," in *Bhagavad Gita* (Bergerfield, NJ: New American Library).

Price, Ira (1907), *The Monuments and the Old Testament* (Philadelphia, PA: American Baptist Publication Society).

Ramm, Bernard H. (1971), *Protestant Christian Evidences* (Chicago, IL: Moody).

Rawlinson, George (1877), *Historical Evidences of the Truth of the Scripture Records* (New York: Sheldon & Company).

Raymo, Chet (1998), *Skeptics and True Believers* (New York: Walker).

Rehwinkel, Alfred (1951), *The Flood* (St. Louis, MO: Concordia).

Ricci, Paul (1986), *Fundamentals of Critical Thinking* (Lexington, MA: Ginn Press).

Ridenour, Fritz (1967), *Who Says God Created?* (Glendale, CA: Gospel Light).

Robertson, A.T. (1932), *Word Pictures in the New Testament* (Nashville, TN: Broadman).

Ruse, Michael and Edward O. Wilson (1985), "Evolution and Ethics," *New Scientist*, October 17.

Russell, Bertrand (1969), *Autobiography* (New York: Simon & Schuster).

Sagan, Carl (1974), s.v. "Life on Earth," *Encyclopaedia Britannica* (London: Encyclopaedia Britannica, Inc.).

Sagan, Carl (1980), *Cosmos* (New York: Random House).

Sagan, Carl and Ann Druyan (1990), "The Question of Abortion," *Parade*, April 22.

Samuel, (1950), *The Impossibility of Agnosticism* [a tract], (Downers Grove, IL: InterVarsity Press).

Sartre, Jean Paul (1961), "Existentialism and Humanism," *French Philosophers from Descartes to Sartre*, ed. Leonard M. Marsak (New York: Meridian).

Sartre, Jean Paul (1966), "Existentialism," Reprinted in *A Casebook on Existentialism*, ed. William V. Spanos (New York: Thomas Y. Crowell Co.).

Sauer, Erich (1962), *The King of the Earth* (Grand Rapids, MI: Eerdmans).

Sayers, Stanley (1973), *Optimism in an Age of Peril* (Delight, AR: Gospel Light).

Schaff, Philip (1910), *History of the Christian Church* (Grand Rapids, MI: Eerdmans).

Schaff, Philip (1913), *The Person of Christ* (New York: American Tract Society).

Schonfield, Hugh J. (1965), *The Passover Plot* (New York: Bantam).

Science Digest (1981), 89[1]:124, January/February.

Simpson, George Gaylord (1949), *The Meaning of Evolution* (New Haven, CT: Yale University Press).

Simpson, George Gaylord (1953), *Life of the Past* (New Haven, CT: Yale University Press).

Simpson, George Gaylord (1964), *This View of Life* (New York: Harcourt, Brace).

Simpson, George Gaylord (1967), *The Meaning of Evolution* (New Haven, CT: Yale University Press), revised edition.

Simpson, George Gaylord, C.S. Pittendrigh, and L.H. Tiffany (1957), *Life: An Introduction to Biology* (New York: Harcourt, Brace).

Sire, James W. (1988), *The Universe Next Door* (Downers Grove, IL: InterVarsity Press).

Smith, David (1910), *Man's Need of God* (London: Hodder and Stoughton).

Smith, F. LaGard (1986), *Out on a Broken Limb* (Eugene, OR: Harvest House).

Smith, George H. (1979), *Atheism: The Case Against God* (Buffalo, NY: Prometheus).

Smith, Huston (1982), "Evolution and Evolutionism," *Christian Century*, July 7-14.

Smith, Nelson M. (1975), "The Case Against Agnosticism," *Firm Foundation*, 92[6]:6,11, February.

Smith, Wilbur M. (1974 reprint), *Therefore Stand* (Grand Rapids, MI: Baker).

Solomon, David (1972), "Procurator," *Encyclopaedia Judaica*, ed. Cecil Roth (Jerusalem: Keter Publishing).

Sproul, R.C. (1978), *If There's a God, Why Are There Atheists?* (Wheaton, IL: Tyndale House).

Sproul, R.C. (1994), *Not A Chance* (Grand Rapids, MI: Baker).

Sproul, R.C., John Gerstner, and Arthur Lindsley (1984), *Classical Apologetics* (Grand Rapids, MI: Zondervan).

Stace, W.T. (1967), *Man Against Darkness and Other Essays* (Pittsburgh, PA: University of Pittsburgh Press).

Stenger, Victor J. (1987), "Was the Universe Created?," *Free Inquiry*, 7[3]:26-30, Summer.

Stoner, Peter W. and Robert C. Newman (1968), *Science Speaks* (Chicago, IL: Moody).

Story, Dan (1997), *Defending Your Faith* (Grand Rapids, MI: Kregel).

Tait, Katherine (1975), *My Father Bertrand Russell* (New York: Harcourt, Brace, & Jovanovich).

Taylor, A.E. (1945), *Does God Exist?* (London: MacMillan).

Taylor, Ian (1984), *In the Minds of Men* (Toronto, Canada: TFE Publishing).

Templeton, Charles B. (1996), *Farewell to God* (Toronto, Ontario, Canada: McClelland and Stewart).

Thaxton, Charles B., Walter L. Bradley, and Roger L. Olsen (1984), *The Mystery of Life's Origin* (New York: Philosophical Library).

Thayer, J.H. (1958 reprint), *A Greek-English Lexicon of the New Testament* (Edinburgh: T. & T. Clark).

Thompson, Bert (1981), "Science in the Bible," *Reason & Revelation*, 1:33-36, September.

Thompson, Bert (1990), "Does Human Suffering Disprove the Existence of a Benevolent God?," *Giving a Reason for Our Hope*, ed. Winford Claiborne (Henderson, TN: Freed-Hardeman College), pp. 280-285.

Thompson, Bert (1993), "Do Natural Disasters Negate Divine Benevolence?," *Reason and Revelation*, 13:65-69, September.

Thompson, Bert (1994), "Famous Enemies of Christ," *Reason & Revelation*, 14:1-7, January.

Thompson, Bert (1995a), "The Case for the Existence of God—[Part I]," *Reason and Revelation*, 15:33-38, May.

Thompson, Bert (1995b), "The Case for the Existence of God—[Part II]," *Reason and Revelation*, 15:41-47, June.

Thompson, Bert (1997), "In Defense of... Christ's Deity," *Reason & Revelation*, 17:89-94, December.

Thompson, Bert (1998a), "In Defense of... Christ's Church," *Reason & Revelation*, 18:1-5, January.

Thompson, Bert (1998b), "In Defense of...God's Plan of Salvation," *Reason & Revelation*, 18:17-22, March.

Thompson, Bert (1999), "The Many Faces of Unbelief—[Part II]," *Reason & Revelation* 19:25-31, April.

Thompson, Bert and Wayne Jackson (1982), "The Revelation of God in Nature," *Reason and Revelation*, 2:17-24, May.

Thompson, Bert and Wayne Jackson (1992), *A Study Course in Christian Evidences* (Montgomery, AL: Apologetics Press).

Thompson, Bert and Wayne Jackson (1996), *The Case for the Existence of God* (Montgomery, AL: Apologetics Press).

Tolstoy, Leo (1964), "Religion and Morality," *Leo Tolstoy: Selected Essays* (New York: Random House).

Trefil, James (1984), "The Accidental Universe," *Science Digest*, 92 [6]:53-55,100-101, June.

Tryon, Edward P. (1984), "What Made the World?," *New Scientist*, March 8.

Turner, Rex A., Sr. (1989), *Systematic Theology* (Montgomery, AL: Alabama Christian School of Religion).

Van Biema, David (1997), "Where's Madalyn?," *Time*, 149[6]:56-60, February 10.

Vine, W.E. (1940), *An Expository Dictionary of New Testament Words* (Old Tappan, NJ: Revell).

Watkin, Edward I. (1936), *Theism, Agnosticism and Atheism* (London: Unicorn Press).

Watson, James D. (1968), *The Double Helix* (New York: Atheneum).

Weinberg, Arthur (1957), *Attorney for the Damned* (New York: Simon & Schuster).

Weinberg, Steven (1993), *Dreams of a Final Theory* (New York: Vintage Books).

Wilson, Edward O. (1975), *Sociology: The New Synthesis* (Cambridge, MA: Belknap Press of Harvard University).

Wilson, Edward O. (1982), "Toward a Humanistic Biology," *The Humanist*, September/October.

Woods, Guy N. (no date), *The Case for Verbal Inspiration* [a tract], (Shreveport, LA: Lambert).

Woods, Guy N. (1976), "Man Created in God's Image," *Gospel Advocate*, 118[33]:514,518, August.

Woods, Guy N. (1982), " 'And be not Conformed to this World,' " *Gospel Advocate*, 124[1]:2, January 7.

Wysong, R.L. (1976), *The Creation/Evolution Controversy* (East Lansing, MI: Inquiry Press).

Young, Robert M. (1982), "The Darwin Debate," *Marxism Today*, vol. 26. NOTE: In this article, in speaking of Harvard evolutionist Stephen Jay Gould, Young has suggested that Dr. Gould is "avowedly non-Marxist." This, however, is incorrect. Gould has admitted, under oath, that he is a Marxist [see: Morris, Henry M. (1982), *Evolution in Turmoil* (San Diego, CA: Creation-Life Publishers), pp. 102-103].

Zerr, E.M. (1952), *Bible Commentary* (Bowling Green, KY: Guardian of Truth).

[AUTHOR'S NOTE: I would like to thank my friend and colleague, Wayne Jackson, for graciously allowing me to use various materials he has written through the years on the inspiration of the Bible, as well as material on God's plan of salvation from the *Study Course in Christian Evidences* that he and I co-authored (see Thompson and Jackson, 1992).]

INDEX

A

B

C

D

E

F

K

L

N

O

P

R

S

T

U